Roadmap to Korean

Roadmap to Korean

Richard Harris

HOLLYM
Elizabeth, NJ·Seoul

Roadmap to Korean

First published in 2003
Second edition, 2005
by Hollym International Corp.
18 Donald Place, Elizabeth, New Jersey 07208, USA
Phone (908)353-1655 Fax (908)353-0255
http://www.hollym.com

Published simultaneously in Korea
by Hollym Corporation; Publishers
13-13 Gwancheol-dong, Jongno-gu, Seoul 110-111, Korea
Phone (02)735-7551~4 Fax (02)730-5149, 8192
http://www.hollym.co.kr e-mail: hollym@chollian.net

ISBN : 1-56591-187-3
Library of Congress Control Number : 2003109608

Printed in Korea

Acknowledgements

This book is not the result of one man's work. There are a lot of people I'd like to thank for helping bring this project to life. Over my years in Korea there have been a great many people—Koreans and non-Koreans alike—who have taken me in, helped me, taught me, tolerated me (a lot), fed me (occasionally), and shown me my way on this slippery path called the Korean language. First and foremost, however, is Eun-ju (은주). Without her I would not be near the level of Korean I am at today. She has put up with my questions, my incessant curiosity, my nagging, my bickering, and my every-once-in-a-while-so-infrequently-that-I-can't-remember tirades into this wonderful language. And through it all she managed to nurture a young man's language capability to a respectable level.

There have been many others, though. I've probably learned more Korean on a quantitative level in my own English classroom teaching at Sungkyunkwan University (성균관대) than anywhere else. For that I owe a debt of gratitude to all the unsuspecting students who put up with my (yet again) endless questions into the Korean language.

My two oldest Korean friends, Kim Ki-young (김기영) and Jung Dae-sung (정대성), also deserve some kind of medal for what they have endured with me, especially in those early days when my Korean was bad to quite bad. Lee Jin-hee (이진희) and her brother, Dr. Lee Chun-goo (이천구), have been an enormous help to me over the years as well.

All through this time, however, there was one person that helped teach me things about Korean that I had never considered, and for that, I owe a huge thanks to Gary Rector, the man who may just be the most knowledgeable person about this language. His weekly columns in the Korea Herald gave me insight and inspiration with Korean on more than one occasion.

With respect to the book itself, *Roadmap to Korean* is an ambitious effort that required the assistance, the foresight, and the dedication of many hardworking and generous human beings. There are many people I need to thank profusely in this regard, but chief among them all is Eun-ju. More than simply provide her time and knowledge, she constantly proofread, constantly edited, and constantly put up with my crap. She was a rock in a time when stormy weather was the norm, and incessant squabbling my favorite pastime.

Equally as dedicated in time and effort, however, was my lifelong editor, best friend, idea bouncer-offer, brother, and all around good guy, Matt Rutledge. He sat through every stage of this book with me and listened patiently as I rambled off about this and that on too many occasions to count. I always told him that it meant a lot for me to have him just listen and let me sound out certain ideas, so now maybe he'll actually believe me. This book would not be as broad in scope or as well researched without him.

Also, my sister, Melanie Rutledge, and her husband, Eric Andrus, gave much too generously of their time to edit this book. They came to Korea on vacation to see their brothers and instead got a *Roadmap to Korean*. This book is immeasurably better because of both their efforts.

Thanks also have to go out to many friends and colleagues. Craig Service was nothing short of brilliant with his suggestions and lightening-fast readings. He read each of the manuscripts and always got back to me in prompt order, with useful advice and constructive criticism. Susan MacDonald was of great help through her vigorous support and professional scrutiny, as was Lieutenant Colonel Brian Douglas, who contributed to this project more than he cares to admit. Sunny Kim (김경선) proved invaluable in bringing certain parts of this book to life. She gave of her time to look over many of the Korean phrases and concepts that were quite difficult, and always provided sound advice. Lee Ji-hyun (이지현) was also selfless in her dedication to *Roadmap*'s slow and laborious birth. She helped a good deal with the grammar while diligently going through the entire verb appendix to make sure everything was in working order. Monica Kim (김귀연) helped provide a lot of insight into the mechanics of Korean and the linguistics of it from a technical standpoint. Drs. Yoon Tae-kyu (윤태규), Lim Jung-ki (임중기), and Im Jee-sun (임지순) were so valuable that they don't even realize it; they are the impetus behind my favorite chapter in this book, All About Rice. Gratitude must also be paid to Lee Sang-hee (이상희) of Sungkyunkwan University's Korean language program, who was kind enough to go over the appendix of verb conjugations with me and offer critical advice where many others could not, and to Hong Joo-hee (홍주희), who provided some very timely advice.

I also feel it necessary to thank one important person that didn't impact this book through her editing or research, but did provide much needed support through an extremely arduous time. Although she never saw one page of this book as a draft, Maria Amore is and always has been a source of incredible drive and support for me. She gave me a boost in my loneliest hour with this book, and for that I will never forget.

Last, but certainly not least (and in fact right near the top of this whole deformed pyramid of thank yous), I wish to thank my editor, Julia Yi (이희정), and Ham Ki-man (함기만), President of Hollym Korea. They both showed an incredible amount of faith in a project that has never been done before, and in a young author trying hard to find his place in this great big world of writing. Thank you for believing in me.

Preface

This language can be learned. Despite what people tell you, despite the rumors and the myths that surround this language, Korean *can* be learned by anyone willing and able to sacrifice the time and energy necessary to do so. I say that to you, the reader, not as someone who has given this language a cursory once-over, but as someone who has dedicated over five years of his life to learning the intricacies and nuances that lie behind the words, the grammar, the culture, and the history of this wonderfully fascinating language. I would never in a million years claim to be fluent, but I can say that after all the time and effort I've put into Korean, I have a great deal to show for it.

To be honest, I love this language as much as I curse at it each and every day of my life. I want to strangle this language on the worst of days and marry it on the best. These are the words that pop into my head when I think of learning Korean: glorious, liberating, stupid, beautiful, ridiculous, dumb, educational, wonderful, amazing, incredible, futile, frustrating. And that's without one single swear word!

The idea for writing this book came to me when shopping for my first Korean language book. I was in a relatively large bookstore and couldn't find a single book that looked complete and comprehensive. What I found that day, and on subsequent days, was that every book about learning Korean was written by a Korean. Now, before you raise your eyebrows and say, Isn't that the way it's supposed to be? let me explain that this language is unlike any other you've seen before. For the novice to Korean, a thorough introduction is necessary to set out the boundaries and limits of where you'll be traversing with this language. That's what I've attempted to do with this book: to make it a roadmap to the language in its entirety.

Don't get me wrong—I'm no expert. I don't have any linguistic degrees or accolades that distinguish me as some great scholar on the Korean language. I'm simply a person that came to Korea over half a decade ago to learn about the country and its language. Since that time, I've fought in the trenches of Korean day in and day out in an attempt to learn what I initially thought would be just another language. I didn't know one single word of Korean before coming to Korea. I didn't know one single person when I arrived, and I certainly had no idea what I was getting myself into at the time.

From the moment I arrived in Mokpo, the city I called home for my first 10 months in Korea, however, I submerged myself in the language and the culture. I lived with a Korean family in Mokpo before coming to Seoul in 1998. I've studied on my own, privately with a tutor, at a *hagwon* (학원)—a private language academy—and at a university. I've made it my mission to unlock the mysteries of this language because it's part of my sadistic personality to punish myself with pain of an intellectual sort. And punished I have been by this language.

Korean is both scientifically precise and wildly erratic; a fantasy for all the science geeks out there who love formulas and straightforward laws; a nightmare for anyone not willing to go through hour after grueling hour of linguistic gymnastics. Why did I (and why do I continue to) put myself through this self-inflicted, pain-inducing exercise? Simply put, this language is the most absorbing, most amazing thing I've ever encountered.

Many people who come to Korea with the intention of living here for any length of time do not learn the language. They justify this apathy in a number of ways: 'I'm lazy,' 'It's too difficult,' 'I don't have any time.' There's also 'I want to help Koreans practice their English,' (altruism at its best) and 'I'm only going to be in Korea for 3 months/1 year/4 years/my entire life.' In truth, there's no excuse for people calling Korea home for however long to not make a basic attempt to learn the language. This book is not a call to arms for all those that have learned Korean to go to the streets to rally the troops, though. Rather, I'd like to inspire all those out there that have not studied the language to do so, and to help others who know a little about the language advance to the next level.

From day one I've asked questions about this language. I wanted to know why certain things happened one way one time, and yet another way other times. I wanted to understand the way Korean worked from its first principles and penetrate this language to the very core. And although many people, both Koreans and non-Koreans alike, will have you believe that you can't learn Korean—that it's too difficult—I have news for you: you can learn this language; this language is within reach.

I wrote this book to help people navigate their way around the mine-infested waters of Korean and to expose the most fascinating aspects of this unique language. I didn't have anything like this book when I first started learning and so as a result, it took me days, weeks, sometimes years, to figure out the most elementary of problems. Koreans have a tendency to just be happy that you've taken the time to learn their language without worrying whether what you're saying is right or not; taxi drivers have been complimenting me on my Korean since the day I learned to say 'Hello,' *an-nyung-ha-sae-yo* (안녕하세요). But I, for one, have never wanted to just speak this language as a mere sojourner to the language.

At the same time, I've written this book for a new generation of Korean language teachers. Through my experiences at *hagwon* and universities, and with private tutors over the years, teachers of the Korean language are guilty of the same thing that many ESL teachers are in Korea: a difficulty in grasping what it is that makes our respective languages so hard to understand for the student. With a teaching aid such as this, it's my sincerest hope that present and future teachers of Korean as a second language learn to approach the language a little more sympathetically.

Anyone can learn Korean. You have to believe this whether you're studying full-time or just here and there a few minutes a day. If you make this your mantra and work at learning the language day in and day out you *will* speak Korean. I believe this book will make it easier for people learning Korean to fit in, to speak properly, and to use more natural phrases and words a lot quicker than ever before.

But for those reading this book only because they're interested in the country and the language from a spectator's point of view, there's a great deal of information in here that will make your head spin, that will make you smile, and that, in the end, will make you happy you read this book. For at the end of the day all we really want is to better understand this esoteric and mysterious language, its roots through history and culture, and its impact on a nation of almost 70 million people. With that in mind, I invite you to turn the page and dive into 22 chapters of knowledge about a brilliant language that most people around the world are not familiar with...

Yet.

Richard Harris
Seoul, December 30, 2002

Contents

Part IV

Studying Korean Formally: Navigating Your Way Through Shark-Infested Waters

Part V

Language in Motion, Cultural Extensions: A World of Knowledge Unraveled

Appendices

Introduction

I've written this book in English with the understanding that the reader may not be able to read Korean or Chinese characters. As such, I've done my best to make every word, every phrase, and every explanation from Korean and Chinese as easy to follow in English as possible. Although the text of this book is written in English, where I include a Korean word or phrase, I also include the Korean word phonetically transliterated into English in *italics* with the Korean character(s) in parentheses (like this). In certain places, where I think the Chinese character(s) proves useful in aiding an explanation, I've also included the Chinese character(s) [漢字] beside the Korean one(s). Thus, a typical phrase that includes Korean and Chinese characters may look something like this:

The concept of *jung* (정 · 情) is difficult to explain in English.

Where Chinese characters have been included without a Korean character to match, I've listed the Chinese character(s) in a different set of brackets [like this]:

The word is derived from the Chinese character for country, *gook* [國]

Another fact the reader may have already noticed is that I'm not using the new method of romanizing words from Korean to English as sanctioned by the South Korean government. I'll let the chapter on romanization (**Chapter 5**) provide the explanation for this, but suffice it to say that I spell words transliterated from Korean in a way that comes closest to preserving the sounds of the word from its original form. By no means am I promoting a new system of transliteration, but I want to make this book as easy to read phonetically as I can. Native English speakers should be able to look at every one of the transliterations and pronounce the word or phrase with nothing more than English as a first language.

Also, I've hyphenated every word from Korean longer than one character so that if you can't read Korean, you'll know where the breaks come between syllables. A good example of this is the word 'hourglass,' which is usually just transliterated into English without any breaks between characters, ***moraesheegae*** (모래시계). I, however, spell it ***mo-rae-shee-gae*** in my book, so that you can be sure of where the stress falls between confusing combinations of letters.

The only exceptions I've made to this rule are internationally recognizable Korean words, names and businesses, as well as all place names and time periods. With these I've decided to use the most common spelling so as not to confuse readers who may be familiar with Korea as a country, but not Korean as a language. Thus, I have kept **King Sejong**, *kimchi*, and **Hyundai**, but to give three examples, exactly as they have been known for years. With regard to place names and time periods, I have opted to use the new romanized names as set forth by the government in 2000, which is why you'll see **Busan** (and not **Pusan**) and the **Silla** dynasty (not the **Shilla** dynasty) spelled the way they are.

Another matter that should be cleared up from the beginning is the fact that the word Korean (as in the language) is expressed several ways in the Korean language. In English, the noun Korean refers to the people and the language, including both the written and spoken portions. The same is not true in Korean, though. For example, the written aspect of Korean is referred to as *Hangeul* (한글), the spoken aspect as *han-goong-mal* (한국말), and the language itself, in a more abstract way, as *han-gook-aw* (한국어). It's important to distinguish between these three words in Korean because not doing so can lead to confusion when discussing different parts of the language that in English are all expressed with the same word.

I know that Korean is an extremely complex language for someone who has never seen it before. Remember, I was once where many of you now are. If you only find yourself asking more questions from the answers and explanations I provide along the way, don't worry—that's completely natural. However, it's my intention that by the end of this book you shall have had all your questions answered. For this book is, as I clearly state on the cover, a roadmap to Korean; everything you ever wanted to know about the language.

Events Associated in the Development of the Korean Language and Printing in Korea

c. 5000 B.C.	Iconified language introduced to East Asia
c. 1800	Evidence of first Chinese characters found in China
c. 800	Chinese characters first standardized, labeled Grand Seal characters
551	Birth of Confucius
c. 200	Chinese characters reduced in number, relabeled Small Seal characters
A.D. 37	Cult of Confucianism first mentioned by a Chinese emperor
c. 105	Paper invented in China by Ts'ai Lun
c. 200	Chinese characters used as national writing system in Korea
372	First evidence of Confucian schools on Korean peninsula
c. 704	Evidence of first document printed on wooden blocks in Korea
868	World's first known printed book made in China (*The Diamond Sutra*)
1087	*Tripitaka Koreana* completed for first time
1234	Metal moveable printing typeface first used in Korea
1239	First document printed with cast metal type made in Korea
1251	*Tripitaka Koreana* completed for second time
1392	Establishment of Joseon dynasty and Annals of the Joseon dynasty
1397	Birth of King Sejong
1398	Korea's longest-standing Confucian academy, Sungkyunkwan, opens in Seoul
1443	*Hoon-meen-jung-eum*—Correct Sounds to Teach the People—written
1446	*Hangeul* codified as an official written language
1714	Chinese character radicals standardized in China under Emperor K'ang-hsi
1910	Japanese annexation of Korean peninsula
1939	McCune-Reischauer System of romanization adopted in Korea
1945	Japanese surrender, Korean once again official language of Korean peninsula
1948	Creation of separate North and South Korean states
1990	UNESCO recognizes *Hangeul* as unique language
2000	New romanization process unveiled by South Korean government

Korean and Chinese
Dynasties and Kingdoms

Korean		Chinese	
Korean		**C**hinese	
Ancient Tribal Period	2333-108 B.C.	Shang	c. 1650-1027 B.C.
Chinese Colonies	108 B.C-A.D. 313	Western Zhou	1027-771 B.C.
Baekje[1]	c. 18 B.C.-A.D. 660	Eastern Zhou	770-221 B.C.
Goguryeo[2]	c. 37 B.C.-A.D. 668	Qin	221-207 B.C.
Silla[3]	c. 57 B.C.-A.D. 935	Western Han	206 B.C.-A.D. 9
Unified Silla	668-935	Xin	9-A.D. 24
Goryeo[4]	918-1392	Eastern Han	25-A.D. 220
Joseon[5]	1392-1910	The Three Kingdoms	220-280
		Western Jin	265-316
		Eastern Jin	317-420
		Southern and Northern	420-588
		Sui	589-618
		Tang	618-907
		Five Dynasties	907-960
		Song	960-1279
		Yuan	1279-1368
		Ming	1368-1644
		Qing	1644-1911

1. This used to be spelled **Paekche**.
2. This used to be spelled **Koguryo**.
3. This used to be spelled **Shilla**.
4. This used to be spelled **Koryo**.
5. This used to be spelled **Chosun**. Sometimes, it's also referred to as the Yi dynasty.

For Eun-ju

If I appear tall it is only because I stand

on the shoulders of giants

생각이 바뀌면 행동이 바뀌고
행동이 바뀌면 운명이 바뀐다

If your thoughts change, your behavior will follow suit;
if your behavior changes, your destiny will follow suit.

Part 1

Background to the Language, Background to the Culture:

Misinterpretations and Misunderstandings

The upper waters must be clear for the lower waters to be clear

윗물이 맑아야 아랫물이 맑다

Chapter 1

A History of the Language and King Sejong the Great
한글의 역사 + 세종대왕

[1] I use the word *Hangeul*, but this word is also variously spelled as *Hanguel, hangul, han-gul, hanguel,* and *hangeul,* depending on which text you happen to be reading. The spelling I use throughout the course of this book is the spelling the South Korean government now recognizes as the official title for the written Korean script.

[2] There have been several invented written languages throughout the course of history, some modern ones that actually created an alphabet. Yet the fact that *Hangeul* is still used to this day, and by so many people worldwide, not to mention the fact that it's the official language of two countries, makes *Hangeul* unique from other invented written languages.

The written form of the Korean language, *Hangeul* (한글),[1] was codified in 1446 during the reign of King Sejong (세종대왕). *Hangeul* is distinct from other written languages in use throughout the world today in two important ways: first, because its codification and mass dissemination can be traced back to a single person at a certain time in history, and second, because it's the only invented language still in use by a government today.[2] Although it's not known to what extent King Sejong participated in writing the *hoon-meen-jung-eum* (훈민정음) treatise—Correct Sounds to Teach the People—or the creation of the Korean alphabet now known as *Hangeul,* there is no doubt that under his reign a Korean writing system was invented with an attendant set of laws and rules governing it.

Koreans had been speaking a language uniquely their own for centuries upon centuries all over the Korean peninsula before *Hangeul* was invented in the 15th century, but there was no written language all their own to express it. Up until then, words and phrases had to be written in Chinese characters. What we know of spoken Korean in its earliest days is the following:

According to early historical records, two groups of languages

2

were spoken in Manchuria and on the Korean peninsula at the dawn of the Christian era; one belonged to the Northern Buyeo group and the other to the southern Han group. Around the middle of the seventh century when the Silla Kingdom unified the peninsula, its language became the dominant form of communication. As a result, the linguistic unification of the peninsula was achieved on the basis of the Silla language. When the Goryeo dynasty was founded in the 10th century, the capital was moved to Gaeseong, located at the center of the Korean peninsula. From that time onward, the dialect of Gaeseong became the standard national language. After the Joseon dynasty was founded at the end of the 14th century, the capital was moved to Seoul. However, since Seoul is geographically close to Gaeseong, the move had little significant effect on the development of the language.[3]

So, when *Hangeul* was unveiled in 1446, it marked a huge step forward for Koreans because it gave the people their own alphabet[4] by which to write the language they had been speaking for well over a millennium.

KING SEJONG THE TRULY GREAT

King Sejong is known in Korean history as the greatest and most benevolent king of the Joseon dynasty (1392-1910). Born in 1397, Sejong acceded to the throne in 1418. Under his reign, many advancements were made in medicine, astrology, science, and farming. Yet no other achievement comes close to matching the effect that the codification of the Korean language has had on the Korean peninsula.

Korea was an agrarian and largely illiterate nation before Sejong came to power in the 15th century. Chinese characters, then, like now, were so difficult to learn that many people never learned them at all. Sejong was determined to alleviate illiteracy upon acceding to the throne in 1418. He believed that education was the key to improving living standards, and thought that if people

[3] See the Republic of Korea's Ministry of Culture and Tourism (MCT) website at *www.mct.go.kr*

[4] Although I constantly refer to *Hangeul* as an alphabet throughout this book, I should point out that, for lack of a better word, *Hangeul* is not exactly an alphabet in the English sense of the word. For a more precise explanation of *Hangeul's* characters, please refer to **Ch. 6**.

could read and write, knowledge would come about as a result. With more knowledge, he reasoned, society prospered, culture flowered, and the country would ultimately become stronger.

In 1443 Sejong published his treatise entitled *hoon-meen-jung-eum* (Correct Sounds to Teach the People). Three years after this, Sejong introduced the Korean alphabet, *Hangeul* (한글), to Koreans. In all probability, Sejong and the court scholars who helped write the Correct Sounds to Teach the People, whom he referred to as *jeep-hyun-jun* (집현전), looked to existing scripts that were geographically close, such as Chinese Old Seal characters, Uighur, and the Mongolian scripts.[5] As much as these court scholars may have done research based on existing languages at the time, however, *Hangeul* was ostensibly based on Sejong's court scholars' own phonological studies.

AN EASY LANGUAGE TO LEARN

Upon its introduction in 1446, *Hangeul* was comprised of 28 characters. These 28 characters, when built one on top of the other, could represent every word that until that time had to be written in Chinese. Koreans finally had a written language to call their own.

The *hoon-meen-jung-eum* explained in clear and lucid terms why the new writing system had been invented, how it was broken down, and listed details about how it could be used. Koreans are naturally extremely proud of the fact that their language came into being accompanied by its own set of rules and instructions governing its use. This not only set *Hangeul* apart from Chinese, but made it unique from other languages around the world.

To Sejong's credit, *Hangeul* is indeed very easy to learn with its strict set of rules. *Hangeul* is a phonetic alphabet like English, in that each character, or *geul-ja* (글자) as they're known in Korean, corresponds to a phoneme (an elementary unit of speech that distinguishes one utterance from another). The modern *Hangeul* alphabet consists of 24 characters, split between 10 'vowels' and 14 'consonants'; the vowels representing the three basic elements in Eastern cosmology (heaven, earth, and humanity), the consonants modeled after pictorial vocal representations. (Please see **Chapter 6** for a clearer definition of

[5] See MCT website.

this concept). Sejong believed *Hangeul* so easy to learn that he wrote in the *hoon-meen-jung-eum*:

> The wise will learn it in one morning; even a fool will be able to learn it in ten days.[6]

Critics of King Sejong's new writing system said *Hangeul* was too easy to learn. So simple was the language to learn, these same critics argued, that it was nothing more than 'morning letters,' *a-cheem-geul* (아침글), because it could be learned in the span of a morning. Others insulted *Hangeul* by calling it 'women's letters,' *am-geul* (암글), a reference to the fact *Hangeul* was so easy that even women could learn the language.[7]

The truth of the matter was that very few people could read Chinese characters in the 15th century. *Hangeul*, on the other hand, was so easy to learn that it was only a matter of time before everyone could read, and they, the critics of *Hangeul* and the guardians of written knowledge, would no longer be the venerated people they once were only because of their ability to read and write.

A UNIQUE LANGUAGE

Unlike other alphabets that have evolved and changed over time, *Hangeul* has changed little in over five centuries. Although originally composed of 28 characters, Korean today makes use of only 24.[8] The only other major change in that time has involved the name linked to the language. People originally referred to written Korean not as *hoon-meen-jung-eun*, but as *awn-moon* (언문). It was only in the early 20th century that Chu Shi-kyung (주시경)[9] first proposed the name *Hangeul.*

The etymology behind the word *Hangeul* is extensive and nothing short of brilliant. The word '*Han*' (in *Hangeul*) was derived from 'one,' *ha-na* (하나), 'great,' *keum* (금), and 'correct,' *ba-reum* (발음), while the word '*geul*' (from *Hangeul*) came from the Korean word used to denote a character, *geul-ja* (글자). In essence, *Hangeul* was then the one great character language.[10]

[6] See
http://korea.insights.co.kr

[7] See the Republic of Korea's website at
www.korea.net/government/government.html

[8] The four characters which were dropped are as follows: △ , ㆆ , · , and ㆁ Also, I've put the words vowels and consonants in quotations because it's the most accepted way by which to differentiate between the two different types of characters in Korean, known as *mo-eum* (모음) and *ja-eum* (자음) respectively. Vowels and consonants in Korean don't follow the same rules of grammar that English ones do, however.

[9] See
http://korea.insights.co.kr

Use of the term *Hangeul* spread slowly over the years, especially so during the Japanese occupation of the peninsula from 1910 to 1945. Yet after the nation's liberation at the end of World War II, the term became incorporated into the vernacular so that now, nearly one hundred years after it was first proposed, Koreans still refer to the written portion of their language as *Hangeul.*

Although a national holiday originally, *Hangeul* Day is now nothing more than an anniversary celebrated every October 9. In 1990, to the great pride of Koreans around the world, the United Nations Environmental, Scientific and Cultural Council (UNESCO) officially acknowledged the uniqueness of *Hangeul* by establishing the King Sejong Literacy Prize to honor people around the world who worked toward the eradication of illiteracy.[11] Thanks in part to the ease by which *Hangeul* can be learned—and aided by a comprehensive elementary school system—Koreans now enjoy one of the highest literacy rates in the world.

OVERCOMING BARRIERS TO MODERN KOREAN

Today, nearly 70 million Koreans living on the Korean peninsula speak Korean as a first language. On top of this number, an estimated five million people speak Korean as a first language outside of Korea.[12] Though alphabetization, spelling and pronunciation differ across the peninsula, Korean is the official language of both North and South Korea. There are six major dialects on the Korean peninsula, one in North Korea and five in South Korea. Even with these differences, however, Koreans can communicate with and understand one another without major difficulty.

The one impediment to Korean for people from Cheju to Pyongyang, though, is the adaptation of English into Korean in South Korea. After the Korean War (1950-53), the two governments of South and North Korea pursued different means by which to incorporate new words and phrases from the global community into Korean. Whereas the North Korean government wished to keep the Korean language 'pure' from outside influences, South Koreans had no problem integrating many new English, French, German, and Japanese words

[10] See
   http://korea.insights.co.kr

[11] See UNESCO's website at
*http://www2.unesco.org:800
0/brx/prizes/Regulations.asp*

[12] See MCT website.

6

into everyday speech. So much so, in fact, that approximately 10,000 English words are now listed in a typical South Korean dictionary[13] (English being the most pervasive of the foreign languages in Korea). Proof of the differences between North and South Korean is no more clearly seen today than when North Korean refugees land in Seoul and are briefed about life in the capitalist South—they are often perplexed by the most basic English terms written in *Hangeul*, such as ice cream, car, printer and soup.[14]

The History of America's Name

There is as much speculation and suspicion surrounding the history of America's name in Korean as there is substance and fact. Almost every country name in Korean is nothing more than a 'Koreanized' word from the country name in its original language. Thus, Italy is *Italia* (이탈리아), Switzerland is *Sweese* (스위스), and Canada is *Kanada* (캐나다). The United States, on the other hand, has its own unique name in Korean, *mi-gook* (미국).

The first and most persistent rumor is that the word *mi-gook* (variously spelled *mi guk* and *mee-guk* in English) is derived from the fact that people in China and Korea think that the Americans are 'beautiful' people, as the Chinese character that America's name is associated with literally means, *mi* (미 · 美). Neither does America's name (as it's expressed in Korean) have anything to do with the fact that America has been a long-standing ally of Korea since the two countries established diplomatic relations in 1882.

The reason that America has a special name in Korean today, (and one with such a splendid connotation) is nothing more fantastic than its phonetic roots. There was a time when both the Japanese and Chinese referred to the Americans by its proper name (in the accent of the language being spoken, of course), but the name was very long, so it was shortened to just one Chinese character. Because of the way America is pronounced in Japanese, though, the 'me' in 'America' was represented by the Kanji character [米] for rice, written as *mi* (미) in Korean. The Chinese, however,

[13] See www.transparent.com

[14] See **Ch. 15** for a more detailed explanation of the use of English in South Korea today.

7

pronounced the middle portion of the word 'America' slightly different than the Japanese, and so shortened America's name to a different character [美], which also happened to be written the exact same way in Korean as the character for rice, *mi* (미).

Initially, when Korea was a Japanese colony (1910-1945), Koreans referred to America by the Japanese Kanji character, rice [米]. But some time either during the Japanese occupation or right after it, Koreans changed the Chinese character by which they referred to the United States. From that time forward, America came to be known as *mi-gook* (미국), stemming from the Chinese characters beautiful [美] and country [國], thus making it the 'beautiful country,' by direct translation, and Americans, 'beautiful people.'

Chapter 2

Writing and Printing in Korean

한글의 발달 + 출판 역사

Even though *Hangeul* wasn't invented until the 15th century, Koreans were busy writing and printing documents long before the language's invention. Though few people outside of Korea know it, Korea played a leading role in the development of the modern printing press centuries ago.

The Chinese are credited with having invented the first form of **paper** in A.D. 105, and the first form of **block printing** in 450.[1] They are also credited with having printed the **first book on paper**, *The Diamond Sutra*, in 868. In 1040, a renowned Chinese alchemist by the name of Li Peng invented the first known **moveable type printing press**.[2] The printing press Peng invented was made out of hardened clay, each Chinese character elaborately drawn on softened pieces of clay, which were later cooled and filled with ink. Although there were significant drawbacks to this type of printing technology—one was the fact that clay was not durable, the second that the characters themselves were time-consuming to draw—there is little doubt that it helped spawn a new era of printing technology.

[1] See *http://inventors.about.com/library/inventors/blprinting.htm*

[2] See *http://www.didyouknow.cd/words/gutenberg.htm*

LITTLE KNOWN KOREAN CONTRIBUTIONS

Most students in the West are taught at an early age that a European by the name of Johannes Guttenberg is credited with having invented the first moveable typeface printing press. However, this fact is somewhat misleading, and increasingly a source of angst for Korean scholars trying desperately to have Korea's name attached to arguably the most important invention in the last millennium.

According to the Korea National Tourism Organization:

> Historical records indicate that woodblock printing was being practiced in Korea at the beginning of the 8th century. A Buddhist scripture printed from woodblocks dating to the Silla period, was retrieved from Bulguksa Temple in Gyeongju. The title of the scripture is Mugujeonggwang daedaranigyeong (*Pure Light Dharani Sutra*). It is presumed to have been translated into Chinese characters by a monk named Mitasan around the year 704. One record also indicates that it was placed within the stone pagoda of Hwangboksa Temple in 706. Others place it as the scripture that inspired the construction of numerous pagodas in Japan. Since the pagoda at Bulguksa Temple from where the scripture was retrieved was built in 751, the scripture itself must have been printed well before that year. Though it is small, the print reveals the characteristics of early woodblock printing in Korea, and attests to the lofty heights in cultural accomplishments that the Korean people at the time reached. It remains the world's oldest printed material.[3]

From what most people are led to believe, the Chinese invented the first moveable clay typeface printing press in the 11th century, while it was Guttenberg who revolutionized the medium by creating metal typeface plates that were moveable. This innovation by Guttenberg both expedited the printing process and saved money.[4]

[3] See the Republic of Korea's National Tourism Organization's (KNTO) website at *www.knto.or.kr*

[4] See the Republic of Korea's homepage at *www.korea.net*

10

Yet this is not what Korean students are brought up to believe when studying in schools from Jeju to Pyeongyang today. Korea claims to have invented the first moveable metal typeface printing press in 1234.[5] Five years later, *nam-myung-chun-hwa-sang-song-jeung-do-ga* (남명천화상송증도가), or Priest Cheon Nam-myung's *A Buddhist Chant*, was the first printed document done with cast metal type in 1239.[6] Furthermore, Korea claims to have printed the world's first book on this same kind of typeface in 1377, when *bool-jo-jeek-jee-sheem-chae-yo-jul* (불조직지심체요절) was published.[7]

What then, you might ask, came of these printing presses that were purportedly invented by the Koreans so many centuries ago? Well, for one, Korean (just like Chinese) was much too complicated to develop on the type of printing presses experimented with in the Middle Ages. Just as Chinese has thousands of characters (and therefore thousands of typeface plates to change), so too does Korean have thousands of possible combinations in which a character can be written. Although only comprised of 28 characters originally (24 today), the permutations and combinations for potential Korean complex characters is staggering.[8] For this reason alone, and without consideration of other political and economic deterrents at the time, the printing press never developed like it did in Europe in the 15th and 16th centuries.

The advantage that the English language had over Chinese and Korean, for example, was that its 26 letters never needed to be changed from the typeface no matter what the document. Once the typeface was set (for size or style, for instance), the printer could go about printing document after document and not have to worry about changing the typeface, creating a new typeface, nor any other time-intensive, costly process.

TWO LONG-LASTING LEGACIES OF KOREAN PRINTING

There are many cultural, scholastic, and religious objects that benefited from Korea's innovation in printing technology during the Middle Ages. Sadly, not all of these treasures are still with us today. While it's true that the centuries have been unduly harsh on many of Korea's historical wonders, Bulguksa (불국사),

[5] Please see the Republic of Korea's National Folk Museum (KNFM) website at *www.nfm.go.kr/folk2002*

[6] See the KNTO's website.

[7] See the KNFM's website.

[8] Because of the nature of how Korean characters are made, the possibilities that a printer would have to take into account when preparing a document would number in the thousands. Thus, the Korean language ensured that it was just as time-consuming as Chinese to print documents with the typeface available at the time.

Changgyeonggung (창경궁), and Gyeongbokgung (경복궁) being but three examples, two artifacts of Korea's rich and distinguished history to have survived the turmoil of modern history are the **Annals of the Joseon Dynasty**, *cho-sun-wang-jo-sheel-lok* (조선왕조실록), and the **Tripitaka Koreana**, *pal-man-dae-jang-gyung* (팔만대장경).

The Annals of the Joseon dynasty were compiled over several centuries from 1392 to 1863, and comprise 1,893 books, from the reign of King Tejo (태조), the founder of the Joseon dynasty, to King Chuljong (철종). To put this number in perspective from a regional point of view, the Authentic Annals of Vietnam, as recorded during the Nguyen dynasty (1802-1945), comprise 548 books, while the official annals of China's Ming dynasty, the Huangming Shilu, comprise 2,964 books.[9]

The *Tripitaka Koreana*, which means Buddhist Canon in English, is another well-preserved piece of history that today sits inside Haein-sa (해인사), or Haein Temple, Buddhist monks first completed the *Tripitaka Koreana* in 1087 on wooden blocks.[10] The monks created the *Tripitaka Koreana* because it was a way of codifying rules that they had to live by, ways of life that were supposed to be adhered to, Buddhist philosophy, and the teachings of the Buddha as passed down through history. Kings during the Koryo dynasty believed that creating such texts would serve as a good luck charm of sorts and repel future invasions from abroad.[11] Unfortunately, the original *Tripitaka Koreana* defended against no such act.

The Mongolians arrived in Korea in the 13th century and set about destroying everything in their path, including the *Tripitaka Koreana*. Four years after the Mongolians destroyed the original *Tripitaka Koreana*, though, Buddhist monks set out once again to re-create it. This was done in 1236 under King Kojong (고종), the king who, during his reign (1213-1259), was determined to bring the *Tripitaka Koreana* back to life after seeing it burned to ashes by the Mongolians. Through diligence, hard work, and an innovative printing press system, the second *Tripitaka Koreana* was completed 15 years after it was begun. Thankfully, this second printing of the *Tripitaka Koreana* remains intact to this day, preserved marvelously through the ages by careful and attendant monks.[1]

[9] See the KNTO's website

[10] See the KNTO's website.

[11] See Life in Korea's Tripitaka Koreana website at *www.lifeinkorea.com/travel/skyongsang/tripitaka.htm*

[12] See the KNTO's website.

CREATION OF *HANGEUL*

King Sejong set out to make *Hangeul* an easy writing system by which to pronounce. Yet at the same time, he also wanted to make it a much easier language to transcribe than Chinese, the written language Koreans had been using to record official court documents since about A.D. 200. Just as King Sejong believed *Hangeul* a simple language to master phonetically, so too did he believe it an easy language to write.

Hangeul, just like Chinese, is governed by a strict set of rules by which the characters are constructed. Every character is to be drawn from up to down and from left to right. Following these two rules of writing ensures that people all draw the same characters in the same fashion, and thus lessens the confusion in how they are drawn from the lowliest citizen to the noblest government official.

For example, take a look at the *mee-eum* (ㅁ) character and the way in which it is drawn:

First Stroke	→	ㅣ	is drawn up to down (left hand side of character)
Second Stroke	→	ㄱ	is drawn left to right, and then up to down, all in one successive motion
Third Stroke	→	＿	is drawn along the bottom from left to right
Final result	→	ㅁ	is created from three strokes

Except for the fact that *Hangeul* has shrunk from 28 to 24 characters over five centuries, Korean is written much the same today as it was five hundred years ago. Interestingly, just as Latin-based languages have both print and script form, Korean has two ways of writing the language as well: print and script.

READING KOREAN

You might remember that I wrote two inscriptions at the beginning of this book, both of which sum up a lot of what I believe went into *Roadmap to Korean*. I'm going to rewrite the second one here for you to look at because there's an important lesson to be learned from it:

행 생
동 각
이 이
바 바
꾸 꾸
면 면
운 행
명 동
이 이
바 바
뀐 꾸
다 고

I first saw this on a traditional scroll, *jok-ja* (족자), years ago and looked at it for a few minutes before I realized that I had no idea how to read it. Actually, I knew how to read Korean quite well by that point, but the trouble was I didn't know whether I should be reading up to down, or down to up; left to right, or right to left; first column then second column, or second column then first column. Even if I did know which direction to read, I mused, how was I supposed to know where the spaces between the words fell? The answer to this riddle, when unraveled and written for the student of Korean horizontally, looks like this:

생각이 바뀌면 행동이 바뀌고 행동이 바뀌면 운명이 바뀐다.
saeng-kak-ee ba-kkwee-myun haeng-dong-ee ba-kkwee-go
heang-dong-ee ba-kkwee-myun oon-myung-ee ba-kkween-da

The answer to the question I posed to myself years ago about how to read this proverb, *sok-dam* (속담), is this: you read the **right column up to down**, and then the **left column up to down**.

Today, Korean is read **left to right, line by line,** from **top to bottom** most of the time. However, there are exceptions to this rule. For example, when watching a film at a movie theatre nowadays, you'll have to pick up a new skill because Korean subtitles there appear on the side of the screen as two vertical columns. The columns are read just like the proverb I used at the beginning of this book, that is, up to down, and from right to left. Also, in your travels around Korea you're bound to see Chinese characters at a lot of famous places like temples and museums. Invariably, these Chinese characters are written horizontally right to left.

WORD SPACING

The second problem I couldn't figure out when reading that proverb years ago was how to separate the words from one another. Though I was pretty sure which words were which, I wasn't *one hundred percent* sure. The positive side to Korean spacing is that it's much more flexible than English. Yet the flip side to this is that reading Korean can sometimes be a tedious act. As if the fact that Chinese characters may be strewn in and among the sentences of written Korean weren't enough, the truth is that words, and sometimes sentences, are not always separated as clearly as you would like them to be. The good news is that newspapers, applications, and reports (three things the average student or business person uses quite a bit in Korea) are almost always written with clear spaces between words.

PUNCTUATION

This is another area where written Korean has taken many liberties from an English perspective. Though originally Korean did not make use of the same punctuation as English, today the written form of the language makes use of a couple of punctuation marks. The first that is *sometimes* used is the period. Just like in English, the period clearly marks the end of a phrase or sentence. Yet it's not always used, so you have to be careful. There are certain verb conjugations, for example, which tell the reader that a Korean phrase is over or a thought completed.

The most confusing of the punctuation marks in Korean today, however, is definitely the comma. The comma is used to separate the subject from the verb in Korean without a phrase in between the two, which looks and sounds very odd in English. Here, for example, are a couple of situations where the comma is used in a strange way:

Korean Phrase	**Literal Translation**
남자, 여자와 사랑에 빠진다. (*nam-ja, yaw-ja-wa sa-rang-ae bba-jeen-da*)	A man, falls in love with a woman.
난, 'XX' 음료수 마신다. (*nan, XX eum-nyo-soo ma-sheen-da*)	I, drink 'XX.'

Because Korean has so many ways to differentiate words and parts of phrases, commas are not usually used as much in written documents as they are in English. Learning to use commas once in a while, like in the two previous examples, is a matter of practice. Though the one piece of advice I might pass on is that commas in Korean usually work in a way that is more auditory than anything; they're placed more where the speaker pauses when saying the phrase out loud than where they should be placed grammatically.

Writing Styles All Our Own

When I first began exchanging e-mails with Koreans, one of the first things I noticed was the way in which people wrote them. In English people write sentences, which form paragraphs, which in the end form the body of an e-mail. With Korean e-mails, however, there is an entirely different structure at work. First of all, there is usually no such thing as a paragraph. Many Koreans simply write one sentence or phrase at a time, line by line, for the length of the e-mail, no matter how long (or short) it is. This isn't a big deal, though it does a lot to explain why most students have a significant number of problems with writing in English. What's more interesting is what a good deal of Koreans do to inundate their e-mails so as to make them more fun or personal. What you may see adorning the average e-mail from a Korean (both professionally and socially) is a series of computer characters that, to my knowledge, have no names, but are supposed to represent people's emotions (much like the *emoticons* on MSN Messenger, for instance). So, for example, after a Korean writes a sentence, you may see one, some, or all of the following configurations: ^-^ or ^__^ or *^^* or --++ or --;;;; or ~~.

In all of these cases, the characters usually signify a smile or a laugh. The point is, it's good to be prepared when your first Korean friend e-mails you, and scattered throughout it are a bunch of indecipherable characters you may take to be nothing more than computer glitches.

WRITING KOREAN

Although written Korean has changed little over the centuries, there's no doubt that the Internet has profoundly changed the Korean language, perhaps much more than many other languages around the world. Languages are evolutionary entities that change with the times, but the speed at which Korean is changing today is unprecedented in its history. The Internet is a vehicle for change in a way that Koreans are not familiar with on a linguistic level—by creating a sense of anonymity, the Internet is breaking down the walls of traditional verb conjugations steeped in thousands of years of Confucian influence. Unlike at any other time in *Hangeul's* history when a person was writing a document with the full knowledge of the intended audience, today the Internet provides a medium by which young boys can converse freely with older men, teachers with students, grandparents with *a-joom-ma* (아줌마), and all with complete secrecy. The effect this has had on the language is profound.

People no longer have to identify themselves based on age, and so can feel freer in molding the language to suit their needs. This means that verbs no longer have to be conjugated like they once were. In a nutshell, Korean has morphed with the Internet. This marks a huge step in another direction for the movement of Korean for two important reasons.

First, it's a clear sign that the walls of Confucianism are being eroded with respect to the language. Second, it's creating a split between generations of Koreans. The young of today write words that look alien to someone studying Korean from a dictionary. Words are inevitably shortened—sometimes hacked would be closer to the truth—because this not only speeds up the typing process, but can at times eliminate the need to conjugate the verb (and thus remain more outside the boundaries of traditional Confucian verb conjugations). As a result, it's not only probable, but a virtual certainty, that an older person born before the Korean War would understand very little, perhaps almost nothing, if he or she were to log onto a popular chat site in Korean today.

This is not to say that generations are not split in other nations and cultures by language. In Korea it has more to do with the fact that the split which has occurred is of an extreme nature. Where slang is one factor among many that separates generations of speakers in English, Internet Korean (for lack of a better title) is now as much a dividing line between generations of Koreans as life experience. Examples of words used in cyberspace today include:

Original Korean/Phonetic Transliteration	**Internet Korean**	**Meaning**
반갑다 *(ban-kap-da)*	방가 *(bang-ga)*	nice to meet you /nice to see you
축하 *(chook-ha)*	추카추카 *(choo-ka choo-ka)*	congratulations/congrats

Original Korean/Phonetic Transliteration	Internet Korean	Meaning
가입 (*ka-eep*)	갑 (*kap*)	sign-in/sign-up
시험 (*shee-hum*)	셤 (*shum*)	test/exam

THE FUTURE OF WRITTEN KOREAN

The Internet will undoubtedly continue to have a significant impact on the Korean language. As Confucianism is one of the most influential aspects on Korean from a linguistic and cultural point of view, it only stands to reason that the more anonymous mediums like the Internet are explored, the more the language will have to grow with it; the laws and codification of *Hangeul* that were set down in the 15th century no longer have as much influence as they once did. That's not necessarily a bad thing, though. Change is always hard to accept, especially for the older and the more conservative, but it doesn't have to be resisted, as some people are doing these days.[13] Personally, the only problem I find is that the changes sweeping through Korean with respect to the Internet today are too much for me, a non-native Korean speaker, to keep up with. As yet, Internet Korean hasn't breached the walls of spoken conversation, however, which is of some consolation; if Internet Korean were as pervasive when people spoke, the language would be even harder to learn for the non-native speaker.

[13] There is an active campaign going on by the government to try and teach students the correct spelling of words in the Korean language, as teachers have begun complaining that spelling among younger students is becoming more and more erratic (presumably because of the Internet).

Chapter 3

Cultural Background: Religion, Confucianism and *Jung*
문화의 배경 : 종교 + 유교 + 정(情)

Korea is a nation steeped in a rich and vibrant cultural history. Unfortunately, it is a history that is at times grossly misunderstood and at other times simply unknown to people in the West. Today's media is not always the most altruistic or innocuous of mediums by which information is exchanged on a global level, and sometimes this comes back to hurt Korea more than it deserves. Stories of 'Crazy Koreans eating dogs,' 'Bear pancreases sought after for medicinal purposes,' and 'Tigers shot dead for their ability to enhance men's sexual stamina' tend to cloud the waters of reality surrounding this country's diverse and unique culture.

Sadly, one of the least talked about and least known cultural entities about Korea for Westerners today remains Confucianism. Though some have heard of a man named Confucius, most are unaware of the impact he had not just on his native China, but on Korea, too.

DIFFERING SENSES OF RELIGION

One of the biggest misnomers that has persisted for some time has to do with Confucianism's label as a 'religion.'[1] Confucius was not concerned with the

---

[1] Through my own research, I saw the word 'religion' attached to Confucianism just as often as I did not, both on Internet websites and in books.

notion of a god or of a higher being. His teachings had everything to do with the earthly, and though people in later ages built temples and shrines to commemorate and to pay homage to the great master himself, Confucianism was never a religion with one person/object the center of devotion or worship.

Part of the misunderstanding and misinterpretation with Confucianism can be derived from a linguistic point of view. In English, religion is defined as, 'the service and worship of God or the supernatural,'[2] so that when English speakers talk about any religion they automatically infer the inclusion of a God or otherworldly being. Such is not the case with Korean, however. In point of fact, actually, the word religion in Korean, *jong-gyo* (종교 · 宗敎), is defined much differently than it is in English. The Korean character *jong* (종) means **ancestral** from its Chinese roots, and the character *gyo* (교) means **teach**, making the definition of religion in Korean 'ancestral teachings,' clearly a step away from the God-centered definition religion is marked by in English.

Take as another example the linguistic roots behind the word Confucianism. The word Confucianism in Korean is *yoo-gyo* (유교 · 儒敎). The characters are derived from Chinese, *yoo* (유) meaning **scholar** and *gyo* (교), meaning **teach**, making Confucianism an ideology that promotes scholarly teaching, if translated word for word. This effectively shows that from a semantic viewpoint Confucianism does not have its roots in religion, acts of worship, God, or the otherworldly. In fact, all religions in Korean are expressed with the *gyo* (교) character, which provides yet a little more insight into the status of religions in Korea. For instance, Buddhism is *bool-gyo* (불교), the two Korean characters meaning **Buddha** and **teach**, and Christianity is *kee-dok-kyo* (기독교), the Korean characters meaning **base, oversee** and **teach** respectively.

CONFUCIUS THE MAN

Confucius was born Kong Qiu, but is known as *gong-ja-neem* (공자님) in Korean. Born in the village of Zou in the country of Lu (modern day Shantung, China) in 551 B.C, Confucius was the tenth of ten children, Confucius's father having sired nine daughters in a row. Legend has it that the day of Confucius's birth was especially auspicious, as mystical music could be heard emanating for

[2] See Merriam-Webster's *Webster's New American Dictionary*, p. 441.

miles around. Two dragons are said to have patrolled the skies warding off evil influences, while five men, representing the five known planets of the time, came down from Heaven.[3]

From his childhood years it was apparent that Confucius was no ordinary young man. He was interested in reading from an early age, and was especially interested in ancient Chinese texts. In fact, Confucius was teaching ethics, philosophy and government by the age of 21. His earliest followers called him Kang Fu-tse (Master Kang), a title that would be romanized to Confucius centuries later by Westerners living in China. (Try saying Kang Fu-tse slowly and you get the picture.)

In his day Confucius was as loved by his disciples as he was hated by jealous bystanders, such as prominent political figures vying for popularity among the people. Yet no matter how popular he was among his pupils, Confucius never enjoyed a fraction of the support and respect for his beliefs and ideologies as when he died. Posterity has treated few others in history with such awe and adulation.

Upon his death in 479 B.C., Confucianism slowly began to take shape around the boundaries of ancient China as an ethical system by which to live one's life. The first people to pay homage to Confucius were members of his own family, but almost 300 years after his death, Confucius's legend had risen from that of being a great scholar among his students to that of a cult-like figurehead.[4]

Confucius wrote and/or edited four books in his lifetime, known today as the **Four Books**: Lun Yu (Analects), Ta Hsueh (The Great Learning), Chung Yung (The Doctrine of the Mean), and Mencius (Book of Mencius). The Four Books, when combined with the **Five Classics**—I Ching (Book of Changes), Shu Ching (Book of History), Shih Ching (Book of Poetry), Li Chi (Book of Rites), and Chun Chiu (Spring and Autumn Annals)—formed the backbone of the principles of what we today know as Confucianism.

A WAY OF ETHICS

In a nutshell, Confucianism was and is a system of ethics developed from the teachings and writings of Confucius. It's concerned mainly with the

[3] See Spencer J. Palmer's *Confucian Rituals in Korea*, p. 97.

[4] See Spencer J. Palmer's *Confucian Rituals in Korea*, p. 17.

principles of good conduct, practical wisdom and proper relationships. The part that is most important for the Korean language today has to do with these proper social relationships. For Confucius, there were five basic relationships that made each person realize their place in society and their place with regards to one another. With each relationship came certain responsibilities and duties, and as a result, an obligation to speak a certain way. These relationships were not only meant to be observed among the average citizen, but among rulers as well. As one historian commented, 'A moral philosopher, Confucius based his social mindedness on a feudal ethic which expected the ruler to act with benevolence and sincerity, avoiding the use of force at all costs.'[5]

CONFUCIUS'S FIVE BASIC RELATIONSHIPS

The five relationships that Confucius espoused were as follows:

The Five Basic Relationships of Confucianism

1. Ruler and Subject

2. Father and Son

3. Elder Brother and Younger Brother

4. Husband and Wife

5. Friend and Friend

Initially, all except the last relationship involved a hierarchy, a superiority of one over the other.[6] However, over time even that last relationship came to bear some kind of hierarchy in Korea, so that today you now have older and younger friends, *sun-bae* (선배) and *hoo-bae* (후배) respectively, that speak to each other with more or less deference depending on one's age.

[5] See Arthur Cotterell's *China: A Cultural History*, p. 68.

[6] See The American Forum for Global Education's China Project website at *www.globaled.org/chinaproject/confucian/reading1.html*

THE RISE OF CONFUCIANISM

Although there has been widespread disagreement over some of the interpretations of Confucius's teachings over the ages, the central tenets of Confucianism are pretty much the same now as they were more than a thousand years ago.

The teachings of Confucius enjoyed some popularity directly after his death, but it took quite a few years before they reached a level of national conscience. Though some claim it took as little as a year after Confucius's death for the sage's teachings to be recognized for the genius they contained, it wasn't until Emperor Han Kao Tsu (206 B.C.-193 B.C.), the first emperor of the Han dynasty (206 B.C.-A.D. 220), visited Confucius's family temple in 195 B.C., though, that we have proof of such a high-ranking official, let alone an emperor, paying his respects to Confucius in any meaningful way.[7] Just over two centuries later, in A.D. 37, the first Chinese court in recorded history commanded that there be a regular cult of Confucius, and in A.D. 59 the court ordered schools in large cities throughout China to offer sacrifices to Confucius. From that time onward, wrote one scholar, 'as long as there were schools, the cult was connected with education; and it was this act which took the worship of Confucius outside [his] family and changed him from the model of scholars into their patron saint.'[8]

COMING TO KOREA

It was probably during this time that Confucianism made its way over to the Korean peninsula. However, no exact date has ever been set, as the first record of Confucianism dates back centuries after its arrival. In all probability, though, Confucianism arrived on the Korean peninsula sometime around the dawn of the Christian era.

Early on, Confucianism's impact was most apparent in the northern and western regions of the peninsula, to the north in Goguryeo (고구려), and to the west in Baekje (백제). The first evidence of institutionalized Confucianism in Korea, however, dates from A.D. 372. At the time, the king of Goguryeo, an

[7] See Spencer J. Palmer's *Confucian Rituals in Korea*, p. 17.

[8] See Spencer J. Palmer's *Confucian Rituals in Korea*, p. 17.

independent state in what is today's North Korea, established a college called *tae-hak* (태학), where the privileged could study Confucian classics. It stands to reason, then, if the first recorded Confucian school was up and running successfully by the 4th century that Confucianism had been circulating in Korea for many years before the establishment of *tae-hak*.

By the end of the fourth century, there were more Confucian academies open for students in Korea. These schools, called *kyung-dang* (경당), grew increasingly popular and ever more influential with the years, so that by the 7th century, King Sinmun (신문) opened a national Confucian school in Gyeongju, the capital of the eastern state of Silla (신라). There was even a central Confucian university in Goguryeo by this time as well, which is more proof of Confucianism's deep roots in Korea from an early age.

DIFFERENT APPROACHES TO CONFUCIANISM

The type of Confucianism that Koreans adopted was a variation of that originally practiced in China. Like other forms of Confucianism that spread in the centuries following Confucius's death, the way Koreans interpreted Confucius's teachings was unique and distinct from other nations and cultures of the time. So strict, for instance, was the Korean interpretation of Confucianism in its early days, that visitors from China commented that Korea was the country of 'Eastern decorum'[9] when they witnessed Confucian doctrine rituals in action. This was a reference to the fact that Koreans taught and followed through with all aspects of Confucius's teachings with rigid inflexibility.

By the time that Silla united the Korean peninsula in the 7th century, the first time in the peninsula's history that any state had succeeded in doing so, Confucianism had only grown greater in importance. So great was Confucianism's importance in society by the time of the Unified Silla dynasty, *tong-eel-sheel-la-shee-dae* (통일신라시대), in fact, that it had become much more than just a system of education; Confucianism was by that point also a system by which to conduct all ceremonies, and a means by which to run the civil administration.

[9] See Sangji University's (상지대학교) Confucianism website at *http://cinema.sangji.ac.kr/WINDOW/window/win00088.htm*

RIVAL BELIEF SYSTEMS: THE RISE OF BUDDHISM

Buddhism was introduced to Korea in A.D. 372 by way of China.[10] From the late fourth century on, there arose a power struggle between those that were faithful to Buddhist ways of thought and those that adhered to Confucian tenets. It was a rivalry that would span centuries. Even though the two schools of thought differed greatly and had different notions of ethics and spirituality, the ideals of each belief system caused a great amount of infighting between clans within Korea and between warring factions vying for power.

When the Silla dynasty collapsed in the early tenth century, Goryeo was quick to pick up the pieces as the unifying political force on the peninsula. By then Buddhism was in great favor among those governing and Confucianism had fallen out of political favor, much as it had in China.[11]

This may have had something to do with the fact that when Buddhism was first introduced to Korea it was through the region then known as Goguryeo, the northern part of the Korean peninsula. Goryeo's capital was located at today's Gaeseong (개성), a city in the south of modern day North Korea. The capital being moved back closer to Buddhism's original roots on the Korean peninsula plausibly helps explain why Buddhism became much more influential during this era.

RESURGENCE OF CONFUCIANISM

That was not to be the end of the power struggle between Buddhism and Confucianism, though. By the time of the Joseon dynasty (조선시대), which unified the peninsula from 1392 to 1910, Buddhism's influence had waned and Confucianism was once again in favor among the power elites. So much so, that state civil service examinations, known as *kwa-gaw* (과거), relied heavily on the teachings of Confucius to test potential civil servants. For the entirety of the Joseon dynasty, Confucianism remained an integral part of the education system, the civil service and of ceremonial practices.

With the Japanese annexation of the Korean peninsula in 1910, parts of Confucian doctrine died, never to be revived again, similar to what would

[10] See L.R. Lancaster and C.S. Yu's *Introduction of Buddhism to Korea: New Cultural Patterns*, p. 4.

[11] In fact, according to Arthur Cotterell's *China: A Cultural History*, Buddhism was brought under control of the Chinese state during the Tang dynasty (618-907), a little earlier than it was in Korea.

happen in China two years later with the rise of the Republic of China (1912-1949). Never again, for example, would Confucianism play such a critical role in the testing of potential civil servants, nor would people perform the ritualistic offerings at temples and shrines in such numbers again. There was one important element of Confucianism that survived the Japanese occupation and still exists to this day, though—the five basic relationships that Confucius set forth two and a half millennia ago.

MODERN LEGACIES OF CONFUCIANISM ON THE KOREAN LANGUAGE

Today, it's difficult to miss the way in which Koreans conduct themselves, the way in which they speak, the way in which they hold a cup when pouring, the way they smile, and laugh, and cry—everything, in short, that defines them on a social level. Confucianism still remains an integral element in the way Koreans act much more than it does in China, for example, where Confucianism died an ugly death in the aftermath of the Communist revolution. Just as centuries ago when visitors from China commented on the fact that Confucianism was a more rigidly respected doctrine in Korea than it was in its founding home, so, too, today does it remain a more important influence on the lives of Koreans.

As will be looked at in subsequent chapters, the notion of Confucian levels of respect and relationships still affects the Korean language deeply. This is most clearly evident in the levels of respect that are given which range from the informal and familiar, *ban-mal* (반말), to the formal and less familiar, *jon-dae-mal* (존대말).[12]

As a cultural influence it is critical to understand the importance that these Confucian levels of respect have on the Korean language. Subsequent chapters will look at this effect from other viewpoints, such as grammar, but before entering that nasty land of verb and adjective conjugation, I can't overstate the importance of keeping these five social relationships in mind when conversing in Korean every minute of every day; failure to do so will inevitably lead to misunderstandings and, worse yet, insults and unintended mistakes. Yet by keeping these social relationships in the back of your mind when speaking, the most difficult and most critical part of the language—conjugation—will become that much easier.

[12] These two concepts will be explained in depth in **Ch. 8**.

THE CONFUCIAN NAIL OF ASSIMILATION

It may be a Japanese proverb, but, 'The nail that sticks out gets hammered down,' is just as relevant to life in Korea as it is to life in Japan. There is another aspect to the social legacy of Confucianism that is not talked about quite as much, but it is just as powerful as the system of ethics on the language: taking care not to rock the boat.

You don't even have to know how to speak Korean to see this part of Confucianism at work in Korea today. The five basic relationships of Confucianism are supposed to be maintained and respected for the betterment of the majority, for the harmony of the whole, as opposed to the individual. This is why most people do not like to break with the times in any way, shape or form, and so the homogeneity of Korean culture is readily evident at almost every turn. If one doesn't want to eat, but the rest of the group is going to eat, tough cookies. If one does not want to go out with his or her co-workers after a long day at work, it's tough beans when it's a *hwae-sheek* (회식), those infamous staff parties that involve a huge amount of drinking. Independent thought, as it were, is a slippery concept in Korea.

Going off and doing your own thing is not only seen as the incorrect way by which to live your life in Korea, it's almost an alien concept. On a linguistic note, this is the clearest example of why the verb 'to endure' is so readily thrown around by Koreans in everyday conversation. Due to the fact that Koreans translate this verb literally, you're able to hear it come out in their discussions in English a great deal of the time. Talk of enduring the test, or enduring a boss's tirade, or enduring the awful situation, is as commonplace in English by a Korean as it is in Korean through the verb *cham-da* (참다).

Lessons in Ordering

With time to burn before our bus left, my girlfriend and I were waiting in front of a Dairy Queen at the bus station and thought a quick bite before

---

our departure would be a wise idea. I walked up to the counter and ordered two hot dogs. However, knowing that Korean restaurants generally load things down with the works, I asked them to put only ketchup and mustard on the hot dogs. The young lady behind the counter nodded like it was an everyday request and went about preparing them for me. A few minutes later she handed me two hot dogs with everything on them: relish, onions, ketchup, and mustard.

I looked down, then looked up. Then I looked down once again. Then up. And then I blinked a couple of times. 'But I ordered them with ketchup and mustard,' I protested.

'Oh, really?' the young lady answered, looking genuinely baffled.

'Yeah. I'm sorry, but could I get two more hot dogs with just ketchup and mustard? I can't eat relish.'

'Okay, sir. I'm sorry.'

A few minutes later

'What's this?' I asked as I looked down upon a fully dressed hot dog.

'It's your hot dog, sir.'

Blink, blink.

'But I ordered it with ketchup and mustard.'

The young lady then blinked. 'What?'

'Ketchup and mustard,' I repeated.

'What do you mean?'

At this point in the conversation I stared at the two girls behind the counter with something akin to great wonder. Mouth fully agape, I couldn't comprehend the situation. On the third try I finally got my two hot dogs with ketchup and mustard, but it was a painful lesson I was to learn that day. Koreans have a certain way in which they do everything it seems, and one of those ways includes the method by which to order fast food. Now me, being ignorant of this, thought that I could order a hot dog with the condiments of my choice, not knowing that every Kim, Lee and Park only took the hot dog as it was given to them.

As soon as I realized that, I started understanding other things that had confused me before, like the fact that waitresses at restaurants never gave me my rice when I asked for it, but rather when they thought it was time (i.e. when the soup was ready). It never mattered that I wanted to eat my rice beforehand, for example. The fact that every Korean eats their rice with their soup meant that I had to do that too.

Once I began to fully comprehend the group mentality and how it functioned in Korea, my days became a lot smoother and the number of misunderstandings I had at places like restaurants decreased substantially.

THE SPIRIT OF *JUNG*

Just as a knowledge of Confucian relationships is beneficial to excelling in Korean, an understanding of *jung* (정) is also helpful in navigating your way through the always challenging waters of the Korean language.

What is *jung* (정 · 情)? Some dictionaries define it as 'feeling,' and nothing more, but I find this definition seriously lacking. My favorite Korean-English dictionary defines *jung* as, 'affection, love, compassion, sympathy, tender feelings, longing, yearning.'[13]

The word *jung* is not well known among many native English speakers living in Korea, but that doesn't decrease or otherwise diminish its importance. *Jung* is one of the hardest words to translate into English, partly because it is so representative of an entire nation's character, which makes finding one word for it in the English language next to impossible.

Jung is a word that describes both a horizontal and vertical system of relationships, depending on the two people involved. For example, it is the horizontal relationship between two friends, but becomes a vertical relationship between parents and children, between the emperor and the subject, and the teacher and the student. *Jung* encompasses all aspects of friendship, but is in no way sexual, nor is it erotic (even between lovers). It is a feeling of deep understanding and compassion towards another person. It's the reason, so some

[13] Minjungseogwan's *Essence Korean-English Dictionary*, p. 1286.

Koreans say, that people in this country are so kind and generous towards people they don't know (e.g. strangers from other countries), and towards those they do know (i.e. friends and loved ones).

It is said that *jung* develops between people on a personal basis, as opposed to a sociological phenomenon in large groups, though that is still possible when the affiliation is strong (such as a group of old high school friends or people from the same office). *Oo-jung* (우정) is the *jung* between friends,[14] while *ae-jung* (애정) is the *jung* between lovers or married couples. However, Koreans will point out that *jung* is in no way homosexualized, which means from a technical standpoint, two homosexuals cannot share *jung* in the traditional sense of the Korean word. This linguistic fact provides another insight into the Korean character by extension; homosexuals still being demonized in Korea, they are not part of one of the defining characteristics of Korean society.

One quaint analogy I heard about *jung* was that it's like water coming up from underneath the ground. Slowly, but surely, the water rises only to eventually reach the surface and spread across the sand. Never too quickly, the water is always rising at a constant pace that is akin to the development of two people's friendship, or love for one another.

Just as an understanding of Western history and the notion of independence is beneficial to understanding a Westerner's character, for example, so too is *jung* important in understanding the Korean character. Opening up to someone and talking in this language is not the same thing as it is in English. Although *jung* is never verbalized, never talked about (like love is, for instance), it is always 'there' in Korea. Two people feel it or they don't. If it's felt, then the relationship blossoms; if it isn't, then the relationship doesn't blossom. That's not to say that there's anything like negative *jung*, though. Rather, it's more like the saying in English, You've either got it or you don't. Once this notion of *jung* is felt, however, the person opens himself or herself up, almost transforming into another person.

[14] The word *oo-jung* (우정) is also the word in Korean for 'friendship.'

Chapter 4

High- and Low-Context Languages

고배경 + 저배경 국어

The title of this chapter may throw some readers off momentarily. To be honest, I had no idea what the terms high-context and low-context meant when I first started learning Korean, and I can only wish I did.

Put simply, Korean is a high-context language. This means that when Koreans speak Korean they do not always look for clear, exact verbal expressions. High-context languages like Korean (and certain other Asian languages, for instance) rely more on an interpretation of shared assumptions, non-verbal signals, and situations to clarify matters that may not be said directly.

English, on the other hand, is a low-context language. This means that people who have English as a mother tongue often say exactly what is on their minds (much to the consternation of their parents). They speak directly, and from the heart. They 'shoot from the hip,' 'let it all hang out,' and a hundred other phrases and idioms that describe the way that people who have English as a first language speak to each other.

For those that have not learned a high-context language this idea may be hard to conceptualize. Basically, the argument goes something like this: the average person who grows up in Canada, for example, will talk candidly with whomever he or she is talking with because it's not only expected, but a natural way of communicating. This may not seem like a big deal to some native English speakers, but I can assure you that it takes readjusting to when learning Korean.

Almost Hard

After realizing that I was going to be in Korea for an extended period of time, I went to the bank one day with the intention of applying for a credit card. I was confident that my Korean was at a level whereby I could perform such an action, but as I was to learn, that was not to be the major problem of the day.

Upon sitting down across from the young man who dealt in the credit card division, he told me that it would be 'almost hard,' *kaw-ee heem-deu-raw-yo* (거의 힘들어요), to get a credit card as a foreigner. I mulled over the words 'almost hard' in my mind before responding. 'Well, that's okay. I'm willing to do whatever it takes to get one,' I said with a smile. He in turn then responded through a thinly disguised nervous laugh, 'But, sir, it is almost hard.'

This was when I still believed that words like 'can' and 'can't' still carried merit, so I figured that because he didn't say directly, 'It's impossible for foreigners to apply for credit cards,' that it was *possible* to get a credit card. I sat and talked with the bank employee for several minutes before asking in a huff, 'Look! *Can* I get a credit card or can I *not*?!' He remained much more composed than me and said simply in conclusion, 'It is almost hard.'

I walked out of the bank in a very bad state, frustrated that I could not get an answer to my question about applying for a credit card. Yet after talking it over with a Korean friend that same day, I realized that 'almost hard' is a more acceptable, more indirect, more high-context way for Koreans to say that it is not possible to do something. There I had been pressuring the man at the bank to say something I could relate to, Yes or No, and he must have been thinking to himself, 'Wow! Some people just don't get it when you tell them it's almost hard!'

READJUSTMENT PERIOD

Being a high-context language, Korean leaves much unsaid. When Koreans talk with each other there is a great deal to be derived from body language, from the relationship of the two speakers, and from the situation surrounding the conversation. To put this a little more simply, Koreans don't always speak their mind (or don't always speak their heart, as they might say). For people just arriving in Korea and learning this esoteric language, this poses a huge stumbling block. Learning to understand the culture here in Korea is imperative to learning the language for this very reason.

To give an example of how and why it's necessary to listen and interpret words differently in Korean, consider the words 'can' and 'cannot.' They are so common in English that most people don't even realize how often they use them. Their usefulness is not at all dulled by their constant use, however. 'Can' and 'cannot' are clear indicators of what is possible and what is not possible, what we are able to do and what we are unable to do, what is within our reach and what is not within our reach. The same *cannot* be said of Korean. That's not to say that the Korean language does not have the auxiliary verbs can and cannot. On the contrary, the language has these two conjugations, *hal soo eet-dda* (할 수 있다), and *hal soo awp-dda* (할 수 없다) respectively.[1] The problem is, unlike English, they're not used by Koreans nearly as often.

I remember learning how to say 'I can' and 'I can't' in Korean years ago and walking around feeling a sense of liberation. This feeling of euphoria waned quickly, though, when I realized that people were not reciprocating its use with the same frequency. Though I didn't know the terms high- and low-context language at the time, this was to be my first insight into the way Korean wasn't as direct linguistically as English. Can you send me the file? we ask our boss at work. Can you speak Spanish? we ask a friend. Can you come to the movies with me this weekend? we ask a classmate. These situations will all be answered with clear answers that divulge the answer we are seeking, Yeah, I can, or Unfortunately, I can't, or some other like-minded answer.

Not only are these questions phrased differently in Korean much of the time,

[1] Actually, the words 'can' and 'cannot' do not necessarily have to be preceded by the verb *ha-da* (하다), but for the sake of explaining this point more easily, I've used the verb *ha-da*. Also, three more common ways to express the ability to do something are *hae-do dwae-da* (해도 되다), *ka-neung-ha-da* (가능하다), and *hal-jool-al-da* (할 줄 알다), usually translated as 'can,' 'possible,' and 'able' respectively.

34

but the answers are as well. When I first started teaching in this country I was baffled by students who responded to questions like, Can you play the piano? with, But I don't play now. When I asked, Can they join us for dinner tonight? people replied, But they are teachers.

At first this may just seem like a grammatical problem, but there is more to this than meets the eye—literally. Look at the following examples of what I mean by this last point of can and can't and see how it works in Korean on a linguistic level:

Korean/Phonetic Transliteration	**Literal Translation**	**Natural Translation**
보이냐? (bo-ee-nya?)	Is it seen?	**Can** you see it?
잘 안 보여요. (chal an bo-yaw-yo)	It is not seen well.	I **can't** see it (very well).
영어 하세요? (yung-aw ha-sae-yo?)	Do you speak English?	**Can** you speak English?
보내 주시겠어요? (bo-nae joo-shee-gaes-saw-yo?)	Will you send it (to me)?	Do you think you **could** send it (to me)?

Another example of Koreans not being direct linguistically is the only-too-common, seemingly ubiquitous 'maybe.' Though some visitors to Korea don't ever pick up on this, even after years of interaction with Koreans, the fact is that the Korean language itself is ladled with grammar structures that imply that something is not definite, when everyone knows it clearly is. That's why Koreans, when speaking English, say things absolutely baffling with regards to the use of maybe. Look at these examples for a better understanding:

Korean Phrase	Usual Translation	Natural Translation
수업에 못 갈 것 같아요. (*soo-awp-ae mot kal kut kat-a-yo.*)	Maybe I can't go to class.	I can't go to class.
누나가 키가 클 거 같아. (*noo-na-ga kee-ga keul-gaw kat-a.*)	Maybe your sister's tall.	Your sister's got to be tall.
아마 (*a-ma*)	Maybe (not)	Yes/No

LEARNING TO DO MORE THAN JUST LISTEN

Sometimes it won't actually be what is said, but what isn't said that you have to read into. I was brought up to believe that when we see people we know, especially those that we consider good friends or colleagues from work, that not saying hello is extremely rude. However, early on in my time in Korea, I confronted friend after friend on the street whom I said, *an-nyung-ha-sae-yo* (안녕하세요) to, only to be greeted with nothing more than a grunt or a nod. At first, this troubled me greatly. Had I upset or offended that person in some way that I was unaware of? I asked myself time after time this happened. It wasn't until I began to understand the intricacies of age as the deciding factor for relationships that it started to make sense.

In Korea, once a relationship is established (i.e. after the first time you meet, for example), it is common for the older person in the relationship to do nothing more than acknowledge someone's presence with a perfunctory nod, perhaps a grunt if the age gap is extreme, but certainly nothing amounting to a full-blown hello. This is in no way rude in the English conception of the word rude or impolite, but merely an understanding of who is older and who is younger. In cases like this, it then becomes very important to read into body language, as opposed to the spoken words you might expect as a Westerner, for instance.

THE SMALLEST HEADACHE

Aside from there being innuendos and connotations in the conjugation of Korean verbs, there is something even more cunning at work within the mechanics of the language: topic markers. With the addition of a single character, an *eun* (은) or *neun* (는) topic marker, there can, at times, suddenly be something assumed about the phrase. What this assumption is depends on the situation and what is actually said, but the point is that what seems like a harmless character is really a major headache when trying to communicate fluently in this language. (The concept of topic markers is explored in depth in **Chapter 7**).

SUGGESTIONS TO THINK ABOUT

Lecturers that prepare business people and diplomats for work in Korea tell them that they should be sensitive to body language, for a smile is not always a smile, a frown not always a frown. That is absolutely true. But in learning the Korean language, it's also important to pick up on clues that are offered through the language itself. These range from the speaker avoiding the subject, to answers and responses that are cryptic and confusing if directly translated into English. For this reason I've put together a short list that new students to the Korean language can keep in mind so as to avert major problems with the high-/low-context language problem in the future:

> **1. Don't be pushy when searching for an answer**. This is especially true if you are older than the person you are speaking with. In cases where there is a significant age barrier, the Korean you're speaking with may simply lower their head for the duration of your questioning, look away, or otherwise be evasive when they don't know the answer to your question.

> **2. Make yourself as clear as possible within the limitations of your linguistic ability**. You may have to rephrase the question for the benefit of the listener, but try as best you know

how to work around the problem instead of bulldozing through it with anger or frustration.

3. A smile on a Korean's face is not always because they are happy. A smile can often times mean the person is embarrassed or shy. This takes a lot of practice because Westerners are so used to smiles being positive and friendly reminders that the person we are with is enjoying himself or herself. Not always so with Korean.

4. Try and learn how to read other signs to communication. This includes everything from the way a Korean **directs their eyes** toward you (or not at you for that matter), to the **amount of laughter** they let out (too much laughter can often be a clear signal that the person has no idea what you just said and is laughing to disguise this), to the way the **person shakes your hand** (a dead fish handshake is not necessarily bad), to the way a **person toasts when drinking together** (the younger person should have their cup or glass lower than the older person), to the way the **person addresses you** (whether the person uses your first name, a title like *sun-saeng-neem* (선생님) or *a-ja-shee* (아저씨), for example, can tell you a lot about the person and the level of respect they are giving you).

These tips will not ensure that there is perfect communication between you and your Korean counterpart, but it will begin to make you, the student of Korean, better prepared for what lies ahead in countless conversations, board room meetings, and classrooms.

BUT WHAT DO YOU *REALLY* MEAN?

I've had a debate with friends before as to whether the greeting 'How are you?' has any substance to it in English. I maintain that it has some intrinsic value, and that if people treat it like a pre-programmed question with a pre-programmed answer (Fine thank you, and you?) then that is more a reflection of their character than the question itself. When people ask me, How are you? I personally try and give an honest answer.

When people greet each other in Korean, though, they never ask, 'How are you?'[2] If you haven't seen someone for a long while, then it's possible that they might ask, *chal jee-naes-saw-yo?* (잘 지냈어요?), 'How have you been?' What is asked in place of How are you? in Korean is usually something totally different: **Where are you going?** or **Have you eaten?** These two common questions are asked in replacement of How are you? when seeing someone on the street, in the hallway at work, or talking with someone on the phone. However, contrary to what I thought initially, these two questions are *not always* meant to be answered. The assumed response (i.e. the pre-programmed answer) in these situations is sometimes more acceptable, especially with large age gaps between people. For instance, the first time I heard a conversation carried out like the following example, I was confused:

Korean Phrase	Phonetic Transliteration	Translation
A: 어디 가세요?	*aw-dee ka-sae-yo?*	Where are you going?
B: 예, 예.	*yae-yae*	Okay.

With regard to the question, 'Have you eaten?' I just thought everybody was interested in my eating habits in the beginning, but then realized over time that it was just a matter of using it as an icebreaker. Simply answering yes or no is sufficient to keep the flow of the conversation going naturally.

[2] No matter what textbooks tell you and no matter what Koreans might believe themselves, there's no such question as 'How are you?' in Korean. Contrary to some opinions, *an-nyung-ha-sae-yo* (안녕하세요) is nothing more than 'Hello,' and *chal jee-nae-da* (잘 지내다) is only used when seeing someone you know after a prolonged absence. Even though a word (or phrase) like *an-nyung-ha-sae-yo* is written with a question mark sometimes, it is not a question in the English sense of the word, which is why someone can respond to your greeting with a cursory nod.

Part 2

Approaches to Korean:

Fundamental Aspects of the Language and the Great
Leviathan Called Verb Conjugation

Like licking the skin of a watermelon
수박 겉 핥기

Chapter 5

Romanization
로마자 표기법

One of the more confusing aspects of the Korean language today is the romanization system, *lo-ma-ja pyo-gi-bup* (로마자 표기법), adopted by the South Korean government in 2000.[1] When the government initially decided to change the romanization process, the bulk of the work fell to the National Academy of Korean Language (NAKL), a research institute under the Ministry of Culture and Tourism.

Although the new transliteration process went into effect right away for all government-related documents, the Ministry of Culture and Tourism allowed more time for different parts of the government to adopt these changes. All publications (including textbooks), for example, were required to use the new romanization process by February 28, 2002, and all public signs were required to abide by the changes by December 31, 2002,[2] a task that has yet to be completed.

AT A LOSS FOR LETTERS

The National Academy of Korean Language (NAKL) was created 'to establish language policies which encourage the Korean people to use their language correctly and appropriately...and other matters which promote the dignified use

[1] Only the South Korean government adopted this new romanization process, so that the spelling of Korean words in English from North Korea is now different.

[2] See the Republic of Korea's Ministry of Culture and Tourism website at *www.mct.go.kr*

42

of the Korean language and contribute to the development of Korean culture.'[3] An extension of the Korean Language Research Institute (KLRI), the NAKL was launched in January 1991.

The reason the old romanization system—known as the McCune-Reischauer System—was changed at all, purports the government, was for a host of reasons that range from the technical (the difference between voiced and non-voiced sounds, the use of the breve above certain letters) to the practical (making it easier to type Korean on a standard computer keyboard).

Essentially, however, the change came about to streamline the whole romanization process so that the Korean language would not be a hindrance in the information age (the breve and the apostrophe were seen as drawbacks). It was also done so that Korean names would become more uniform. Finally, the new romanization process was introduced so that consonants and vowels would be readily identifiable (for Koreans).

While it's true that Koreans need to have an efficient and streamlined way of romanizing words from their own language, it's equally true that but for a fraction of visitors to this country, no one is able to read *Hangeul.* This means that visitors from around the world now come to Korea and pronounce words like *Silla* (신라), *Daecheon* (대천), *Gimpo* (김포), and *Jamsil* (잠실) incorrectly.[4]

Romanization is most visitors' lifeblood to understanding anything in Korea. The old system for transliterating Korean into English was far from perfect, but in terms of the phonetic sounds being transliterated into Latin letters, they were closer, in my opinion, with most words. Now, however, even someone like myself who speaks Korean and who has access to both pronunciation patterns, has trouble understanding newcomers to Korea because the words they are reading in English often come out sounding completely unlike their Korean counterparts.

FROM OLD TO NEW AND EVERYTHING IN BETWEEN

The old McCune-Reischauer (M-R) System of romanization for the Korean language was developed in 1939. Until 2000, the M-R System was the romanization system most identifiable throughout the world. Maps, dictionaries, encyclopedias, and newspapers made use of this system of transcribing Korean into English.

[3] See the National Academy of Korean Language's (NAKL) website at *www.korean.go.kr/eng/intro/intro1.html*

[4] This, in fact, was an exact point some of the foreign press picked up on when reporting from South Korea during the 2002 FIFA World Cup. Some travelers complained of not being able to identify major cities and towns because official tourist maps had places spelled differently than travel guides.

The old M-R System was clearly imperfect, not least because it had funny looking symbols laden throughout the transliterations, but it served its purpose usefully and consistently in other areas. The following is a table of how the old transliteration system was derived:

McCune-Reischauer Romanization System for the Korean Language

Korean Vowels, *mo-eum* (모음)	Romanized Letter(s)	Korean Consonants, *ja-eum* (자음)	Initial Position	Medial Position	Final Position
ㅏ	a	ㄱ	k	k, g (between vowels and after m, n, g, l), ng (before m, n, l)	k
ㅑ	ya	ㄴ	n	n, l (when preceded or followed by l)	n
ㅓ	o	ㄷ	t	t, d (between vowels)	t
ㅕ	yŏ	ㄹ	n	r (between vowels), l (before all other consonants, and after n, l), n (after other consonants)	l
ㅗ	ŏ	ㅁ	m	m	m
ㅛ	yŏ	ㅂ	p	b (between vowels), m (before m, n, l), p (before and after all other consonants)	p

Korean Vowels, *mo-eum* (모음)	Romanized Letter(s)	Korean Consonants, *ja-eum* (자음)	Initial Position	Medial Position	Final Position
ㅜ	u	ㅅ	s, sh (before wi)	s, sh (before wi), n (before m, n, l)	t
ㅠ	yu	ㅇ	SILENT (not romanized)	not romanized, ng (after syllabic final)	ng
ㅡ	u	ㅈ	ch	j (between vowels, and after m, n, ng), ch (after all other consonants)	t
ㅣ	i	ㅊ	ch′	ch′	
ㅐ	ae	ㅋ	k′	k′	
ㅒ	yae	ㅌ	t′	t′	
ㅔ	e	ㅍ	p′	p′	
ㅖ	ye	ㅎ	h	h	
ㅚ	oe	ㄲ	kk	kk	kk
ㅟ	wi	ㄸ	dd	dd	
ㅢ	ŭi	ㅃ	pp	pp	
ㅘ	wa	ㅆ	ss	ss	
ㅙ	wae	ㅉ	tch	tch	
ㅝ	wŏ				
ㅞ	we				

While attempting to streamline the vowels and consonants of the Korean language, on top of doing away with the breves and the apostrophes, the Ministry of Culture and Tourism released the following table in 2000:

New Romanization System (Simplified Table)

ㅏ	ㅓ	ㅗ	ㅜ	ㅡ	ㅣ	ㅐ	ㅔ	ㅚ	ㅟ	ㅑ	ㅕ	ㅛ	ㅠ	ㅒ	ㅖ	ㅘ	ㅙ	ㅝ	ㅞ	ㅢ
a	eo	o	u	eu	i	ae	e	oe	wi	ya	yeo	yo	yu	yae	ye	wa	wae	wo	we	ui

Initial	Initial	ㅇ	ㄱ	ㄴ	ㄷ	ㄹ	ㅁ	ㅂ	ㅅ	ㅈ	ㅊ	ㅋ	ㅌ	ㅍ	ㅎ
Final[5]	Final		g	n	d	r	m	b	s	j	ch	k	t	p	h
ㄱ	K	g	kg	ngn	kd	ngn	ngm	kb	ks	kj	kch	kk	kt	kp	kh(k)
ㄴ	N	n	ng	nn	nd	ll(nn)	nm	nb	ns	nj	nch	nk	nt	np	nh
ㄹ	l	r	lg	ll	ld	ll	lm	lb	ls	lj	lch	lk	lt	lp	lh
ㅁ	M	m	mg	mn	md	mn	mm	mb	ms	mj	mch	mk	mt	mp	mh
ㅂ	P	b	pg	mn	pd	mn	mm	pb	ps	pj	pch	pk	pt	pp	ph(p)
ㅇ	ng	ng	ng	ngg	ngn	ngd	ngn	ngm	ngb	ngs	ngj	ngch	ngk	ngp	ngh

Here are some words that compare the old McCune-Reischauer System to the new government-sponsored one:

Korean Name	M-R System	New System	Korean Name	M-R System	New System
부산	Pusan	Busan	대구	Taegu	Daegu
광주	Kwangju	Gwangju	대전	Taejŏn	Daejeon
인천	Inch'on	Incheon	전주	Chonju	Jeonju
제주	Cheju	Jeju	청주	Ch'ŏngu	Cheongju
경주	Kyŏngju	Gyeongju	김포	Kimp'o	Gimpo
고구려	Koguryŏ	Goguryeo	동대구	Tongdaegu	Dongdaegu

THE MISSING 'H'

One of the most conspicuously missing letters from the new romanization process is the letter H from six specific Korean characters, *shee* (시), *shwee* (쉬), *sho* (쇼) *sha* (샤), *shoo* (슈), and *shaw* (셔). As a result, today's government-sponsored romanization system includes words and phrases like Silla (신라), as in the dynasty that unified the Korean peninsula over a thousand years ago (properly pronounced as *Shilla*), *si* (시), as in the word that means 'city' and 'poem' in Korean, and is properly pronounced *shee*, and *bosyeosseoyo?* (보셨어요?), as in the question that means, Did you see it? and is properly pronounced *bo-shaw-saw-yo?*

I believe that the letter H needs to be reintroduced to the romanization

5 'Final' refers to the final position character in a Korean block character. 'Initial' refers to the first position character in a Korean block character. When the final position character of one syllable is followed by the first position character of the next, the phonetic value of either or both characters changes in a limited number of cases, as demonstrated here.

process. For me, and others like me who are concerned about the future of the Korean language, there is no bigger misunderstanding with the transliteration process than the fact that the government does not recognize an H sound in certain Korean characters. The longer it's omitted, the longer Korean will be a mishmash of broken sounds and phonemes when transliterated in English. (For more information on the pronunciation of Korean, please see **Chapter 6**.)

Origins of the Name Korea

Although there is no empirical evidence of exactly when and from where the country name Korea derived its origins, we do have some idea of its early roots.[6] The first non-Orientals to conduct trade with the Koreans were probably either the Persians or the Arabs sometime around A.D. 1000. Aside from Japan, Korea really was the farthest trading outpost that Europeans, Arabs, or Persians could venture to. Thus, it's no wonder why it remained a secret to the Western world for so long.

As most accounts go, the Arabs or Persians that arrived in Korea a thousand years ago were told that the name of the ruling dynasty over the peninsula was Goryeo (고려), the dynasty that we now know ruled from the 10th to 14th centuries. When the traders from the far west left and brought back their newfound knowledge of the boundaries of Asia, they recounted their tales about a land far past the great riches of India and China, a land, they said, called 'Corre.'

Over the centuries this name would change form in the Latin script to the point when it became 'Coree' (from the French, who also left us the modern day spelling of Seoul). English speakers from Britain and the United States eventually changed this spelling slightly, so that they commonly referred to 'Coree' as 'Korea.' It wasn't until the establishment of the Republic of Korea on July 17, 1948, though, that the controversy was settled once and for all. From that time on, the country that is famous for *kimchi* and *soju* has been known as Korea with a capital K.

[6] See the Korea National Tourism Organization's (KNTO) website at *http://english.tour2korea.com/html/main/basic_info/basic_history.html*

IS THERE A MIDDLE GROUND?

While the new system of romanization is excellent in some ways, such as the fact that it is now easier to transcribe Korean characters onto a computer, there are still serious flaws with it. If it were possible to do anything else in the future, I would propose keeping the new system developed by the government with the *exception* of all family names, business names, and proper nouns. This would mean that corporations (e.g. Hyundai, Samsung, Daewoo, etc.) to personal names (e.g. Mr. Park, Mrs. Chung, Ms. Seo, etc.) to cities and villages (Inchon, Kwangju, Taegu, etc.) would be spelled as they were before 2000, and as they were written for most of the 20th century.

Chapter 6

Pronunciation

발음

Pronunciation is one of the toughest parts of Korean. Newcomers to the language almost invariably have the same reaction, How do you pronounce that? Although many of the sounds are *similar* to ones in English, there are a few sounds in Korean that simply don't exist in English, and so people learning Korean, especially those that do so outside of Korea, have a heck of a time wrapping their tongue around the language.

Linguists rave about the orthography (spelling) and phonetics (sounds) of Korean. Originally designed to be very scientific in nature, *Hangeul*'s 24 characters all correspond to one phoneme (an elementary unit of speech that separates one utterance from another) that almost never change. Unlike English, scholars point out, where one letter can have several different sounds, in Korean, each character, called a *geul-ja* (글자), corresponds to one sound (with a few exceptions).[1] Vowels always have the same sound, it's just the consonants that change depending on where they are placed, respective to the other characters.[2]

Hangeul is very unique in that it combines elements of two different systems. On the one hand *Hangeul* has an alphabetic system (each character representing a phoneme), which includes, for example, characters like ㅂ, ㅁ,

[1] In Korean, the term *geul-ja* (글자) refers both to the single character (e.g. ㄱ, ㄹ, ㅗ) and to the block character (e.g. 잔, 강, 벼).

[2] See the Republic of Korea's Ministry of Culture and Tourism (MCT) website at *www.mct.go.kr* for more information about the pronunciation of *Hangeul* according to the government. The way I think Korean characters are pronounced is slightly different and explained in detail in subsequent sections of this chapter.

and ㅏ. Yet *Hangeul* also combines elements of a syllabic system (each syllable easily recognizable by its separation from another set of characters), such as 비, 운 and 가.

A HEAVENLY LANGUAGE

King Sejong wrote in the preface to *hoon-meen-jung-eum* (훈민정음):

> The sounds of our language differ from those of Chinese and are not easily communicated by using Chinese ideographs. Many among the ignorant, therefore, though they wish to express their sentiments in writing, have been unable to do so up to now. Considering this situation with compassion, I have recently devised 28[3] characters. I wish only that the people will learn them easily and use them conveniently in their daily lives.[4]

Even though the written language created under Sejong's reign would derive most of its meaning from Chinese characters, the sounds by which Koreans spoke these words changed after the release of the *hoon-meen-jung-eum* (Correct Sounds to Teach the People).

The 24 characters that today make up the written portion of the Korean language have an extremely interesting history with regards to the sounds that are associated with each one. The ten basic vowels, called *mo-eum* (모음), of today's *Hangeul* (ㅏ, ㅑ, ㅓ, ㅕ, ㅗ, ㅛ, ㅜ, ㅠ, ㅡ, ㅣ) are derived from three basic geometric shapes (ㅣ and · and ㅡ), which represent the three fundamental elements of Eastern cosmology:

ㅡ　is based on earth
ㅣ　is based on humanity
·　is based on heaven[5]

By combining any or all of these three basic shapes, every vowel is created.

[3] As explained in **Ch. 1**, Korean now only makes use of 24 characters, though originally there were 28 characters to *Hangeul*.

[4] See
http://korea.insights.co.kr

[5] See
http://korea.insights.co.kr

50

Linguistic scholars claim that this feature of combining basic vowels to create further vowel character blocks corresponds to generative theories of modern mathematics and science.[6]

The fourteen consonants, called *ja-eum* (자음), (ㄱ, ㄴ, ㄷ, ㄹ, ㅁ, ㅂ, ㅅ, ㅇ, ㅈ, ㅊ, ㅋ, ㅌ, ㅍ, ㅎ), were developed in strict scientific accordance just like their vowel counterparts. The five basic consonants (ㄱ, ㄴ, ㅁ, ㅅ, ㅇ) were created from the shapes of vocal organs in mind, while the rest of the consonants were made by either adding a stroke or slightly altering the shape of one of the five basic consonants. The five basic consonants were formed by the following principles:

ㄱ depicts the root of the tongue blocking the throat
ㄴ depicts the outline of the tongue reaching the upper palate
ㄷ depicts the outline of the mouth
ㅅ depicts the outline of the incisor (front teeth)
ㅇ depicts the outline of the throat

Basic vowels and consonants are then combined to form more complex characters, referred to sometimes as block characters, which have exactly one syllable. So, for instance, in the case of *dak* (닭), ㄷ is combined with ㅏ and ㄹ and ㄱ to form a word which means chicken, *dak*.[7]

SIMILARITIES TO THE LATIN ALPHABET USED TODAY

Like English, Korean characters have names for the characters themselves, some having independent sounds from the way in which they are pronounced when used to form words. Just as the letter A is pronounced one way as a letter in English and uttered differently when used to form a word like 'apple,' characters in Korean often function in a similar way. Korean vowels are the only exception to this rule. All vowel names and vowel sounds (i.e. the way they are pronounced), be they simple or in block form, are exactly the same in Korean. Only consonants and complex consonants have names to the characters that are different from their phonetic sounds. For example, the simple

[6] See *http://korea.insights.co.kr*

[7] Block characters may have several meanings, sometimes upwards of 20 or 30 meanings that are spelled the exact same way in Korean. See the insert in **Ch. 21** for an example of this.

character, ㅏ, is called *ah,* while the block character 아 is also pronounced *ah.* Alternatively, the simple character ㄱ is called *gi-awk,* while the block character 가 is pronounced *ka.* Take a look at the following table for a complete listing of Korean simple and complex character names:

Simple Character Names

Korean Character, geul-ja (글자)	Phonetic Transliteration of Character's Name[8]
ㄱ	*gi-awk*
ㄴ	*nee-eun*
ㄷ	*dee-geut*
ㄹ	*lee-eul*
ㅁ	*mee-eum*
ㅂ	*bee-eup*
ㅅ	*shee-ot*
ㅇ	*ee-ng*
ㅈ	*jee-eut*
ㅊ	*chee-eut*
ㅋ	*kee-euk*
ㅌ	*tee-geut*
ㅍ	*pee-eup*
ㅎ	*hee-eut*
ㅏ	*a*
ㅑ	*ya*
ㅓ	*aw*
ㅕ	*yaw*
ㅗ	*o*
ㅛ	*yo*
ㅜ	*ooh*
ㅠ	*yoo*
ㅡ	*eu*
ㅣ	*ee*
ㅐ	*ae*

[8] It's impossible to capture the names of Korean characters in English, so this table should only be used to serve as a rough guide to the sounds.

52

Complex Character Names

Korean Character, *geul–ja* (글자)	Phonetic Transliteration
ㅒ	*yae*
ㅔ	*ae*
ㅖ	*yae*
ㅘ	*wa*
ㅙ	*wae*
ㅚ	*wae*
ㅝ	*waw*
ㅞ	*wae*
ㅟ	*wee*
ㅢ	*eui*
ㄲ	*ssang gi-awk*
ㄸ	*ssang dee-geut*
ㅃ	*ssang bee-eup*
ㅆ	*ssang shee-ot*
ㅉ	*ssang jee-eut*

The Name Game

I have a difficult name to pronounce in Korean. Between my given and family names there are three R's, a letter with a sound that is not very compatible in Korean. Koreans tell me that for the most part my Korean accent is excellent, and I believe that with Korean words this is true. However, give me a word transliterated from English into Korean and people always double-take with me. 'Yea?' they ask me, sometimes more than once. 'What was that you said?'

Chief among all these foreign words that cause me considerable angst and pain is my own name. After years in this country—and tons of practice —I still can't get people to understand it all the time. 'What was that you said?' people ask me on the phone more often than not.

'Richard Harris.'

'Lee-coo-du He-ree?'

'No. My name is Richard Harris.'

'What?'

'Richard Harris', I say again, patiently

'I'm sorry. I have no idea what you just said.'

'Right. Lee-cha-de Hae-ree-se.'

'AH, YES! I see. I see. How are you Lee-cha-de?'

For the first few years this really got me down, especially on the phone when I couldn't write my name down for the listener to see in plain view. Yet after a while it got me thinking that I had to make more light of the situation. On good days, I have people fooled that they're talking with a native Korean speaker, but on the bad days, I inevitably have to go through the linguistic gymnastics of saying my name over and over and over …

A DIFFERENCE IN OUTLOOK

When the government changed the official romanization process, they not only changed the way in which Korean words are spelled in Latin letters, but the way in which the words are pronounced in English. Although I believe some of the sounds that the government now recognizes from Korean (when transliterated phonetically into English) are correct, I still think there are flaws. That's why I've created my own transliteration tables. The following tables, unlike the ones offered previously, do not list the name of a character but its sound when combined to make a word as a part of a block character:[9]

[9] Please see the MCT's website at *www.mct.go.kr* for the South Korean government's own chart on pronunciation.

54

Vowels, *mo-eum* (모음)[10]

Korean Character, *geul-ja* (글자)	Phonetic Transliteration
아	*ah* (as in, 'Ah! This hurts')
야	*ya* (as in 'yahoo')
어	*aw* (as in 'awful')
여	*yaw* (as in 'yawn')
오	*o* (as in the letter 'O')
요	*yo* (as in 'yo-yo')
우	*oo* (like the 'u' in 'super')
유	*yoo* (as in the pronoun 'you')
이	*ee* (as in the letter 'E')
으	There's no sound for this character in English, but it sounds something like 'eung,' minus the 'ng' sound

Complex Vowels

Korean Character, *geul-ja* (글자)	Phonetic Transliteration
ㅐ	*ae* (as in the letter A)
ㅒ	*yae* (as in the first syllable of the country 'Yemen')
ㅔ	*ae* (as in the letter A)
ㅖ	*ae* (as in the letter A) when preceded by any consonant except the ㅇ character, *yae* (as in Yemen) when preceded by the 'ㅇ' character
ㅘ	*wa* (as in the group Wham!)
ㅙ	*wae*
ㅚ	*wae*
ㅝ	*waw* (as in 'wash')
ㅞ	*wae*
ㅟ	*wee*
ㅢ	*eui* (there's no sound in English that matches this very well. It's a combination of the sounds 'eu,' as in 'eung,' and 'E,' as in the letter E.)

[10] Vowels always go in the second position of a Korean block character.

55

CONSONANTS: FIRST POSITION [11]

The way you pronounce certain Korean consonants depends on whether it's in the first or the final position of the block character, the first position being defined as the character in the upper left hand part of the block character. Therefore, if you consider an example such as *dan* (단), the first position character is the ㄷ character. On the other hand, the final position character is defined as the character at the bottom of the block character. So, using the same example as before, the final position character is the ㄴ character. Here's a breakdown of the sounds associated with consonants in the first position:

Korean Character, *geul-ja* (글자): First Position	Phonetic Sound in English
ㄱ	Somewhere between a soft 'K' sound and a hard 'G' sound
ㄴ	'N' sound
ㄷ	Somewhere between a soft 'T' sound and a hard 'D' sound
ㄹ	Sometimes an 'L' sound, sometimes an 'R' sound. It depends on the situation
ㅁ	'M' sound
ㅂ	Somewhere between a soft 'P' sound and a hard 'B' sound
ㅅ	'S' sound
ㅇ	SILENT
ㅈ	Somewhere between a soft 'CH' sound and a hard 'J' sound
ㅊ	'CH' sound (as in 'cheese')
ㅋ	'K' sound (as in 'kit')
ㅌ	'T' sound (as in 'tiger')
ㅍ	'P' sound (as in 'pipe')
ㅎ	'H' sound (as in 'help')

[11] There's always a consonant in the first position of a Korean block character. Sometimes, though, there may also be a consonant in the third position. Occasionally, there is even a consonant in the fourth position as well.

COMPLEX CONSONANTS: FIRST POSITION

Complex consonants have two of the exact same characters beside one another. There are only five complex consonants, but they manage to be a source of great angst for many people learning Korean. Officially, the South Korean government does not recognize the fact that the Korean language has tones, which means that for the above mentioned, Koreans think the characters are simply double consonants. The problem with that explanation is that in English there is no difference in pronunciation between 'sshark' and 'shark'; no difference between 'ddate' and 'date.' For that reason, the traditional explanation is confusing.

There is no way to explain double consonants justly without hearing how a native Korean speaker pronounces them. When I write that they are high pitched, I say that because I know of no other way to describe the sound you make when trying to distinguish the complex consonants from the simple ones. Take a look at the following table:

Korean Complex Character, ssang-geul-ja (쌍글자)	Phonetic Sound in English
ㄲ	a high pitched 'K' sound
ㄸ	a high pitched 'T' sound
ㅃ	a high pitched 'P' sound
ㅆ	a high pitched 'S' sound
ㅉ	a high pitched 'J' sound

CONSONANTS: FINAL POSITION

Consonants that are located in the final position of a block character, the ㅊ character in the case of soot (숯), for example, sometimes change sounds. When pronouncing a word in Korean with a consonant in the bottom position, you have to be careful in certain circumstances not to pronounce it the same way you would if it were in the first position. For a complete breakdown of the sounds associated with final position consonants, take a look at the following chart:

Korean Character, *geul–ja* (글자): Final Position	Phonetic Sound in English
ㄱ	'K' (as in 'mark')
ㄴ	'N' (as in 'man')
ㄷ	'T' (as in 'mat')
ㄹ	'L' (as in 'low') or 'R' (as in 'rap')
ㅁ	'M' (as in 'mom')
ㅂ	'P' (as in 'pope')
ㅅ	'T' (as in 'mat')
ㅇ	'NG' (as in 'making')
ㅈ	'T' (as in 'mat')
ㅊ	'T' (as in 'mat')
ㅋ	'K' (as in 'mark')
ㅌ	'T' (as in 'mat')
ㅍ	'P' (as in 'pope')
ㅎ	SILENT

To give you an idea of how these characters sound with real words, consider the following examples:

Korean	Phonetic Transliteration	Korean	Phonetic Transliteration
옷	*oat*	넣	*naw*
갑	*kap*	싱	*sheeng*
숯	*soot*	찾	*chat*
일	*eel*		

COMPLEX CONSONANTS: FINAL POSITION

Complex consonants (ㄲ, ㄸ, ㅃ, ㅆ, ㅉ) are rarely used in the final position of a Korean character. Fortunately, though, when they're used in the final position, their sound doesn't change from that of being in the first position. So, for example, in the case of *bak-kae* (밖에), the K sound stays the same as if it were in the first position.

TWO CONSONANTS: FINAL POSITION

Korean characters that have two consonants in the final position can be really difficult for new students to the language. The reason they're more difficult than the average block character is that there's no set rule on how to pronounce the character. No single Korean character is more than one syllable, which means trying to pronounce these kinds of words is challenging, even to students that have been studying the language for a long time. The best approach is, of course, to ask a Korean how to pronounce the word, but short of having a Korean to ask, the next best thing to do is to sound out the word. If it sounds awkward, chances are it's not the right pronunciation. If the word flows, however, then chances are you're pronouncing the word correctly. Look at the following examples:

<u>Korean</u>	<u>Phonetic Transliteration</u>	<u>Meaning</u>
늙다	*neuk-dda*	to be old
읽다	*eek-dda*	to read
뚫다	*ddool-ta*	to master, to pierce
값	*kap*	price
젊다	*jum-dda*	to be young (i.e. people)
짧다	*jjal-dda*	to be short (i.e. objects, not people's height)
넓다	*nul-dda*	to be wide/spacious

The only way this kind of Korean character is made easier to pronounce is when it precedes a vowel. In cases such as these, the first of the two consonants is pronounced with the first block character, and the second of the bottom two consonants is pronounced along with the second block character. Take a look at some examples:

Proper Korean	**How It Sounds in Korean**	**Phonetic Transliteration**	**Meaning**
늙은 사람	늘근 사람	*neul-geun sa-ram*	an old person
읽어야지	일거야지	*eel-gaw-ya-gee*	you should read it
값이	갑씨	*kap-sshee*	price
젊은 여자	절믄 여자	*jul-meun yaw-ja*	a young woman
짧은 머리	짤븐 머리	*jjal-beun maw-ree*	short hair

EXCEPTIONS TO THE RULE

As scientific as *Hangeul* is with its rules and laws of pronunciation, there are some exceptions that have to be kept in mind. These exceptions can be tricky, as they become exceptions only after a combination of certain characters (i.e. it's not the block character itself that is the exception, but the fact that one certain character precedes or follows another certain character). The following table details the exceptions to pronunciation:

Korean Word/Phrase (Incorrect Pronunciation)	Exception to the Rule	Correct Pronunciation
신라 (*sheen-ra*)	ㄴ precedes ㄹ	실라 (*sheel-la*)
음력 (*eum-ryuk*)	ㅁ precedes ㄹ	음녁 (*eum-nyuk*)
명륜동 (*myung-ryoon-dong*)	ㅇ precedes ㄹ	명뉸동 (*myung-nyoon-dong*)
국민 (*kook-meen*)	ㄱ precedes ㅁ	궁민 (*koong-meen*)
금리 (*keum-ree*)	ㅁ precedes ㄱ	금니 (*keum-nee*)
독립문[12] (*dok-reeb-moon*)	ㄱ precedes ㄹ	동님문 (*dong-neem-moon*)
독립문 (*dok-reeb-moon*)	ㅂ precedes ㅁ	동님문 (*dong-neem-moon*)
받는 (*bat-neun*)	ㄷ precedes ㄴ	반는 (*ban-neun*)
좋다 (*cho-da*)	ㅎ precedes ㄷ	조타 (*cho-ta*)
좋기도 (*cho-gi-do*)	ㅎ precedes ㄱ	조키도 (*cho-kee-do*)
익히다 (*eek-hee-da*)	ㄱ precedes ㅎ	이키다 (*ee-kee-da*)
받히다 (*bad-hee-da*)	ㄷ precedes ㅎ	바치다 (*ba-chee-da*)

[12] While not the norm, a word like *dong-neem-moon* (독립문) is extremely difficult for students to pronounce properly because it contains not one, but two exceptions to the rule.

Korean Word/Phrase (Incorrect Pronunciation)	Exception to the Rule	Correct Pronunciation
십리 (*sheep-ree*)	ㅂ precedes ㄹ	심니 (*sheem-nee*)
합니다 (*hap-nee-da*)	ㅂ precedes ㄴ	함니다 (*ham-nee-da*)
먹는다 (*mawk-neun-da*)	ㄱ precedes ㄴ	멍는다 (*mawng-neun-da*)
밟히다 (*balb-hee-da*)	ㅂ precedes ㅎ	발피다 (*bal-pee-da*)

DICTIONARIES

So, you're a little confused about a word in Korean and want to look it up in your trusty Korean-English dictionary, do you? There's a problem, though. How do you look up a word in a Korean dictionary? That's a good question and fortunately the answer is relatively easy. Like English, *Hangeul* is a collection of characters, the characters being listed in a specific order. Therefore searching for a word in Korean is just like searching for a word in English: follow the order to the Korean alphabet, after you've memorized it, of course, and find the word in no time flat. Korean consonants fall in order as listed here:

ㄱ(ㄲ), ㄴ, ㄷ(ㄸ), ㄹ, ㅁ, ㅂ(ㅃ), ㅅ(ㅆ), ㅇ, ㅈ(ㅉ), ㅊ, ㅋ, ㅌ, ㅍ, ㅎ

You can search for a word by looking at the first character of the word (which will always be a consonant) and then flipping to the part of the dictionary where that character lies. Therefore a word like *hae-hwa* (혜화) comes at the back of the dictionary and a word like *kee-reum* (기름) falls somewhere near the beginning.

VOWELS

Due to the fact that Korean block characters build upon themselves, the process of searching for a word becomes a little more complicated. Listed below is the order in which vowels fall in the dictionary:

ㅏ, ㅐ, ㅑ, ㅒ, ㅓ, ㅔ, ㅕ, ㅖ, ㅗ, ㅘ, ㅙ, ㅚ, ㅛ, ㅜ, ㅝ, ㅞ, ㅟ, ㅠ, ㅡ, ㅢ, ㅣ [13]

Following this order then, a word like *a-ma-do* (아마도) would be found early in the ㅇ section, whereas a word like *eep-da* (입다) would be found at the back of the ㅇ section.

ONE MORE INGREDIENT IN THE LINGUISTIC STEW

Unfortunately, that's not where all the fun stops on the whirlwind tour of the Korean-English dictionary. There is still the matter of the double consonants, *ssang-geul-ja* (쌍글자). These always come at the end of the same character section. Consequently, ㄲ comes at the end of the ㄱ section, and ㄸ comes at the end of the ㄷ. Other consonants that have the *ssang geul-ja* capability (i.e. ㅂ, ㅅ, and ㅈ) fall at the end of their respective sections.

MAKING SENSE OF ALL THE WORDS

As I mentioned before, you need to keep two things in mind when searching for a word: the placement of the consonant and the placement of the vowel. To put this in simple terms, consonants always come first and vowels always come second. Let's take a look at an example.

Take the word *sa-jun* (사전), which means dictionary, for example. The first character is the ㅅ character. If you look at the list I provided on consonants, you'll see that the ㅅ character falls between the ㅂ and ㅇ characters, somewhere near the middle of the dictionary. The next character in the word 사전 is the ㅏ character. Now the ㅏ character is at the beginning of the vowel list, so we've stumbled upon a piece of good luck. However, unless 사전 is the only word in Korean that starts with 사, you're going to have to continue your search, this time using the ㅈ character as your next point of reference. Following this through, the complete breakdown of the word 사전 looks like this:

ㅅ →ㅏ →ㅈ→ㅓ →ㄴ

[13] Although I've listed the vowels here without any accompanying consonants, Korean vowels as a rule have to be preceded by a consonant when used to form block characters. For the sake of making the vowels easier to recognize, I've taken the preceding 'ㅇ' character away.

To give but two more examples to look at, consider the words *kawm-pyu-taw* (컴퓨터) and *kwaen-chan-ta* (괜찮다). In the first case, you can find the word toward the end of the dictionary (between the ㅊ and ㅌ characters). A breakdown of the Koreanized version of 'computer,' *kawm-pyu-taw* (컴퓨터), looks like this:

$$ ㅋ → ㅓ → ㅁ → ㅍ → ㅠ → ㅌ → ㅓ $$

Subsequently, a breakdown of the next word, *kwaen-chan-ta* (괜찮다), looks like this:

$$ ㄱ → ㅙ → ㄴ → ㅊ → ㅏ → ㄴ → ㅎ → ㄷ → ㅏ $$

Truthfully, it does take some time to get used to this way of searching for words, but it eventually gets easier (I promise), so don't worry. You'll get the hang of it once you start using a Korean-English dictionary with any amount of regularity.

AND WHEN YOU FIND THE RIGHT WORD IN THE DICTIONARY...

Once you've figured out how to read a Korean dictionary, the next thing that may surprise you is the translation itself. You hear a word in Korean used over and over, look it up in your trusty dictionary, and discover the translation to be a word or a phrase that you rarely ever use in English. You understand the meaning, but you can't understand why the translation was written just so. This is, sadly, a sign of things to come.

Translations of Korean words into English in dictionaries are usually awkward (sometimes wrong, in fact) for three main reasons. First, Koreans wrote many of the dictionaries, and so people who speak English as a second language wrote the translations. Second, many dictionaries are archaic. My favorite dictionary, and the one I use to this day, was printed almost 30 years ago. The reason I continue to use it is because it is nothing if not detailed in its explanations in both Chinese and Korean. However, with an outdated dictionary, I get translations like 'salacious,' 'hoodwinked,' and 'unsavory,' three words I, personally, never use. Third, no dictionary that I've come across properly documents the word in Korean with a situational description. As you've seen through this whole book, Korean words are extremely complicated, usually backed by a long history, and tied to a complex system of cultural beliefs.

What this all means is that you have to take dictionary translations with a pinch of salt, a dash of pepper, and a touch of patience. Find the word you're looking for, read the word or phrase that you think comes closest to describing it (there will be a more detailed explanation with more complicated words), and then make a note of it, especially if it's really complicated. After you've done all this, ask a Korean for a more elaborate explanation. Chances are that the word you want to know from Korean, or vice-versa for that matter, isn't completely and exactly explained in a standard dictionary. However, the more you take this thorough approach to finding definitions, the clearer you're going to understand each one you come across.

Chapter 7

Grammatical Structure
문장형식

Although the written form of the Korean language is replete with evidence backing up its origins, the spoken form of the language remains much more mysterious. Although modern science is yielding more insight into the inhabitants both on and off the Korean peninsula, documentation about Korean's early roots is still a dark shadow. According to the South Korean government:

> The origin of the Korean language is as obscure as the origins of the Korean people. In the 19th century when Western scholars "discovered" the Korean language, from what family of languages the Korean language derived was one of the first questions posed about the language. These scholars proposed various theories linking the Korean language with Ural-Altaic, Japanese, Chinese, Tibetan, Dravidian Ainu, Indo-European and other languages. Among these theories, only the relationship between Korean and Altaic (which groups the Turkic, Mongolian and Manchu Tungus languages) and the relationship between Korean and Japanese have continuously attracted the attention of

comparative linguists in the 20th century.

Altaic, Korean and Japanese not only exhibit similarities in their general structure, but also share common features such as vowel harmony and lack of conjunctions, although the vowel harmony in old Japanese has been the object of dispute among specialists in the field. Moreover, it has been found that these languages have various common elements in their grammar and vocabulary. Although much work remains to be done, research seems to show that Korean is probably related to both Altaic and Japanese.[1]

THOSE GHASTLY VERBS

English and Korean differ in a number of ways.[2] The first thing that many native English speakers find great difficulty adjusting to is placing the verb at the end of the sentence in Korean. Moreover, verbs are memorized in English, whereas they are conjugated depending on the verb in Korean, so there's no memorization in the same sense as there is in English. On top of that, verbs are conjugated for situation in Korean (i.e. social situation and relation of speakers).

AND A KNOWLEDGE OF GRAMMAR!

Another difficult aspect of Korean that drives many people crazy is the fact that it demands a thorough knowledge of grammar. Unlike English where people simply make a sentence and have the contents of its parts understood by each word's placement in a phrase, Korean requires subject and object markers, as well as something called particles, which can loosely be translated as prepositions, and in the case of adverbs, an adverb marker. So, for instance, whereas in English the speaker puts the words where they 'feel right' most of the time, not necessarily knowing if what they're saying or writing is a noun, adverb, adjective, pronoun, subject, object, or the like, in Korean, almost every word is marked for the role it plays in the phrase. For example, the following sentence, **I learned Korean this morning**, when translated directly into Korean comes out as:

[1] See the Ministry of Culture and Tourism's (MCT) website at *www.mct.go.kr*

[2] This chapter is intended to serve as nothing more than an introduction to Korean grammar. For those interested in understanding more complex grammar in a wider range of areas, please refer to a comprehensive book on Korean grammar.

Today morning (particle) **I** (subject) **Korean** (object) **learned**
(past tense verb, conjugated for situation and level of respect).[3]

Added on top of all this is the fact that Korean often drops the subject of the phrase if it is understood between those taking part in the conversation. Thus, if you're joining a conversation after it's begun, you might find yourself lost and bewildered. For example, a sentence directly translated from Korean could look something like this in English:

So went to store and bought drink because wanted to have good time with older friend who came with younger friend.

However, that's not to say that the subject is always dropped. Another tough aspect of the Korean language is the inclusion of titles in replacement for names (a theme explored in more detail in **Chapter 17**). This means that even if a subject is used, it is not always clear who exactly the subject is.

Let me provide a few examples of how this mysterious language functions on a basic level before I go any further:

Korean	**Direct Translation**	**Proper Translation**
1. 어디 가요? (*aw-dee ka-yo?*)	Where go?	Where are you going?

In the first example, you see one of the most common questions used when greeting someone in person. *Aw-dee* (어디) means 'where,' while *ka-yo* (가요) means 'go,' but there is no inclusion of a subject, namely, the person being spoken to.

| **2.** 밥 먹었어?
(*bam maw-gaws-saw?*) | Rice ate? | Have you eaten?/Did you eat? |

[3] In this example, the speaker would literally be including the words 'object' and 'subject' in their speech.

67

In the second example we get a peek at another common greeting used in Korean. In this question, *bap* (밥) means 'rice,' and *maw-gaws-saw?* (먹었어?), means 'Did you eat?' Put together, the question is meant to inquire whether or not you've eaten a meal. (i.e. breakfast, lunch, dinner)

3. 저는 버스를 탔어요.   I bus took.   I took the bus.
(*jaw-neun bu-se-reul tas-saw-yo.*)

In the third example you see some of the more complicated aspects of Korean grammar come to the forefront. Here *jaw* (저) means 'I,' *neun* (는) being a topic marker, which tells us that the speaker is the subject of the phrase. *Bu-se* (버스) means 'bus' (literally), *reul* (를) is an object marker that signifies the use of it as the object of the phrase, and *tas-saw-yo* (탔어요) means 'took' or 'rode.' So, even though you have a subject and an object (whoopee!), you now have to distinguish them from each other with separate markers, using both sides of our brain to put the sentence together, while thinking of the grammar at the same time (boo!).

4. 나는 중국에 갔다왔어.   I China to went and came.   I went to China.
(*na-neun choong-gook-ae*
kat-da-was-saw.)

In the fourth example, *na* (나) means 'I' (in a more casual form than the previous example), *neun* (는) is again used as a topic marker, *choong-gook* (중국) means 'China,' *ae* (에) is a particle which refers to movement (like 'to' might be used in English in this case), and *kat-da-was-saw* (갔다왔어) means 'to go and come' in the past tense, or simply 'went' in everyday English.

MORE GRAMMAR (THE FUN NEVER STOPS!)

As you can see from the examples previous, not only is it imperative that you learn to manipulate language in a new way, but that you understand grammar at a fundamental level. This is not to say that learning Korean requires a rocket scientist's knowledge of grammar and structure and predicates and so on and so forth. What it means is that the student of this marvelous language need only learn how to build sentences with one, two and three verbs, identify the subject and the object in a phrase, and learn to use particles.

SUBJECT AND TOPIC MARKERS

Marking the subject of a phrase (or the topic as the case may be) is a real challenge in Korean. Just locating the subject of a basic sentence can be a real challenge for some native English speakers; learning to distinguish between a topic marker and a subject marker can turn this into an even bigger conundrum for many.

THE ONLY EASY PART TO IT

Although there is a difference between a topic marker and a subject marker in Korean, there is rarely a difference in the English translation, which makes defining the differences in English that much harder. Technically, subject markers (S.M.) are *ee* (이) and *ga* (가), while topic markers (T.M.) are *eun* (은) and *neun* (는). In truth, however, the differences can seem very complicated to someone just starting their studies in Korean.

The only easy thing to remember about both sets of markers is that once you've decided on which marker you're going to attach, there are strict rules about which one is chosen, depending on the final character of the preceding character; *ee* and *eun* only come after final-character consonants; *ga* and *neun* only come after final-character vowels. For example,

Korean Word	Subject/Topic Marker	Reason	Phonetic Transliteration
지하철[4]	이	final character ㄹ, from 철	*gee-ha-chu-ree*
잔	은	final character ㄴ, from 잔	*jan-eun*

[4] This example is slightly different in pronunciation than most other examples because of the inclusion of the ㄹ character. When a vowel follows right after the ㄹ character (in the final position), the pronunciation changes slightly.

Korean Word	Subject/Topic Marker	Reason	Phonetic Transliteration
컴퓨터	가	final character ㅓ, from 터	*kawm-pyu-taw-**ga***
자전거	는	final character ㅓ, from 거	*ja-jun-gaw-**neun***

ARE THEY REALLY THAT DIFFERENT?

Although there are basic laws which govern when to use a topic marker and when to use a subject marker, it is extremely difficult for many Korean language students (even people who have been working with the language for years) to master the nuance of when to use one and not the other. The basic differences can be summarized as follows, though:

1) Subject Markers: 이/가

a) When a subject is introduced, the subject marker is usually used to distinguish it in the phrase or sentence. So if, for example, you were to make a random comment about the sky, it might look like this:

The sky is beautiful.   하늘이 아름다워요.   *ha-neu-ree a-reum-da-waw-yo.*

b) If answering a who/what/where/which question, the subject marker is once again used. For example:

Which one is the book? 어느 것이 책입니까? *aw-ne gaw-shee chaek-eem-nee-kka?*

This one is the book. 이것이 책입니다.   *ee-gaw-shee chaek-eem-nee-da.*

2) Topic Markers: 은/는

a) On the other hand, if the subject you're talking about is relaying information which has already been mentioned, then the topic marker is used. For example:

Where's the phone? 전화가 어디에 있어요?   *jun-hwa-ga aw-dee-ae ees-saw-yo?*

It's beside the store. 전화는 가게 옆에 있어요. *jun-hwa-neun ka-gae yawp-ae ees-saw-yo.*

In this example, the phone, *jun-hwa* (전화), is the subject of the sentence and is introduced (we assume) in the question because the *ga* subject marker is attached to it. In the answer, however, because we now know that we're talking about a telephone, the *neun* topic marker is used (which implies old information).

b) In instances where the subject of the sentence is described as the topic word of the sentence (e.g. when the verb 'to be' is used in many cases), then the 은/는 topic marker is used, even when the subject is new information that we're just being introduced to. For example:

I'm a student.   나는 학생이에요.   *na-neun hak-saeng-ee-ae-yo.*

c) When contrasting information (in an abstract way) between a subject that was previously mentioned, the topic marker will also be used. Sometimes this means that the topic maker will replace an object marker (you should definitely be shaking your head at this time and saying to yourself, Could this get any harder??). Thus, the following example appears grammatically wrong (in English), but is correct nonetheless because it shows a contrast of information.

I like dogs.   개를 좋아합니다.   *kae-**reul** cho-a-ham-nee-da.*

But I don't like cats.   그렇지만 고양이는 *ke-raw-chee-man go-yang-ee-*
(and I'm not talking about dogs) 안 좋아합니다.   ***neun** an cho-a-ham-nee-da.*

In this example, the dog, *kae* (개), is the object, *reul* (를), of the person's first sentence, while in the second sentence, cat, *go-yang-ee* (고양이), is the topic, *neun* (는), when it is clearly the object of English translation. Also, the contrast given here implies that although the person doesn't like cats, this has no bearing on whether or not he likes dogs.

d) With sentences where there is a vague contrast, the 은/는 topic marker is used once again. Cases like this have no structural connection between the topic and the subject, but a slight connection means that both sets of markers may be used in the same sentence. Look at the following example:

I feel great today.   오늘은 기분이 좋아요.   *o-neu-reun kee-boon-ee cho-a-yo.*

This last example is particularly confusing because both markers are used in the same sentence, thus creating the illusion that there are two subjects (from an English point of view). The truth of the matter is that Korean is a little more subtle than English in this case because the Korean sentence tells us that we're only talking about 'today' (the topic), but that 'I' (the subject) 'feel great' (as opposed to yesterday). Lastly, in this previous example the thing that makes it even harder to understand in English is that 'I' is the subject in English, whereas your 'feeling,' *kee-boon* (기분), is the subject in Korean.

HONORIFIC SUBJECT MARKERS

Finally, if showing another person (as a subject) a high degree of respect, the subject marker is changed to *ggae-saw* (께서), irregardless of the final subject character, as shown in the following examples:

If you're free…   선생님께서 시간 있으시면⋯ *sun-saeng-neem-ggae-saw shee-gan ees-se-shee-myun⋯*

Mr. Kim is really nice. 김선생님께서 아주 친절해요. *Kim-sun-saeng-neem-ggae-saw a-joo cheen-jul-hae-yo.*

In the first example a final-character consonant (ㅁ) precedes the subject marker, where the subject might be a second person teacher (you) or a third person teacher (Mr. Kim, for instance). In the second example a final-character vowel (이) precedes the subject marker.

HOW AM I EVER GOING TO WRAP MY HEAD AROUND THIS?

As if learning Korean were not hard enough, the introduction of subject and topic makers seems to make this whole thing even more complicated than you had ever imagined. Don' t fret, though. Because both sets of markers (이/가 and 은/는) can technically distinguish the subject of the sentence, it' s not critical that you use one or the other for a Korean to understand you. Though there can be slight differences in the connotation of the sentence when one is used and not the other, you will in most likelihood be understood by a Korean as long as you're using one of the markers to distinguish the subject of the phrase or sentence.

In researching this book I asked many Koreans, including many Korean language teachers, if it was a matter of strict importance whether students at a low level or just getting started with the language used one set of markers over the other. Invariably, the answer was no, it was not absolutely critical that one be used over the other. The thing that they told me was what I would also tell you when considering which marker to use for the subject or topic of a sentence: as long as you're marking the subject with an 이, 가, 은, or 는 character you'll be safe in most instances.

DROPPING MARKERS

This title may seem like a cruel statement after everything I've written about subject, object and topic markers, but the fact of the matter is that they're not always needed. You read that correctly. You *may not* need them in certain circumstances; it always depends on the situation. Subject, object and topic markers can be dropped at will by the speaker when the situation permits it. When does the situation permit it? Good question.

Usually when the subject/object/topic is clearly understood between the two speakers the marker can/will be dropped. Not only that, the entire subject may be dropped in some instances. For example:

Wow, I'm/it's cold.	아~ 추워	*ah~ choo-waw.*

In this example, we can safely assume that the room or weather is cold (we'd need to know more information or have a visual to know for sure) and that the subject is the person saying this statement or the weather/temperature.

Bad Boy

Sitting around talking to a close friend of mine in Korean some years ago, his girlfriend made some witty remark that made me laugh. I, thinking the remark was decidedly sexual, then turned to my friend's wife and said, 'You *bad* girl,' which I took to be *na-ppeun-nyun* (나쁜년) in Korean. At the time, everyone at the table stopped talking and looked at me with grave fear on their faces, eyes bulging out of their sockets.

The smile was still on my face when my friend explained to me that I had just called his wife a 'bitch.' After hastily trying to explain what I had meant, I thought to myself, 'No, this is okay. I'm getting used to embarrassing myself like this. I like it. It humbles me.' A simple mistranslation was all it took in this case to momentarily offend my close friend's wife and put me in the doghouse. What else was I to think, though? *Na-ppeun* (나쁜) means 'bad' in Korean, and *nyun* (년) means 'girl' or 'woman,' thus making what I assumed was 'bad girl.' Foolish me. Whatever could I have been thinking trying to translate directly from English!!

OBJECT MARKERS, *MOK-JUK-KYUK JO-SA* (목적격 조사)

The next part of one's grammar that must be revisited is the object of a phrase. Although Korean has a few exceptions where the object in English is not the object in Korean (see **Chapter 8** for more on this), the two languages usually see eye to eye on this point. An object is distinguished in Korean by one of two markers, an *eul* (을) or a *reul* (를). The first object marker, *eul* (을), is used when the last character of the object ends in a consonant, while the second marker, *reul* (를), is used when the last character of the object ends in a vowel. Here are a few examples with object markers (O.M.):

Korean Phrase (Consonant as Final Character)	**Object Marker**	**Phonetic Transliteration**
한국**말**을 배웠어요. I('ve) learned **Korean**.	을	*han-goong-ma-**reul** bae-wus-saw-yo.*
사**전**을 읽어요. I'm reading a **dictionary**.	을	*sa-jun-**eul** eel-gaw-yo.*
컴퓨**터**를 썼어요. I used the **computer**.	를	*kum-pyu-taw-**reul** ssus-saw-yo.*
차를 가지고 왔어요. I brought my **car**.	를	*cha-**reul** ka-gee-go was-saw-yo.*

PARTICLES, *JO-SA* (조사)

The last item of grammar that you'll need is the **particle**. The particle is loosely translated as a preposition, however there is one fundamental difference between a Korean particle and an English preposition: Korean particles can be dropped in conversation. This is yet another example of how written and spoken Korean differ.

Particles are similar to prepositions in that they attach themselves to nouns and pronouns to form phrases. All particles are used both in *ban-mal* and *jon-dae-mal* situations except *ggae* (께), which is the honorific way of saying *ae-gae* (에게), and so is only used in *jon-dae-mal*.

In written Korean, particles basically serve the same function as prepositions in English, but when speaking Korean there is a lot more flexibility to drop the particle(s). For a rough translation of the major particles, look at the following:

Korean Particle	English Preposition(s) Used in Same Situation(s)
에[5] *ae*	**to/on/at**
에서 *ae-saw*	**from/at/for/on**
에게 *ae-gae*	**to/from**
께 *ggae*	**to** (honorific)
에게서 *ae-gae-saw*	**from** (this particle isn't used a lot in conversation, as it's replaced by *ae-gae* (에게) on most occasions)
(으)로[6] *(e) ro*	**to/by/through/on/in**
한테 *han-tae*	**to/from**
한테서 *han-tae-saw*	**from** (this particle isn't used a lot in conversation, as it's replaced by *han-tae* (한테) on most occasions)
부터 *boo-taw*	**from**
까지 *kka-gee*	**until/till/by**
사이 *sa-ee*	**between**
(이)랑 *(ee)rang*	**with**

Here are some example sentences to see how particles are used in everyday Korean:

Korean	Phonetic Transliteration	English
한국말로 하세요.	*han-goong-mal-**lo** ha-sae-yo.*	You can say it **in** Korean
인터넷으로 못 찾았는데.	*een-taw-nae-**se-ro** mot cha-jan-neun-dae.*	I couldn't find it **on** the Internet.
싱가포르에 가요.	*sheeng-ga-po-re-**ae** ka-yo.*	I'm going **to** Singapore.
선생님께 보내드릴께요.	*sun-saeng-neem-**ggae** bo-nae-de-ree-ggae-yo.*	I'll send it **to** you.

[5] Particles, like *ae* (에), though usually attached to nouns, can sometimes be attached to words that in English are already prepositions, such as *dwee* (뒤), *meet* (밑) and *wee* (위).

[6] This particle can also be added to a noun turning it into an adverb. Please see the next sub-section, **ADVERBS**, for more on this.

Korean	Phonetic Transliteration	English
너에게 보낼께.	*naw-**ae-gae** bo-nael-ggae*	I'll send it **to** you.
학원에서 공부해요.	*hagwon-**ae-saw** gong-boo-hae-yo.*	I'm studying **at** a *hagwon*.

ADVERBS, *BOO-SA* (부사)

Adverb markers are fairly easy to recognize and work with in Korean. Either the *gae* suffix (-게) is attached to the word, serving roughly the same function as the -ly suffix does in English (i.e. modifying verbs and adjectives) or the *ha-da* part of a *ha-da* verb is conjugated to a *hee* character (e.g. 확실하다→확실히), or the (e)ro ((으)로) particle is added to a word (e.g. 전체→전체적으로). The twist with Korean is that adverbs are sometimes used in the most unlikely of places (from an English point of view) and can sound awkward when translated directly. Take a look at the following examples for a better clue:

Korean	Literal Translation/ Phonetic Transliteration	Proper Translation
맛있게 먹어.	Eat deliciously. (*ma-sheet-gae maw-gaw.*)	Have a good breakfast/ lunch/dinner.
예쁘게 해주세요.	Please do prettily. (*yea-ppe-gae hae-joo-sae-yo.*)	Can you make it look nice, please? (e.g. wrapping a present)
확실히 모르겠어요.	Don't know entirely. (*hwak-shee-ree mo-re-gaes-saw-yo.*)	I'm not entirely sure.

Korean	Literal Translation/ Phonetic Transliteration	Proper Translation
재미있게 놀아.	Play interestingly. (*jae-mee-eet-gae no-ra*)	Have a good time/ Enjoy yourself.

ARTICLES (I FINALLY HAVE GOOD NEWS FOR YOU!)

The Korean language makes no use of articles (i.e. 'a,' 'an,' 'the'). I'll limit my explanation to that. Hallelujah.

Chapter 8

Verb and Adjective Conjugation
동사 + 형용사 변화

This is what it all comes down to. This is the crux, the heart, the centerpiece, the veritable pinnacle of all pinnacles. That's why, in part, this is the longest chapter in the whole book. In all seriousness, conjugating a verb in Korean is what separates the men from the boys, as the adage goes, in this linguistic marathon. People who have lived here for years can often times only conjugate words in one of two ways —basic *jon-dae-mal* (존대말) or simple *ban-mal* (반말)—and not know that between those two ledges lies an entire world of communication.

What I try to do in this chapter is deconstruct Korean verbs from their basic roots to their most complex and obsequious endings. If you're still at a loss for words when you finish this chapter, don't despair. Years into my own encounters with this language, I still learn new things about verbs every day.

VERBS ARE WHERE IT'S AT

The first thing to know when considering verb conjugations is that Korean works with two kinds of verbs: **action verbs** (the only verbs in English) and **descriptive verbs** (otherwise known as adjectives), commonly referred to as **A.V.s** and **D.V.s** respectively.[1] For the sake of convenience, I will refer to both

[1] In English, a verb is defined as 'a word that is the grammatical center of a predicate and expresses an act, occurrence, or mode of being.' (*Webster's New American Dictionary*, p. 579).

D.V.s and A.V.s as simply 'verbs' throughout the course of this chapter, so as to not further complicate matters.

The second thing to keep in mind is that, contrary to popular opinion, there are more than two ways to conjugate a verb in Korean. The words *jon-dae-mal* (존대말) and *ban-mal* (반말), two words that denote levels of respect given in accordance with conjugation of the verb, might lead you to believe there are only two ways, but that's not true. These two words are the end points, if you will, that border a world of possibilities between the two extremes of verbs. Learning to use all the different endings, and doing so without batting an eyelash, is the true art of mastering Korean to a level whereby Koreans can look at you and say, 'Wow! Your Korean's awesome!'

WHAT MAKES A VERB SO SPECIAL?

Verbs aren't particularly special entities in the English language. The only significant way they differ from any other part of speech in the grammatical toolbox is that they're conjugated for tense. Still, with so many verb tenses to deal with, English isn't the easiest body of water to navigate if you're not a native speaker.

Korean verbs are much more unique than their English counterparts. Not only are Korean verbs conjugated for tense, but they are also conjugated for 'situation.' And within these so-called situations are thousands of years of history at work, the legacy of Confucianism, the weight of an entire nation's cultural beliefs, and its traditions all rolled up into one. Yet I hear my persistent reader yelling into my ears from point blank range, What ever are you talking about? Let me explain.

JON-DAE-MAL (존대말) AND *BAN-MAL* (반말)

Jon-dae-mal[2] and *ban-mal* are not scientific principles that adhere to one rule and one rule only. Much to the consternation and confusion of students learning Korean, they're not static entities that are only used with one specific person or group of people. For lack of a better translation, I've translated *jon-dae-mal* as 'honorific,' and/or 'polite' throughout this book, while translating *ban-mal* as 'familiar' and/or 'casual.'

[2] The term *jon-dae-mal* (존대말) is sometimes replaced with the term *no-peem-mal* (높임말), literally, 'high or heightened speech.' For the sake of simplification, however, I'll only refer to honorific speech as *jon-dae-mal*.

80

Truthfully, *jon-dae-mal* and *ban-mal* are very hard to quantify in English because there is nothing like them in the English language. In a nutshell, *jon-dae-mal* and *ban-mal* are ways by which you conjugate a verb in Korean. However, more than just reveal the tense of the verb, they do so much more. With a verb conjugation (or lack of it), a relationship between the speakers is established (or not established, as the case may be if there's no conjugation. See the **CAUTIOUS TO CONJUGATE** subsection in this chapter for more on this). A great deal about the speakers can be surmised from listening to the verb conjugations.

Most strangers use *jon-dae-mal* with each other until a firm relationship is established. However, an older man speaking with a student won't necessarily use *jon-dae-mal*. Younger friends usually use *jon-dae-mal* with older friends, but not always; it depends on the situation. Teachers teach school children in *jon-dae-mal*, but when speaking to individual students may switch into *ban-mal*. People may be referred to in the third person with *jon-dae-mal* if they are of an advanced age or of significant social rank, but not if it's an abstract statement in the third person.

At the same time, using *ban-mal* is just as sorted and mind-boggling. For instance, if I were to use anything but *ban-mal* with my close friend who is a few years younger than me, it would be completely unnatural. Alternatively, if I were to use *ban-mal* with a co-worker who is older than me or higher on the corporate ladder, it would be seen as extremely rude and offensive.

A major misconception of *ban-mal* is that it's akin to swearing in English. This is not true. When Koreans get in arguments they do not wield *ban-mal* (usually) like a weapon of mass destruction. Although it sounds strange to a non-native Korean's ears (or at least it did to mine in the beginning), even when Koreans get in fights or arguments the social relationship is still respected so that the younger person uses *jon-dae-mal* and the older person *ban-mal*.

This whole concept of *jon-dae-mal* vs. *ban-mal* might seem hopelessly confusing, but I promise you that once you start using Korean day-to-day it becomes easier. Because the concepts of 'honorific' and 'casual' ways of speaking are extremely intricate, it takes more than one lesson or one night to adjust to properly.

AN INTRODUCTION TO QUESTIONS

How you construct the most elementary of phrases is determined by the person(s) you are talking with. This means that even if I want to say 'I'm hungry,' me as the subject, keep in mind, I have to consider the age, sex, status, and relationship I share with the other speaker. Are we close friends? Is he/she younger? Am I trying to win them over (as a salesman)? Are they related to my wife/husband? All of these questions, whether consciously or sub-consciously, go through the speaker's mind as soon as you gain the power to change the value of a verb from a static root to a living, breathing grammatical object.

Before this explanation gets any more complicated, let me indulge you with a basic example of how a question may be posed in Korean. This list of conjugations does not demonstrate every single type of conjugation possible in Korean from a grammatical point of view,[3] but it does cover the majority of the conjugations for a basic, everyday question, Do you know (something)? in the second person. For the serious student of Korean, I've highlighted the question forms most common in everyday speech:

al-da (알다): to know

Korean	English	Situation Used
1. 알고 계십니까? (*al-go kae-sheem-nee-ka?*)	**Do you know?**	**formal, honorific (extremely polite, common)**
2. 알고 계세요? (*al-go kae-sae-yo?*)	**Do you know?**	**formal, honorific (extremely polite, common)**
3. 알고 계시나요? (*al-go kae-shee-na-yo?*)	**Do you know?**	**formal, honorific (common)**

[3] Depending on the verb, the conjugation can sometimes change. The conjugations I include here are those that fit for the verb *al-da* (알다). Different conjugations fit for different verbs. It always depends on the verb in question.

Korean	**English**	**Situation Used**
4. 알고 계신가요? (*al-go kae-sheen -ka-yo?*)	Do you know?	honorific (common)
5. 아십니까? (*a-sheem-nee-ka?*)	Do you know?	formal, very polite (not common)
6. 압니까? (*am-nee-ka?*)	Do you know?	formal, very polite (not common)
7. 아세요? **(*a-sae-yo?*)**	**Do you know?**	**formal, very polite (very common)**
8.* 아시죠? **(*a-shee-jo?*)**	**Do you know?**	**formal, very polite (very common)**
9. 아시나요? (*a-shee-na-yo?*)	Do you know?	formal, very polite (not common)
10. 알고 있으세요? (*al-go ees-se-sae-yo?*)	Do you know?	formal, very polite (common)
11. 알고 있으신가요? (*al-go ees-se-sheen-ka-yo?*)	Do you know?	polite (somewhat common)
12. 알고 있어요? (*al-go ees-saw-yo?*)	Do you know?	very polite (common)
13. 알고 있나요? (*al-go eet-na-yo*)	Do you know?	very polite (not common)

Korean	English	Situation Used
14.* 알고 있죠? (*al-go eet-jo?*)	Do you know?	polite (common)
15. 알아요? (*a-ra-yo?*)	Do you know?	polite (common)
16.* 알잖아요? (*al-jan-a-yo?*)	Do you know?	polite (not common)
17. 아나요? (*a-na-yo?*)	Do you know?	polite (not common)
18. 알죠? (*al-jo?*)	Do you know?	casual, between friends (common)
19.* 알지? (*al-gee?*)	Do you know?	casual (very common)
20. 알아? (*a-ra?*)	Do you know?	casual (very common)
21.* 알잖아? (*al-jan-a?*)	Do you know?	casual (not common)
22. 아나? (*a-na?*)	Do you know?	casual (not common)
23. 아니? (*a-nee?*)	Do you know?	casual (common, especially to children)

* These questions assume the listener knows something, which is why they're sometimes translated as, 'Don't you know?'

There are 23 ways to pose the same English question in Korean with the verb *al-da* (알다), Do you know? If that doesn't make you shake your head and grin at the craziness of it all, I don't know what will. Just writing out all those questions makes me laugh. The funny thing is that all those conjugations are only done for second person in the present tense! When you conjugate *al-da*, like any other verb in Korean, for first person in another tense there are a lot more ways to do it. (Please see the appendix entitled **Verb and Adjective Conjugations** for a more detailed list of verb conjugations).

You can memorize a thousand different verbs with thousands of other nouns and think you're off to the races, that you're ready to have a simple conversation, only to find out that as soon as someone asks you a question, you're as lost as if you had never studied this labyrinth-like language. As you learn more about the Korean language and become more fluent, it's imperative to master the ability to conjugate verbs.

AN INTRODUCTION TO STATEMENTS

Like asking a question, making a basic statement is a hemorrhage-inducing procedure laced with booby traps and hidden ditches. You think you're making a basic statement about yourself only to discover from your friend that you're talking about the other person; you're talking with your boss at work and realize seconds after making a statement about him that he has no idea what you're talking about because you've just conjugated the sentence for the first person with the subtraction of one character. This is tough stuff.

Here's a list of ways by which you may conjugate the verb *ka-da* (가다), in the first person and *ha-da* (하다), in the second person. Again, like the last example with questions, I highlight the most common sentences used in everyday speech with respect to the verb conjugated:

ka-da (가다): to go

First Person

Korean[4]	English	Situation Used
1. 학교에 갑니다. (***hak-kyo-ae kam-nee-da***.)	**I'm going to school.**	**formal (common)**
2. 학교에 가고 있습니다. (*hak-kyo-ae ka-go ees-seum-nee-da.*)	I'm going to school.	formal (never used)
3. 학교에 가고 있거든요. (*hak-kyo-ae ka-go eet-kaw-deun-yo.*)	I'm going to school.	polite (somewhat common)
4. 학교에 가고 있잖아요. (*hak-kyo-ae ka-go eet-jan-a-yo.*)	I'm going to school.	polite (rare)
5. 학교에 가거든요. (*hak-kyo-ae ka-kaw-deun-yo.*)	I'm going to school.	polite (uncommon)
6 학교에 가잖아요. (*hak-kyo-ae ka-jan-a-yo.*)	I'm going to school.	polite (rare)
7. 학교에 가요. (***hak-kyo-ae ka-yo***.)	**I'm going to school.**	**polite (common)**
8. 학교에 가는데요. (*hak-kyo-ae ka-neun-dae-yo.*)	I'm going to school.	polite (rare)
9. 학교에 가고 있어요. (*hak-kyo-ae ka-go ees-saw-yo.*)	I'm going to school.	polite (never used)

[4] As with the last example, *al-da* (알다), these verb conjugations are only for the specific verb in question, and may not represent every conceivable verb conjugation in the given tense and situation.

Korean	**English**	**Situation Used**
10. 학교에 가고 있는데요. (*hak-kyo-ae ka-go een-neun-dae-yo.*)	I'm going to school.	polite (never used)
11. 학교에 가는데. (*hak-kyo-ae ka-neun-dae.*)	I'm going to school.	casual (not used)
12. 학교에 가고 있는데. (*ha-kyo-ae ka-go een-neun-dae.*)	I'm going to school.	casual (not used)
13. 학교에 가고 있어. (*hak-kyo-ae ka-go ees-saw.*)	I'm going to school.	casual (sometimes used)
14. 학교에 가고 있잖아. (*hak-kyo-ae ka-go-eet-jan-a.*)	I'm going to school.	casual (not used)
15. **학교에 가.** (***hak-kyo-ae ka.***)	**I'm going to school.**	**casual (common)**
16. 학교에 가거든. (*hak-kyo-ae ka-kaw-deun.*)	I'm going to school.	casual (uncommon)
17. 학교에 가잖아. (*hak-kyo-ae ka-jan-a.*)	I'm going to school.	casual (uncommon)
18. **학교에 간다.** (***hak-kyo-ae kan-da.***)	**I'm going to school.**	***ban-mal* (common)**

[5] This sentence is sometimes translated from Korean as 'You speak Korean well,' but for the interest of keeping translations as natural as possible, I've changed this one somewhat.

ha-da (하다): to do

Second Person

Korean	**English**	**Situation Used**
1. 한국말을 잘하십니다.[5] (*han-goong-ma-reul chal-ha-sheem-nee-da.*)	Your Korean's really good.	very polite (uncommon)
2. 한국말을 잘하시네요. (*han-goong-ma-reul chal-ha-shee-nae-yo.*)	**Your Korean's really good.**	**very polite (the most common phrase used by Koreans)**
3. 한국말을 잘하신다. (*han-goong-ma-reul chal-ha-sheen-da.*)	**Your Korean's really good.**	**very polite (common)**
4. 한국말을 잘하시네. (*han-goong-ma-reul chal-ha-shee-nae.*)	**Your Korean's really good.**	**polite (extremely common for Koreans to use with foreigners)**
5. 한국말을 잘합니다. (*han-goong-ma-reul chal-ham-nee-da.*)	Your Korean's really good.	polite (uncommon)
6. 한국말을 잘해요. (*han-goong-ma-reul chal-hae-yo.*)	**Your Korean's really good.**	**polite (common)**

Korean	**English**	**Situation Used**
7. 한국말을 잘하는데요. (*han-goong-ma-reul chal-ha-neun-dae-yo.*)	Your Korean's really good.	polite (somewhat common*)*
8. 한국말을 잘하는데. (*han-goong-ma-reul chal-ha-neun-dae.*)	Your Korean's really good.	casual (uncommon)
9. 한국말을 잘한다. (***han-goong-ma-reul chal-han-da.***)	**Your Korean's really good.**	**casual (commom)**
10. 한국말을 잘하네. (*han-goong-ma-reul chal-ha-nae.*)	Your Korean's really good.	casual (somewhat commom)
11. 한국말을 잘해. (***han-goong-ma-reul chal-hae.***)	**Your Korean's really good.**	**casual (common)**

CONJUGATION (ACT I: THE ROOT THAT LED TO THE GIANT BEANSTALK)

In the beginning, there was the word. And the word was a verb. Inspiring stuff, but really, it all starts with the root of the verb. In English the root of 'play' may be 'to play,' but no one really cares about that, because as soon as you open your mouth and make a sentence, the root disappears. Thus, we can say something like, I play hockey, and not have to worry about what it's little brother, the 'to,' is doing. Making a sentence such as, Let's to play! or We to play a game, or Together to play! would only make you laugh. Not so with Korean.

From the root itself, verbs can be laid down in a phrase and brought to life.

Therefore, a descriptive verb in root form like *cho-ta* (좋다) can be said simply as *cho-ta*, and have perfect, even colloquial meaning, to a native Korean speaker. However, there are three important things to keep in mind when not conjugating a verb and using it as its root. First, roots are not used in conversation as questions or answers, more as responses or observations about something. Second, roots have to be considered for the situation. You would not, for instance, use a root adjective in front of your boss or someone of advanced age. Third, roots can be used as questions and responses in hypothetical, imagined, or educational situations. Examples of this range from a practice dialogue to an advertisement to a newspaper headline. In cases such as these, where no one person is directly being addressed, the root can and will be used constantly in question and answer format.

CONJUGATION (ACT II: THE THREE WISE VERBS)

There are three kinds of verbs in Korean: something loosely referred to as regular verbs (all verbs with final vowel *oh* (오) or *ah* (아) endings, not including the last 다 part, as in 오다 or 가다), known as *o-ah dong-sa* (오/아 동사), *ha-da* (하다 동사) verbs (i.e. all verbs ending in *ha-da* (하다)) and irregular verbs (i.e. every other verb that does not fall into one of the first two categories), known as *bool-kyu-cheek dong-sa* (불규칙 동사). Fortunately, most verbs in Korean end in *ha-da* (하다), and as these verbs happen to be the easiest to conjugate, you've stumbled upon one piece of good fortune.

Now that you know the three distinct kinds of verbs, what are you supposed to do with them? As we saw in **Chapter 3**, Confucianism still plays a dominant role in Korea's social relations. This pertains to language in the way Koreans speak with one another, the verb being the centerpiece of the sentence. Older people get more respect (*jon-dae-mal*) from younger people, and conversely, older people give less respect (*ban-mal*) through their conjugations.[6]

The same hierarchy that was outlined in **Chapter 3** is useful to understand verb conjugations. It's vital to recognize where you find yourself in one of these five relationships, then conjugate the verb appropriately. Naturally, this takes a lot of practice. In the beginning, the average Korean student uses *ban-mal*

[6] As I've said before in this book, I use the words 'honorific,' 'polite,' 'casual,' and 'respect' when describing *jon-dae-mal* and *ban-mal* not because they are true representations of their Korean counterparts, but because there is no way to translate these concepts into English perfectly. These words are the closest I can come to capturing the differences.

phrases with his bosses and older friends (a big no-no), and *jon-dae-mal* with his younger friends (something that is alien to Koreans in a situation like this). Expect to make some big mistakes in the beginning, but to learn from those mistakes at the same time. For a quick recap, here's an outline of Confucius's five major social relationships:

1. Ruler and Subject
2. Father and Son
3. Elder Brother and Younger Brother
4. Husband and Wife
5. Friend and Friend

CONJUGATION (ACT III: GIVING THE BEAST A FACE)

While it's true that the root form of the verb in Korean can be a phrase in and of itself, this is usually not the case.[7] By conjugating the verb for tense (generally simple past, present, or future), and for situation (i.e. anywhere in that huge chasm between the high of *jon-dae-mal* (존대말) and the low of *ban-mal* (반말)), you effectively bring a verb to life. And once your verbs are living, breathing grammatical entities, you're officially speaking Korean! You're taking part in conversations, and you're one step closer to your end goal of speaking Korean with confidence.

Without putting any fancy bells or whistles on your verbs, there are a few basic ways in which they can be conjugated. Schools in Korea only tend to teach the most deferential of verb conjugations, and though it's important to know these verb endings, it's also important to know the other ones.

Statements

Statements end in a variety of ways, among these, *-yo* (요) being the best known and most common (especially for non-native Korean speakers). While it's true that the *-yo* (요) ending is extremely useful and polite in everyday conversation, it doesn't represent the only way to conjugate a verb as a

[7] Korean verbs can be expressed by their root when writing Korean. Except for this, the root is rarely used in conversation form. When it is used in conversation, it's usually used in the abstract (e.g. 'it's cold,' 'that's expensive,' etc.).

statement in the first person. Here's a list of present tense conjugations for the three different types of verbs, *ha-da* (하다), *oh/ah* (오/아), and irregular:

	TO STUDY *gong-boo-ha-da* (공부하다)	**TO COME** *oh-da* (오다)	**TO EAT** *mawk-da* (먹다)
very polite	공부합니다.	옵니다.	먹습니다.
polite	공부해요.	와요.	먹어요.
casual	공부해.	와.	먹어.

Questions

Just like statements, the *-yo* (요) ending is a very common ending attached to verb conjugations for questions. As before, I'll provide a list of the same three verbs in **present tense**, conjugated for common situations with respect to questions:

very polite	공부합니까?	옵니까?	먹습니까?
polite	공부해요?	와요?	먹어요?
casual	공부해?	와?	먹어?

You'll notice from the previous examples that the **polite** and **casual** ways to conjugate verbs ended up being the same in **statements** and **questions**. This should naturally bring a good question to the forefront of your mind: How can you tell when someone is making a statement and when they're asking you a question? Often it's just a matter of intonation.

A MATTER OF INTONATION

Although some Korean verb conjugations can be expressed independently in question and statement form, some are expressed the exact same way for both. The first way to get around this problem is to master the intonation of asking questions and making statements. Are you asking me a question, or are you making a statement? you might hear someone ask you, your intonation not yet perfect in Korean. In instances like this, the rising or falling intonation can become absolutely critical. Look at the following example where two Korean sentences are written the exact same way:

Korean Sentence	Phonetic Transliteration	English Translation
모자 썼어요?	*mo-ja ssaws-saw-yo?*	Are you wearing a hat?
모자 썼어요.	*mo-ja ssaws-saw-yo.*	I'm wearing a hat.

Two sentences written the exact same way have completely different meanings. One is meant as a question (in the second person) and the other is meant as a statement that provides information (in the first person). However, the only thing that separates them in spoken conversation is the intonation: either the rising tone (in the question), or the falling tone (in the statement). Although intonation is important, there is a way around it in polite speech.

CONJUGATION (ACT IV: MAKING YOURSELF CRYSTAL CLEAR)

In formal or polite situations the addition of certain characters before the ending of the conjugation can make the sentence clear as to whether you're speaking in the first, second or third person, whether you're asking a question or making a statement. Also, especially if talking with someone much older or of considerable social rank, it's not considered very polite to simply use intonation as a means of distinguishing a question from a statement. This is where we have to bring in some of the extra characters that are going to make your Korean more polite and more conversational (by virtue of the fact that you will now be understood one hundred percent of the time).

The *shee* (시) and *sae* (세) characters are the best way to distinguish between first and second person because they're only used in the second and third person. These two characters will be a valuable addition to your verb conjugation arsenal. The characters *shee* and *sae* don't actually mean anything by themselves; they only grow to have honorific meaning as an attachment to a verb conjugation. That's why they're not used when talking about yourself in the first person.

The *shee* (시) character is used in second and third person statements (past, present, and future), and second and third person questions (past, present and future), and the imperative (present tense). Let's take a look at a few examples and see how this character works:

Potentially Confusing Statement		**Crystal Clear Statement**
한글 잘 써요.	→	한글 잘 쓰시네요.[8]
Hangeul chal ssaw-yo		*Hangeul chal sse-shee-nae-yo.*
You write Korean really well.		You write Korean really well.
(or I write Korean really well)		

Another potentially confusing sentence is fixed in the same way:

Potentially Confusing Statement		**Crystal Clear Statement**
콜라 두개 주고...	→	콜라 두개주시고요...
kol-la doo-gae joo-go		*kol-la doo-gae joo-shee-go-yo*
Can you give me two cokes and...		Can you give me two cokes and...
(I'll give you two cokes and...)		

Here are a few more examples using the *shee* character in past, present and future conjugations:

Korean (unclear)	**Korean** (clear/more polite)	**English**
메일 받았어요?	메일 받으셨어요?	Did you get my e-mail?
(*mae-eel ba-das-saw-yo?*)	(*mae-eel ba-de-shaws-saw-yo?*)	
운동 할 거에요?	운동 하실 거에요?	Are you going to work out?
(*oon-dong-hal gaw-ae-yo?*)	(*oon-dong ba-sheel gaw-ae-yo?*)	

[8] In this statement, the addition of *nae* (네) emphasizes how well you think the person writes Korean.

Korean (unclear)	**Korean** (clear/more polite)	**English**

잘 했어요.   잘 하셨어요.   Good work.
(*chal haes-saw-yo.*)   (*chal ha-shaws-saw-yo.*)

With respect to the *sae* (세) character, it isn't used with quite as much versatility as *shee* (시), but it's useful nonetheless. *Sae* is used in present tense questions and statements and in the imperative (i.e. orders, suggestions, advice, etc.). Just like before, a potentially confusing phrase is remedied more polite with one character:

Potentially Confusing Question   **Crystal Clear Question**

자취해요?   자취하세요?
ja-chwee-hae-yo?   *ja-chwee-ha-sae-yo?*
Do you live on your own?   Do you live on your own?

When offering a little advice to an older friend, you can turn an unclear sentence into a clear one with the same character:

Potentially Confusing Phrase   **Crystal Clear Phrase**

푹 쉬어요.   푹 쉬세요.
pook shee-aw-yo   *pook shwee-sae-yo.*
Get some rest now.   Get some rest now.

WHO, ME?

Even after learning how to alter verbs so that the first and second person is well established, you'll continue to experience an apparent misunderstanding in communication, something that to this day I still get a kick out of: the confirmation of the person you are speaking to. I've asked Koreans a question on many occasions using a polite (sometimes honorific) ending, and had them ask me back, Who, me? Are you asking me? At first, I attributed this to my bad accent, my bad grammar, or my dumb question—anything, but the person I was talking to. Over time, though, I started to see a pattern. No matter who I was talking to, no matter how clear my question, and no matter how many people were in the room, Koreans often times responded to my questions with, *jaw-yo?* (저요?), Who, me? Or, in *ban-mal, na?* (나?).

This confused me to no end until I realized that it was a natural reaction on the part of many Koreans and had nothing to do with the accent, verb conjugation, or speaking ability of the non-native Korean speaker. Koreans do it with other Koreans all the time.

CONJUGATION (ACT V: SPECIAL SUBJECT VERBS)

There are a host of exceptions and special-circumstance verbs that you need to know. The first set of verbs has to do with special subject verbs. Korean sentences may seem crazy in their wording and their order, but they follow the same basic guidelines as English most of the time: the subject in an English sentence is usually the subject in Korean, the object, the object. There are, however, four major exceptions to this: the verbs 'to have,' *eet-dda* (있다), 'to not have,' *awp-dda* (없다), 'to need,' *pee-ryo-ha-dda* (필요하다), and 'to not need,' *pee-ryo awp-dda* (필요 없다). In all four cases, no matter what you're saying, the object in English becomes the subject in Korean. Sound weird? Just memorize it and get it ingrained in your head because it's not going to change no matter how much you will it. Here's a look at some examples sentences:

Korean	**Literal Translation**	**Proper Translation**
돈이 있어요? (*don-ee ees-saw-yo?*)	Is money have?	Do you have any money?
여자친구가 없어요. (*yaw-ja-cheen-goo awp-saw-yo.*)	Girlfriend not have.	I don't have a girlfriend.

Korean	Literal Translation	Proper Translation
도움이 필요해요. (*do-oom-ee pee-ryo-hae-yo.*)	Help needs.	I need help.
새 옷이 필요 없어요. (*sae o-shee pee-ryo awp-saw-yo*)	New clothes not need.	I don't need any new clothes.

CONJUGATION (ACT VI: HONORIFIC VERBS)

You may be saying to yourself, 'But I thought *jon-dae-mal* (존대말) was the honorific way of conjugating a verb!' It's true that conjugation can be honorific, but Korean doesn't stop there. When you *really* want (or have) to show respect, there is an entirely different set of verbs that you use in the common ones' place. You now have something to keep in mind when you speak to someone much older than you: **how you conjugate the verb** and **which verb you use**. The following examples should help you understand this a little better:

Ban-mal	*Jon-dae-mal*	Honorific *Jon-dae-mal*	English Translation
잘 자. (*chal ja.*)	잘 자요. (*chal ja-yo.*)	주무세요. (*joo-moo-sae-yo.*)	Have a good sleep.
먹어. (*maw-gaw.*)	먹어 보세요. (*maw-gaw bo-sae-yo.*)	드세요. (*de-sae-yo.*)	Go ahead and eat.
줄께. (*jool-ggae.*)	줄께요. (*jool-ggae-yo.*)	드릴께요. (*de-reel-kkae-yo.*)	I'll give you (something)

On a technical level, there are no set rules governing when to use *ban-mal* and when to use *jon-dae-mal* because it's not always just a matter of who's older and who's younger, a common mistake some native English speakers make when learning Korean. *Ban-mal* is generally used when speaking to children (in private), when speaking to a close friend (whom you feel comfortable speaking to and vice-versa) and when speaking to underlings (in a business setting, assuming that the person is also younger than you). *Jon-dae-mal* is generally used when meeting someone for the first time (assuming the age gap is not extreme), when speaking to superiors or equals (in a business setting) and when speaking to people who are older than you (and who you're not close with). If ever you're unsure which type of verb conjugation to use, be safe and use *jon-dae-mal.* Although it may seem strange in some circumstances, you're being polite with your use of language and that's the most important thing.

There are two types of special verbs connected with *jon-dae-mal* that you need to be aware of. One is honorific doubles,[9] which are used only in the second and third person, and the second is polite doubles, which are used in the first, second and third person.

The honorific double is used when speaking to a person much older than yourself (e.g. seniors, parents) or when wanting/needing to be very polite (e.g. speaking to a company boss, meeting an older person for the first time). The following is a list of the honorific doubles. For a look at how they are conjugated, please refer to the appendix titled **Verb and Adjective Conjugations.**

Common and Honorific Verbs

English	Common Verb	Phonetic Transliteration	Honorific Verb	Phonetic Transliteration
to be	있다	*eet-dda*	계시다	*kae-shee-da*
to die[10]	죽다	*chook-da*	돌아가시다	*do-ra-ka-shee-da*
to drink	마시다	*ma-shee-da*	드시다	*de-shee-da*
to eat[11]	먹다	*mawk-da*	잡수시다	*jap-soo-shee-da*
to not be	없다	*awp-dda*	안 계시다	*an kae-shee-da*
to sleep	자다	*ja-da*	주무시다	*joo-moo-shee-da*

[9] I use the word "double" here in reference to the pairs of words in Korean that mean the exact same thing, but are used situationally. See **Common and Honorific Verbs** and **Common Polite Verbs** for a complete list of these doubles.

[10] Although *do-ra-ka-shee-da* (돌아가시다) is most common, other honorific verbs for the same situation include *ta-gae-ha-shee-da* (타계하시다), *oon-myung-ha-shee-da* (운명하시다) and *oon-myung-eul dal-lee-ha-shee-da* (운명을 달리하시다).

[11] The honorific verb for 'eat' is *jap-soo-shee-da* (잡수시다), but it's much more common to use *de-shee-da* (드시다). Also, when talking about liquids with common verbs, especially alcohol, the verb *mawk-da* (먹다) is used in place of *ma-shee-da* (마시다) in many instances.

98

Polite doubles are different from honorific doubles in that they can be used about yourself (i.e. in the first person). The following is a list of the major polite doubles used in everyday Korean:

Common and Polite Verbs

English	Common Verb	Phonetic Transliteration	Polite Verb	Phonetic Transliteration
to ask	묻다	*moot-dda*	여쭈다	*yaw-jjoo-da*
to bring	데려오다	*dae-ryaw-o-da*	모셔오다	*mo-shaw-o-da*
to give[12]	주다	*joo-da*	드리다	*de-ree-da*
to see	보다	*bo-da*	뵙다	*bwaep-dda*
to speak/say	(말)하다	*(mal)ha-da*	말씀하다	*mal-sseum-ha-da*
to treat	사주다	*sa-joo-da*	대접하다	*dae-jawp-ha-da*

CONJUGATION (ACT VII: SITUATIONAL VERBS)

Korean Verbs are not only conjugated for situation, but the verbs themselves are often chosen for situation differently than in English. Think of verbs like 'go,' 'come,' 'take,' or 'get.' These are the very embodiment of versatile verbs in a grammatical sense, as they are not limited to one situation or event. Unfortunately, Korean verbs are not usually as versatile with different situations, which makes learning verbs an exhausting process. A good example of this is the verb 'to wear.' Although it comprises everything and anything you put on your body or head (from shoes to hairpins) in English, the verb *eep-dda* (입다) in Korean only covers the bare minimum amount of clothing. Here's a summary of how the English verb 'to wear' is broken down in Korean:

Korean	Phonetic Transliteration	Situation(s) Used
입다	*eep-dda*	pants, dresses, shirts, sweaters, *hanbok* (한복)

[12] *De-ree-da* (드리다) is a very special verb in Korean that has more than one function. For more information on it, please refer to the end of the appendix **Verb and Adjective Conjugation.**

99

Korean	Phonetic Transliteration	Situation(s) Used
쓰다	sse-da	eye glasses, sunglasses, hats, tuques, caps
차다/하다	cha-da/ha-da	belts, girdles, watches, bracelets
신다	sheen-dda	shoes, sandals, socks, pantyhose
하다	ha-da	watches, jewelry, hair accessories (e.g. hair pins)
묶다	mookk-dda	hair (e.g. a ponytail),
매다	mae-da	scarves, ties, bowties.
끼다	ggi-da	rings, earrings (also used with ha-da), bracelets (sometimes)
뿌리다	bboo-ree-da	colognes and perfumes (i.e. things you spray)
달다	dal-da	broach, earrings, ribbons

The lesson to draw from this is that it's always prudent when asking for translations to inquire as to which situations the verb is used in Korean. Your question may seem like it has an obvious answer, but as this last example illustrates, the act of asking that one simple question can save you weeks of headaches, as dictionaries do not always clarify such matters.

CONJUGATION (ACT VIII: VERB TENSES)

As tedious as it is to memorize English verbs for the non-native English speaker, I believe that with the rare exception verb tenses make a great deal of sense. Korean, however, doesn't always make as much sense from an English point of view. Korean does have a present continuous tense, for example, but it's rarely used. There are clear distinctions between past and present tense in conjugation, but they're not always as clear in conversation. There is something of a present perfect tense, yet it's almost never used. And although there is something like a present perfect tense in Korean, there isn't a separate past perfect or a future perfect tense independent of other tenses. Tenses take practice and nothing more. Here are just a few examples:

Korean	Literal Translation	Proper Translation
1. 어디 가요? (*aw-dee ka-yo?*)	Where **go**?	Where are you **going**?
2. 뭘 좋아하세요? (*mol cho-a-ha-sae-yo?*)	What **like**?	What **would you like**? (ordering food, say)
3. 뭐 해요? (*mo hae-yo?*)	What **do**?	What **are you doing**?
4. 타이타닉 봤어요? (*ta-ee-ta-neek bwas-saw-yo?*)	**Saw** 'Titanic'?	**Have** you ever **seen** 'Titanic'?
5. 어제밤 내가 술 먹고… (*aw-jae-bam nae-ga sool mawk-go…*)	Last night I **drink** and…	I **drank** last night and…

As is seen with these examples, sometimes it's not only the tense that changes, but the meaning as well. In example 3, for instance, the meaning of the literal translation is not only different grammatically, but in context as well. What do you do? refers to work or occupation, whereas the proper translation shows that the person is asking what action you are performing at the present moment. As I said earlier, the only way to get a hold of the tense problem is to listen carefully to Koreans speak and see which situations they choose to use different tenses; past is present, present is past, present is future. Don't worry. You'll get the hang of it after a while. It just takes practice.

CONJUGATION (ACT IX: ONE MORE TIME, BABY!)

So far, I've explained that you need to conjugate verbs when speaking Korean and though this is true, there is one more situation you need to be mindful of that is essential in formal speech. When meeting someone older than yourself or someone you don't know similar in age, it's important to not just conjugate the verbs and adjectives, but conjunctions and phrases as well. I know, I know, this makes less and less sense with each passing page. Remember, though, I'm on your side and just trying to alert you of the pitfalls.

So, here's the situation: you're meeting someone for the first time and the person is older than you. You're wondering how to be polite with respect to conjugations. Well, the thing is, when you start and stop your phrases in Korean, you should probably be conjugating those parts with a *-yo* (요) at the end, too. Before I go off any further and lose you completely, I'll give you an example. Someone asks you a question, such as, Why did you come to Korea in the first place? and you say:

Korean Phrase	**English Translation**
왜냐면**요**, 그냥 동양에 가고 싶어서요. *(wae-nya-myun-**yo**, ke-nyang dong-* *yang-ae ka-go sheep-aw-saw-yo.)*	Simply because I wanted to go to the Orient.

Although the word 'because' is no more than a conjugation in English, it is conjugated for respect in Korean sometimes. This is not a super-huge point that has to be followed if you're scared of disrespecting the person you're speaking with. However, it is a point that shows a very real command of the language. Here are two more examples:

Korean Phrase	**English Translation**
근데**요**, 저 못 해요. *(keun-dae-**yo**, jaw mo-tae-yo.)*	But I can't do it.
그러면**요**, 그렇게 합시다. *(ke-raw-myun-**yo**, ke-raw-kae* *hap-shee-da.)*	Well in that case, let's do it/that.

102

CAUTIOUS TO CONJUGATE

Koreans don't always use a verb when speaking. It took me years to figure out, but when I finally stumbled upon it, it was like seeing a great white light at the end of the verb tunnel. On many occasions, I would listen to Koreans talk away in my classroom over break or between classes (in Korean) and be baffled by something: they weren't getting to the part of the phrase where the verb was, and so didn't ever conjugate it. Even when they were conjugating the verb, they were doing it through laughter or as quiet as a whisper.

People in Korea that don't know each other well face a difficult problem, especially when the two people are very similar looking in age: how to conjugate the verb. Obviously everyone in my English class, for example, is roughly the same age, but someone is older and someone is younger and this makes speaking a little complicated. So, most students, unless there is a clear age difference, will be innovative with their language. Instead of just making a sentence and conjugating the sentence into *ban-mal* or *jon-dae-mal,* they'll start a sentence and let it hang in mid-air, a noun with no accompanying verb; they'll start a sentence and then trail off like the verb is understood and let the thread be picked up by another speaker. Women, always the more polite of the sexes, will do something equally as innovative in that they'll cover their mouth (sometimes they're genuinely laughing, other times not so much) as they squeeze out the verb that is barely audible to anyone except the verbaholic teacher standing nearby waiting to learn from them.

In situations like this (and others where people are just introduced and look the same age), you can see a lot of this going on. Koreans could simply use *jon-dae-mal* and assure politeness; they could use *ban-mal* and assume age superiority. However, the truth is that Korean is much more developed, much more complicated, and much more of a game in this sense.

I think of it as playing cards. The conjugation of the verb is the absolute last step in playing—the veritable showing of the cards that leaves no room for mystery or possibility. By not conjugating the verb and doing other neat little things to get around it, you effectively keep your cards close to your chest, not giving anything away. This may seem like a lot to go through (and a huge headache when communicating), but if you want to speak Korean naturally, then it's just another part of conjugating verbs that you have to deal with.

First Impressions Last a Lifetime?

All right. The big night is finally here for me. I'm finally going to meet my girlfriend's parents after having waited almost three long years for the chance. I've practiced what I'm going to say with friends, memorized certain phrases so I don't screw them up, and thought about possible responses to a whole range of questions. I've prepared like this so I make the best first impression in a language that is still alien to me.

My girlfriend and I arrive early at the restaurant. No big deal, I say to myself as I take off my blazer and see that I've already sweated through my dress shirt and the parents have yet to arrive. The parents arrive shortly thereafter and I flash them a smile as I welcome them in. So far so good, I murmur to myself, wiping another thick layer of sweat from my forehead, arms, hands, ears.

We sit down and the father orders some *kalbi*. The waitress now out of the room, he begins the first series of questions (no, of course it didn't feel like an interrogation), and I handle myself pretty well. My girlfriend is silent throughout this whole ordeal, leaving me to fend for myself. The trusty bottle of *soju* arrives (at least there's always one constant at a Korean dinner), and I ask the father, *sool chal maw-gaw-yo?* (술 잘 먹어요?) Oh, crap! I say to myself as the words roll off my tongue and become forever condemnable in the court of popular dinnertime opinion. I screwed up. I asked him a normal question by Korean standards, but I didn't conjugate the verb with the honorific verb (absolutely necessary in this case, as it's the first time I'm meeting my girlfriend's parents). I merely conjugated it for tense and politeness—with respect to the verb I chose—and so feel like a total heel. What I should have said is, 술 잘 드세요? (*sool chal de-sae-yo?*)

A couple of hours later while reminiscing about the dinner, I asked my girlfriend what she thought of my linguistic faux pas. 'Don't worry about it. It's no big deal,' she responded.

Not believing her, all I could think was, Freaking language! I hold my own as well as I know how, and though I was doing admirably, all things considered, I inadvertently insulted the man of the hour with the wrong choice of honorific verbs. Such is the life of the conjugation game around this neck of the woods.

Chapter 9

Questions and Statements
질문 + 대답

Asking a question or making a statement in Korean is not all that straightforward. With both questions and statements, there is always the matter of conjugating the verb, like we saw in the last chapter. This chapter, however, is more concerned with the idea of asking questions and making statements in a more general way, not just from a verb point of view.

WHEN A QUESTION JUST ISN'T A QUESTION

In English, Yes/No questions are answered, for the most part, with the first verb in the question. Thus, Do you know the time? is answered with, Yes, I do or No, I don't. Of course, in spoken conversation there are exceptions to this rule with words lopped off, words added, and sometimes just grunts and snarls for answers, but what we're talking about here is the philosophy and grammar behind these things.

Alternatively, asking Yes/No questions in Korean does not require the same thought pattern for answers. In Korean, the verb you're repeating in the answer is the second verb or participle from an English question. For example:

Example 1

Korean/Phonetic Transliteration	Direct Translation	Proper English Translation
A: 조깅 좋아하세요? (*jo-ging cho-a-ha-sae-yo?*)	**like** jogging?	**Do** you like to jog?
B: 예, 좋아해요. (*yea, cho-a-hae-yo*)	Yeah, **like**.	Yeah, I **do**.

This change in thought pattern is not incredibly difficult to adjust to, but there is something else to keep in mind with questions in Korean. The way in which non-Yes/No questions (i.e. who, what, where, when, why, how) are answered also differs. As we saw in **Chapter 8**, there are times when honorific verbs are used to show respect for the person being addressed. In cases like this, the answer will not look anything like the question and vice-versa. This makes high-speed conversation a bit of a minefield when posing questions and giving answers quickly. Whereas in English the verbs almost always match from the question to the answer, it's not always so in Korean. Look at the following example:

Example 2

Korean Question	Translation
A: 뭐 드셨어요? (*mo de-shaw-saw-yo?*)	What did you **have** (for dinner)?[1]
B: 김치볶음밥 먹었어. (*kimchi-bok-keum-bap maw-gaws-saw.*)	I **had** some fried rice with *kimchi* (for dinner).[2]

[1] The word 'dinner' is not used in the Korean phrase here, but we assume that the person is asking about one of the three meals. The meal is not always specified in Korean, which is why in this example I've put 'dinner' in brackets.

[2] Although the verbs *de-shee-da* (드시다) and *mawk-da* (먹다) both mean 'to eat,' I've decided to translate what I believe a more natural question and response for this situation. Even with the translation, though, the same discrepancy appears between Korean and English with regards to the change in verbs.

You can see from the highlighted portions of the question and answer that although the same verb appears in the English question and answer, the Korean sentences use two different verbs (meaning the same thing). The question has *de-shee-da* (드시다), while the answer has *mawk-da* (먹다).

The reason this is important is that unlike English where you can listen carefully and repeat the verb from the question in the answer, in Korean you can't always do that. In the last example, if you were to answer the question with the verb *de-shee-da*, it's highly probable that the other person wouldn't understand you.

WHAT WAS THAT YOU SAID?

There's something much harder than the previous examples of asking and answering questions that very few people learn when studying Korean: repeating questions and statements once again because you may not have heard what exactly was said or you simply want to make sure what you heard is correct. In English, both of these situations are fairly straightforward. For example:

Repeating a Question

Speaker 1: Did **you** get home late last night?
Speaker 2: Did **I** get home late last night?

Repeating a Phrase

Speaker 1: **I'm** having a tough time studying.
Speaker 2: **You're** having a tough time studying?

In the **Repeating a Question** example, there's no special conjugation needed. All that's necessary is to switch the subject from 'you' to 'I.' With the **Repeating a Phrase** example, all you have to do is flip the subject and change the verb so it matches the new subject. This is pretty elementary stuff if you've practiced English long enough and can repeat phrases after hearing them just one time.

With Korean, much more needs to be done. First of all, the conjugation of the verb completely changes when you repeat questions and answers. This means that on top of all the conjugation you learn to speak the language, there is another step necessary to become fluent in conversation. Depending on whether the person you are speaking with is asking a question or making a statement, you will flip the sentence around in your head and then re-conjugate it for the situation. Consider the following examples:

Repeating a Question

Speaker 1: 미국에 **가보셨습니까?**
(*mee-gook-ae ka-bo-shaws-seum-nee-ka?*)

Have you ever been to the States?

Speaker 2: 미국 **가봤냐고?**
(*mee-gook ka-bwan-ya-go?*)

Have I ever been to the States?

Repeating a Phrase

Speaker 1: 나는 컴퓨터 **샀는데요.**
(*na-neun kawm-pyu-taw san-neun-dae-yo.*)

I bought a computer.

Speaker 2: 컴퓨터 **샀다고요?**
(*kawm-pyu-taw satt-da-go-yo?*)

You bought a computer?

A COMMON MISTAKE

When you want to clarify something in any language, repeating questions or statements is a natural way to do it. Native English speakers who learn Korean try and do this much of the time, often to the bewilderment of Koreans. This has everything to do with the fact that most people don't know how to conjugate a phrase for repetition, and so, do the only thing that comes to mind:

repeating the question or statement verbatim. It's at this point that the average Korean looks at you with amazement and wonder, for they have no idea what you mean. Look at the following examples to get a better idea of what I'm talking about here:

Example 1

Incorrect Way To Repeat a Question	Translation
A: 밥 먹었어요? (*bap maw-gaws-saw-yo?*)	Did **you** eat yet?
B: 밥 먹**었어요**? (*bap maw-gaws-saw-yo?*)	Did **you** eat yet?

Example 2

Incorrect Way To Repeat a Statement	Translation
A: 2년 동안 영어 배웠어요. (*ee-nyun dong-an yung-aw bae-wus-saw-yo.*)	**I studied** English for two years
B: 2년 동안 영어 배웠어요? (*ee-nyun dong-an yung-aw bae-wus-saw-yo?*)	**Did you study** English for two years?

In **Example 1**, the person asking the question would obviously be thoroughly confused because the question is being asked right back again without an answer being provided first (the subject wasn't changed). In **Example 2**, the first speaker may not be as confused, but because one small conjugation was not made, the second speaker looks as if he is deaf, asking a question anew instead of confirming what was said. This makes it incredibly

110

useful (not to mention important) to learn the different conjugations for questions and answers in Korean. The correct way to express the repetition of the question and statement in the two previous examples is done as such:

Example 1

Correct Way To Repeat a Question	**Translation**
A: 밥 먹었어요? *(bap maw-gaws-saw-yo?)*	Did **you** eat yet?
B: 밥 먹**었냐고요**? *(bap maw-gawn-ya-go-yo?)*	Did **I** eat yet?

Example 2

Correct Way To Repeat a Statement	**Translation**
A:. 2년 동안 영어 **배웠어요**. *(ee-nyun dong-an yung-aw bae-wus-saw-yo.)*	**I studied** English for two years.
B: 2년 동안 영어 **배웠다고요**? *(ee-nyun dong-an yung-aw bae-wut-da-go-yo?)*	Oh, **you studied** English for two years, **did you**?

RULES TO LIVE BY

Before you look at any more examples, keep in mind the following two general rules when wanting to repeat a question or statement:

- When **repeating a question**, take the root verb, conjugate it for tense, and then add *nya-go-yo* (냐고요)? Some people today in spoken and written Korean change the *go* (고) character to a *goo* (구) character, but that's more a matter of style than anything else.

• When **repeating a phrase**, the same basic rules apply as for a question, except for the model of the conjugation itself. In terms of phrases being repeated, the root (in proper tense) is lifted from the phrase and then outfitted with a new ending, *da-go-yo?* (다고요?) Like the last rule, the *go* (고) character will occasionally be replaced with it's upside down brother, *goo* (구). Look at the following examples for a better idea of how this actually works:

	Korean	**English**
1.	A: 밥 **먹었니**? *(bap maw-gawn-nee?)*	Have **you** eaten?
	B: 밥 **먹었냐구**? *(bap maw-gawn-ya-goo?)*	Have **I** eaten?
2.	A: 어디 **가세요**? *(aw-dee ka-sae-yo?)*	Where are **you** going?
	B: 어디 **가냐고요**? *(aw-dee ka-nya-go-yo?)*	Where am **I** going?
3.	A: 돈 **있어**? *(don ees-saw?)*	Do **you** have any money on you?
	B: 돈 **있냐고**? *(don een-ya-go?)*	Do **I** have any money on me?

This should all seem nothing less than completely confusing. It took me years to use this effectively in conversation, and to be honest, even Koreans are impressed when you can use this in conversation without batting an eyelash. To make it easier on yourself, though, you might want to make the following checklist to help you remember how to correctly repeat a question or statement:

- **Remember** what was just said and be able to recall it quickly.
- Consider the **relationship** you have with the speaker.
- Keep in mind the **verb** at the end of the sentence and decide if it has to be changed from honorific to common, from polite to casual, from casual to polite, or whether it doesn't need to be changed at all.
- Keep in mind the **tense** you're dealing with as you conjugate- don't change it from the original when you're repeating a question or statement.
- **Don't tear your hair out** when you discover that the person you're speaking with doesn't understand you because you made one tiny error in conjugation.

When Asking Questions Drives You Nuts

I was at a music store in Gangnam some years ago and wanted to listen to a CD before I bought it. Walking up to one of the assistants in the store I asked him, 'Can you try and listen to this, please?' The young man looked at me quizzically and asked me to repeat myself. Thinking my accent fine, and trusting my question, I asked him again, 'Can you try and listen to this, please?' The young man then said something I didn't understand. Growing agitated and impatient, I took the CD and put it to my ear, like I was listening to the disc itself. At this, the sales assistant finally understood what I was trying to say and the problem was solved.

However, after leaving the store I couldn't help feeling that I was missing something. As usual, I asked my girlfriend about the scenario and what I had done wrong. The problem was that I had made a mistake in the conjugation of the verb, stemming from the fact that I had learned *hal-soo-ee-se-sae-yo?* (할 수 있으세요?) as a polite way to ask if something could be done. Not wanting to be anything but polite, I put the correct verb in place and asked if I could listen to the CD, *ee shee-dee-reul de-raw bol-soo-ees-se-sae-yo?* (이 시디를 들어 볼 수 있으세요?). The problem, however, is that the verb conjugation *ee-se-sae-yo* (있으세요?) is only used in the second person as a question. And though the pronoun 'you' has several meanings in English, one of which being the universal everybody, in Korean, the use of 'you' is much more limited in scope, and thus the confusion on the sales assistant's face. You want *me* to listen to this thing, buddy? the young man must have been thinking.

What I should I have said instead was, *ee CD-reul de-raw bol-soo-een-na-yo?* ('이 시디를 들어 볼 수 있나요?') That *ee-se-sae-yo?* verb conjugation caused me enough angst in one conversation to never let me forget the lesson.

ANOTHER WAY OF REPEATING: CLARIFICATION

When you need to do more than simply repeat a question or statement, that is you need to clarify something the other person said because you're not sure you heard correctly, or you're taken aback with what someone said, there are a few ways by which you can do this. This includes using the verbs *mal-ha-da* (말하다), *mal-sseum-ha-da* (말씀하다), *moot-dda* (묻다), and *ke-raett-dda* (그랬다).[3]

If you've lived in Korea for any length of time, you've probably heard this type of verb conjugation thrown at you hundreds of times, but not realized what it was the person was saying to you. Because few people who study Korean are actually fluent in it, Koreans often want/need to make sure they understand you, the non-native Korean speaker, clearly, so they use a particular kind of conjugation with one of the four above-mentioned verbs.

Yet this is not to say that non-native Korean speakers can't use this

[3] The verb *mal-ha-da* (말하다) means 'to say' while *mal-sseum-ha-da* (말씀하다) also means 'to say.' The verb *moot-dda* (묻다) means 'to ask.' The verb *ke-raett-dda* (그랬다) is usually defined as 'is that so?' but when attached to sentences for clarification, it comes to mean something closer to 'is that what you said?'

conjugation, too. In fact, quite the opposite. I like to use this neat little conjugation as a way by which to tell the person I'm speaking with that I can in fact speak Korean (while at the same time clarifying what it was the person just said to me). Though most people won't blink if you pull this particular tool out of your linguistic toolbox, I can assure you that it not only proves useful getting around day-to-day in Korea, but demonstrates a solid command of the Korean language. In the following examples, the phrase I've included in parentheses is the non-stated, understood meaning of the conjugation:

Example 1

A: Did you find an umbrella by any chance?

혹시 우산 찾았어요?
hok-shee oo-san cha-jas-saw-yo?

B: Oh! Did I find an umbrella?
(is that what you're asking)?

아! 우산 찾았**냐고 말씀하
셨어요**?
*ah! ooh-san cha-jan-**ya-go
mal-sseum-ha-sshaw-saw-yo**?*

Example 2

A: I'd like to buy some film.

필름 사고 싶어요.
peel-leum sa-go-sheep-aw-yo.

B: Oh! You'd like to buy some film
(is that what you said)?

아! 필름 사고 싶**다고 그랬어**?
*ah! peel-leum sa-go-sheep-**da-go ke-raes-saw**?*

Example 3

A: Do you know where City Hall
Station is?

시청역 어디인지 아세요?
shee-chung-yawk aw-dee-een-gee a-sae-yo?

B: Do I know where City Hall
Station is?
(is that what you mean?)

시청역 어디**냐고 말했어요**?
shee-chung-yawk aw-dee-
nya-go mal-haes-saw-yo?

Example 4

A: Are you studying Korean these days?

요즘 한국말을 공부하세요?
*yo-jeum han-goong-ma-reul
gong-boo-ha-sae-yo?*

B: Am I studying Korean these days?
(is that what you're asking me?)

요즘 한국말을 공부**하냐고
물었어요**?
*yo-jeum han-goong-ma-reul
gong-boo-**ha-nay-go moo-
raws-saw-yo**?*

In all four examples, the B speaker is just confirming what he thinks he heard, or otherwise making sure that he got the facts straight the first time. Although all four verbs in the previous examples are used in conversation (i.e. 말하다, 말씀하다, 묻다, 그랬다), the only major difference between them is that *mal-sseum-ha-da* (말씀하다) is the more honorific version of *mal-ha-da* (말하다), the latter being used more between friends, and the former being used more in business, when meeting strangers, or when wanting to be polite.

Chapter 10

Pronouns

대명사

No matter what anyone tells you and no matter what you see translated throughout Korea, pronouns are *not* nearly as common in Korean as they are in English, save the pronouns 'I' and 'we' (and even then they're not nearly as common as they are in English). Pronouns do exist in Korean, but aside from inanimate objects ('this,' 'that,' 'it'), where pronouns are extremely common in Korean, they are rarely used. Understanding this fact and working around it takes many students a great deal of time. This is mostly because until you start learning Korean you won't realize how much you depend on pronouns for sentence clarity.

WHO, THEN, ARE YOU TALKING ABOUT?

Undoubtedly the biggest source of confusion with pronouns has to do with the use of 'you.' In English, the use and inclusion of pronouns (as subjects) is absolutely essential to communicate effectively and clearly. In Korean, the inclusion of the subject is not always essential and often assumed to be understood between the speakers. Even when a subject is included in the phrase (grammatically), the meaning of the subject might be unclear (in real terms) because of Koreans' reluctance to use people's names in conversation.

When the subject is clearly understood (and sometimes even when it's not) and the second person pronoun is dropped altogether, the sentence has the ability to be little more than a verb conjugated for tense and relationship with the other speaker. To use an example that many students of Korean are familiar with:

Korean	Literal Translation	Proper Translation
어디 가? (aw-dee ka?)	Where go?	Where are you going? /Where are you off to?

However, the dropping of the subject is not exclusive to the second person *you*. The subject can be dropped at will when the speaker feels comfortable knowing that the subject is understood with the other speaker. Hence, those of you that have asked a Korean friend to translate something you heard may have been surprised when your friend replied, But I don't know who he/she is talking to/about. Consider the following example:

Korean	Literal Translation	Proper Translation
뭐라고 했어요? (maw-ra-go haes-saw-yo?)	What said?	What did you/he/she/it say?

This example provides clear enough proof that if you are entering into a conversation well under way, it might be impossible to understand the context. This is why it's often necessary to listen for a short while before concluding anything about the nature of the conversation or speech.

BUT I'VE SEEN 'YOU' WRITTEN ALL OVER THE PLACE!

I've been guilty of this statement on numerous occasions: 'But I've seen pronouns used in advertisements, on TV, and in movie subtitles all the time! If they can do it there, why can't I use it when I speak?' Good question. But you may not like the answer.

As will be discussed in more depth in **Chapter 13**, sometimes words, phrases and conjugations are only used in the written or the spoken form, but not both. With regards to the use of 'you,' it, unfortunately, falls into this last category much of the time. This sly pronoun has several translations in Korean that range from the formal (and sometimes matrimonial, sometimes antagonistic) *tang-shin* (당신), to the often-seen-in-subtitles *ja-nae* (자네), to the occasionally-used-between-married-women *dae-geun* (댁은), to the informal *nawn* (넌), *naw-neun* (너는), *naw* (너), *nee-ga* (니가), and *nae-ga* (네가), to the classical and more literary *ke-dae* (그대), to the friendly/romantic, but sometimes abstract *cha-gi* (자기), to the most infrequently used in conversation, *gwee-ha* (귀하).

In almost all of the translations of 'you,' the word is not used in spoken Korean nearly as much as it is in English. Also, the rules and laws governing each word's use is not clear-cut, and therefore, not easily explained. The easiest advice I can give on this point would be to not use 'you' in Korean, except in situations when you are speaking *ban-mal* with a close friend, in which case the use of *naw* (너) is completely acceptable.

Don't say 'you!'

When I first moved to Seoul and found my own place, I naturally had a landlady, *jeep-joo-een* (집주인), as opposed to a landlord, like almost every other tenant in this country. My landlady was particularly gregarious and we would often try and strike up a conversation in my limited Korean. At the time, I was studying the language but still did not have a firm grasp on addressing people. I, like many before me, refused to believe that I couldn't use the pronoun 'you' at will. As a result, I often said *tang-sheen* (당신) to my landlady when asking her a question. I could tell that she was never really comfortable with my use of it, but until I was told how awkward I sounded from close friends, I kept up with it. 'Just drop the subject and speak to her without one,' my friends urged me.

'No subject when speaking to my landlady?' I asked back.

'Yeah, you don't need it,' they assured me. 'If you want to call her anything, call her *a-joo-maw-nee* (아주머니),' they went on.

'So let me get this straight,' I fired back. 'I can refer to my landlady in the third person when talking with her directly, but I can't refer to her in the second person when talking with her.'

'Right.'

'Okay. That makes a lot of sense. Thanks for clearing that up,' I said as I took a deep breath.

To this day I still get a chuckle out of the fact that I was making someone uncomfortable by using the respectable pronoun 'you.'

THE ROLE OF THE SPEAKER

The first of two exceptions to the pronoun rule in Korean is 'I.' This pronoun is expressed several ways in Korean: *chae-ga* (제가), *jaw-neun* (저는), *jawn* (전), *jaw* (저), *nae-ga* (내가), *na-neun* (나는), and *nan* (난). The important thing to keep in mind is that once you've established the fact that you're the subject of the phrase or discussion, it's not necessary to keep putting the pronoun 'I' in your sentences. Look at the following example comparing a random sentence from English and Korean:

> **I** went to the store to buy some milk, but before **I** got there, **I** ran into a few friends, so **I** took off with them to play some pool.

In that one sentence, the pronoun 'I' is used **four times**. If that same sentence were to be said in Korean, though, the pronoun 'I' would only be used once. Take a look at the translation below (in *ban-mal*):

> **나는** 우유 사러 가게에 가는 길에 친구들을 몇 명 만나서 같이 당구 치러 갔어.
> (**na-neun** oo-yoo sa-raw ka-gae-ae ka-neun-kee-rae cheen-goo-deu-reul myun-myung man-na-saw ka-chee dang-goo chee-raw kas-saw.)

EVERYONE IS JUST ONE BIG, HAPPY FAMILY

The other exception to the pronoun rule is the word 'we,' which is expressed as *oo-ree* (우리), *oo-ree-ga* (우리가), *oo-ree-neun* (우리는), or *oo-reen* (우린). In more formal situations you would say *jaw-eui* (저희), *jaw-eui-neun* (저희는), or *jaw-eui-ga* (저희가), *jaw-euin* (저흰).

However, there are two things you should know about the word 'we' as it's used in Korean. The first is that it's both a pronoun and an adjective (i.e. 'we' and 'our'); the second thing is that it's not always meant to be plural and inclusive of the other speaker. The most common situation where this is evident is when Koreans talk about their family and refer to their mother as 'our mother,' *oo-ree awm-ma* (우리 엄마), or 'our parents,' *oo-ree boo-mo-neem* (우리 부모님), for example. What the speaker means to convey in situations like this is merely 'my mother' and 'my parents.'

FROM LANGUAGE TO CULTURE

I've read many times how some people cite the fact that Koreans use the words *oo-ree* (우리) and *jaw-eui* (저의) as proof that the group mentality dominates over the individual in Korea. From a linguistic and historical point of view, I tend to agree with this sentiment. Classic examples that scholars cite are the fact that Koreans don't usually say 'Korean' when talking about their own language, but *oo-ree mal* (우리말), 'our language'; when talking about their country, they often replace 'Korea,' *han-gook* (한국) with *oo-ree na-ra* (우리나라), 'our country.'

AND THE OTHER PRONOUNS...

Technically, pronouns exist for 'he,' *ke* (그), and 'she,' *ke-nyaw* (그녀), but like the use of 'you,' they are used mostly in a written context. There is a word for 'they,' *ke-deul* (그들), but it is not used nearly as much as it is in English.

Titles, on the other hand, like *a-joom-ma* (아줌마), or *a-jaw-shee* (아저씨),

are much more common and natural in Korean when referring to 'he' or 'she' much of the time. (Please see **Chapter 17** for more on this) Alternatively, the pronouns for 'it' and 'these,' *e-gawt* (이것), and 'that' and 'those,' *ke-gawt* (그것), are common within Korean speech.

A BRIEF SUMMARY OF THE PRONOUNS

I know how confusing this must look, so let me try and make this a bit easier by breaking down the pronouns in a simple chart. In spaces where there is no word, it means that there is either no word for it in Korean, or it's not appropriate to use the word in that situation:

English	Informal Korean Word	Formal Korean Word
I	*na* (나)	*jaw* (저)
You	*naw* (너), *nee* (니)	
He	*ke* (그)	
She	*ke-nyaw* (그녀)	
We	*oo-ree* (우리)	*jaw-eui* (저희)
They	*ke-deul* (그들)	
It	*ee-gawt* (이것), *ke-gawt* (그것)	

And for the adjectives, the same rules apply as did for pronouns:

English	Informal Korean Word	Formal Korean Word
My	*nae* (내), *na-ae* (나의)	*jae* (제)
Your	*naw-ae*(너의), *nae* (네)'	
His	*ke-ae* (그의)	
Her	*ke-nyaw-ae* (그녀의)	
Our	*oo-ree* (우리)	*jaw-eui* (저희)
Their	*ke-de-rae* (그들의)	
Its	*ee-gawt-de-rae* (이것들의), *ke-gawt-de-rae* (그것들의)	

¹ The words 'my,' *nae* (내), and 'your,' *nae* (네), are written differently in Korean, but pronounced exactly the same way. That's why it can be extremely difficulty for non-native Korean speakers to understand what the other person is talking about when the other speaker uses one of these two words.

Chapter 11

Chinese Characters
한자

I think Chinese characters rank right up there with the coolest things in the world. Before I studied any Chinese, everyone told me that I had to study *han-cha* (한자) if I really wanted to improve my Korean. Though there's a lot of truth to that on a linguistic level, there's so much more to Chinese characters that make them endlessly fascinating for the typical native English speaker.

A LONG AND DISTINGUISHED HISTORY

The first notion of an iconified written language was introduced to East Asia about 7000 years ago.[1] However, the earliest archaeological evidence there is of written Chinese dates back to approximately 1800 B.C. At the time, the only people that used the written form of the Chinese language were government officials and record scribes. Inscriptions found on tortoise shells and flat cattle bones reveal ancient China's first signs of the writing system we know of today as Chinese, or *han-cha*, as it's called in Korean.[2]

By about 800 B.C. Chinese characters were finally standardized, and a corresponding catalogue created to go along with them.[3] These characters were

[1] A monk by the name of Fu-Hsi is actually credited with having brought iconified language to China about 5000 B.C. *See Chinatown.org's website at www.chinatown.org*

[2] See *www.chinatown.org*

[3] See *www.chinatown.org*

from that time on referred to as Grand Seal characters. At the beginning of the Han dynasty (206 B.C-A.D. 220), Emperor Chin Shih-Huang had his court officials set about standardizing the language once again. The roughly 3,500 Chinese characters in use throughout the kingdom then were simplified and labeled Small Seal characters, with all other characters being deemed illegal to use after the introduction of Emperor Chin's Small Seal characters.[4] Although Chinese has evolved as a written language since that time over 2,000 years ago, the written Chinese language in use today is a variant of the same standardized Small Seal characters that Emperor Chin brought about more than two millennia ago.[5]

COMING TO KOREA

Similar to Confucianism, the exact date at which Chinese characters arrived on the Korean peninsula is unknown to this day. However, it's a safe bet that Chinese characters probably arrived on the peninsula sometime during China's Han dynasty, the dynasty whose outer limit borders stretched as far as today's North Korea. Although we don't know the exact date that Chinese characters arrived on the Korean peninsula, we do know that Koreans used Chinese characters as a national writing system from approximately A.D. 200.[6]

Interestingly enough, it was Chinese characters that facilitated some of the first discussion and bargaining between Westerners and Koreans. Even after *Hangeul* was invented in the 15th century, Chinese characters continued to play an important role in Korean society. Some of the first Western traders and missionaries to Korea had no ability to speak or write Korean, but they often had people with them that were fluent in Chinese and Chinese characters. As a result, the two peoples from opposite sides of the planet communicated in a written dialogue: Chinese characters.

MODERN CHINESE CHARACTERS

Chinese characters have gone through many changes in more recent times.

[4] See *www.chinatown.org*

[5] See *www.chinatown.org/culture/chinese_characters/chinese_characters.htm*

[6] See the *Korea Herald*, p. 10, Friday October 4, 2002.

This was never so pronounced as when Mao Tse-tung, or *Mo Taek Dong* (모택동) as he's known in Korean, came to power in 1949. Upon the founding of the People's Republic of China (PRC), Mao attempted to do what King Sejong had in mind five hundred years before—eradicate illiteracy by simplifying the language. However, unlike Sejong, Mao did not create an entirely new language. Instead, he made characters easier to write by reducing the number of strokes in many of the more complicated characters. He also simplified the radicals that make up individual characters, which made it easier for the hundreds of millions of poor, illiterate farmers in his country to learn the written form of their mother tongue. From the thousands upon thousands of characters that existed in one form or another (there were over 50,000 in one of the earliest dynastic dictionaries), 4000 characters were ultimately simplified by the 1950s.[7]

Korea, on the other hand, never altered Chinese characters as much as the Chinese. Consequently, today Chinese characters in Korea are closer to what they were originally in China hundreds of years ago. In yet another ironic twist of fate, just as the notion of Confucianism grew to be stronger in Korea than in China, so too did the written language of Chinese remain closer to the original in Korea.

LEARNING *HAN-CHA* TODAY

Back to the original question, though, is *han-cha* necessary to learn Korean? No, it's not. Is *han-cha* helpful in learning Korean? No doubt about it. Most of the Korean language derives its meaning from Chinese, and so as a result, learning Chinese allows the student to notice patterns and roots much quicker than the student who has no knowledge of Chinese.

There is also a practical side to this that one has to consider, though. Chinese is used—however sparingly—throughout many newspapers and advertisements today in South Korea. This means that if you wish to read a Korean newspaper (save the Hankyoreh (한겨레), the only major newspaper printed in South Korea without any *han-cha*) you need a working knowledge of *han-cha*.

[7] See *http://zhongwen.com/faq.htm* for more information.

125

NOT LATIN!

My father always used to tell me that to study Latin was to study the roots of English, and that a thorough knowledge of Latin made you a better English speaker. In many ways, the same can be said for learning Chinese with regards to Korean. Although a knowledge of *han-cha* does not facilitate a greater understanding of Korean grammar, it does provide the student with a dearth of new information and knowledge about two cultures steeped in thousands of years of history, tradition and culture. However, if studying Chinese isn't appealing enough, consider the more artistic version of simple Chinese characters: Chinese calligraphy, *saw-yae* (서예). Not only is Chinese calligraphy more fun than learning Chinese through rote memorization, but it will allow you to learn a whole new set of vocabulary associated with calligraphy.

Who Would Have Thought There Would Be Chinese in China!

When I first went to China, I'd been in Korea a grand total of three and a half years and I had studied enough *han-cha* up to that time to remember some of the more useful characters. This was a fact that would come to help me greatly on my trip.

Upon my arrival in Beijing, I quickly realized that the average person in China was in no position to have a conversation with me in English. Later on in the trip, while trying to buy a train ticket in the far western town of Jiayuguan, I found myself in an incredibly tough bind—the person selling tickets didn't understand any English and I didn't speak any Chinese. I thought quickly, though, and realized that I had the ability to write the Chinese characters of the place I was going, Lanzhou.

As people were pawing and grabbing at me, I took a piece of paper out and wrote the Chinese characters of my destination. Just as the scene was turning ugly (scores of people wanting to get one of the few remaining seats on the train all pushing me out of the way), the man behind the counter handed me my ticket and I sighed a huge breath of relief; *han-cha* had saved the day!

CHINESE CHARACTERS VS. CHINESE PICTOGRAMS

Some people refer to the written form of the Chinese language as Chinese pictograms. While it's true that some characters in the Chinese language do have a pictographic history, most do not. Chinese characters are just that: characters. In certain characters, for instance, it's still possible to see the meaning of the word from the character, like 'tree,' *mok* (목 · 木), and 'rice,' *mæ* (미 · 米), clearly resembling the etymology behind the character.[8] Other characters, though, resemble an idea in an abstract form, such as 'one,' *eel* (일 · 一), 'two,' *ee* (이 · 二), and 'three,' *sam* (삼 · 三). However, most characters' meaning is not readily identifiable from the character itself, as it may be a combination of pictures (pictographs) and ideas (ideographs). Examples of this are 'horse,' *ma* (마 · 馬) and 'story,' *cheung* (층 · 層). To learn Chinese characters today you have to be much more scholastic in your approach than merely trying to guess the meaning through a series of pictographs; the radical is now every student's means to learn the language.

Radicals are the small components of the word (i.e. the character), which as a sum combine to form one meaning. Thus, most words in Chinese have several radicals (meanings), which come together to form one separate meaning distinct unto itself. For example, consider the Chinese character for **love** [戀], which is *yun* (연) in Korean. The Chinese character is derived from three radicals (from upper left to upper right and then down): **silk/word/silk over heart**. Now it might help to know that silk also means rope in Chinese, so, effectively, the meaning of *yun* from the original Chinese is **the rope binding the word** (or commitment, as it may be seen in love) **to the heart**. Many characters in Chinese tend to have meanings that are as thought provoking and interesting as the last example.

CHINESE-KOREAN DICTIONARIES

Like most things in the Korean language, the word for Chinese-Korean dictionary, *oak-pyun* (옥편), has an interesting story behind it. *Oak-pyun* is derived from the Chinese characters jade (玉) and book (篇). It's important to note here that for most of Chinese history the gemstone jade was considered to

[8] In the case of the word 'rice' [米], the character is derived from the rice paddy sprouting up from the fields around it, the roots dangling below water level. With respect to the word 'tree' [木], the tree has roots below the surface and a body above it.

be the most valuable and precious of all gemstones. Emperors in China would go as far as spending an entire reign trying to amass as much jade as possible. And in a fitting twist of language, the word for king in Chinese, *wang* (왕 · 王), is almost identical to that of jade, *oak* (옥 · 玉), this telling you something of how close the two were thought of in ancient China.

As cool as the meaning behind the word *oak-pyun* might be, though, you needn't worry yourself with learning how to get around one unless you plan on making Chinese characters a part of your study routine; just recognizing the basic *han-cha* characters used in everyday life is hard enough without having to sift through a Chinese-Korean dictionary. For those intent on studying *han-cha*, though, there is a systematic way by which to look up words in a dictionary that has no alphabet.

TWO WAYS TO LOOK UP WORDS

The list of Chinese radicals was finally (and thankfully, I'm sure) standardized in China in 1714 under the reign of Emperor K'ang-hsi.[9] This standardization then provided the basis by which people could look words up in a dictionary. Amazingly, the same system of radicals is in use today in China, Korea and Japan. However, as mentioned above, the PRC has changed the Chinese characters themselves somewhat, so that a Korean looking up a Chinese radical in Beijing or a Chinese person looking up a radical in Seoul might be in for a bit of a loop.

Using these radicals, you can search for a word in an *oak-pyun* in one of two ways: **by counting the number of strokes needed to make the character** (which in itself is a skill) or **by looking under the relevant radical**. Each system of looking up words in an *oak-pyun* is fraught with challenges, though.

The first method—stroke counting—is the longest, and therefore the most difficult and time-consuming, not to mention the most unreliable. Although Chinese characters may look very similar in China, Korea, and Japan, they do not always have the same number of strokes.

The problem with the second method of searching for words—looking for radicals—can be problematic because the first radical (generally defined as the

[9] James C. Whitlock Jr., *Chinese Characters in Korean*, p. 11.

128

radical in the uppermost left corner of the character) is not always clearly evident.

HOW MANY RADICALS CAN THERE BE?

Today, there are approximately 214 accepted basic radicals separating the thousands of Chinese characters.[10] These 214 radicals, when built one on top of another, form the basis for almost every word you will ever come across in newspapers and books. Each radical, like many Greek and Latin roots, has a meaning that not only makes sense, but is connected to other radicals (and thus other words). With that in mind, it's possible to learn Chinese characters through their basic radicals and thus increase your knowledge of the Korean language, while learning a lot of interesting historical and cultural information about ancient China. Though most radicals are not incredibly complicated in and of themselves (relative to the language they are derived from, mind you), the ideas or pictures that they come to form are nothing less than daunting to someone who has never studied *han-cha* before.

SURGICALLY MODIFYING CHINESE-DERIVED NOUNS

As discussed in **Chapter 7**, one of the three types of Korean verbs is the *ha-da* (하다) verb. What many students of Korean don't know, though, is that almost every *ha-da* verb is an extension of a Chinese-derived noun.[11] Adding *ha-da* to the end of a Chinese-derived noun changes the role of the word grammatically to that of a verb. It's that straightforward and easy. Honest. I know you're shaking your head and saying to yourself, There's no way anything in this language can be that easy, but I'll give you a few examples so you believe me. You know the words 'choice,' *sun-taek* (선택), 'washing,' *bbal-lae* (빨래), and 'publishing,' *chool-pan* (출판), but you don't know how to use them as verbs. No problem. 'To choose' becomes *sun-taek-ha-da* (선택하다), 'to wash' becomes *bbal-lae-ha-da* (빨래하다), and 'to publish' becomes *chool-pan-ha-da* (출판하다). This might be clearer if it's all shown in one direct line:

[10] James C. Whitlock Jr., *Chinese Characters in Korean*, p. 8.

[11] Though the far majority of *ha-da* (하다) verbs are derived from Chinese nouns, there are some words, such as *soo-go-ha-da* (수고하다) and *kawl-lae-jeel-ha-da* (걸레질하다), for example, that are pure Korean, otherwise known as *soon han-goong-mal* (순 한국말).

choice	(선택)	→	**to choose**	(선택하다)
washing	(빨래)	→	**to wash** (i.e. laundry)	(빨래하다)
publishing	(출판)	→	**to publish**	(출판하다)

Alternatively, whenever you see a verb that's not connected with *ha-da*, you know that it's derived from pure Korean (i.e. it has no Chinese root). Examples of this are 'to eat,' *mawk-da* (먹다), 'to cut,' *ja-re-da* (자르다), and 'to be easy,' *shweep-da* (쉽다).

THE COOLEST OF THE COOL

I don't think I'm that different from many other people that come to Korea and find a lot that has to do with the Korean language fascinating, enriching, and entertaining. As I keep reiterating throughout this book, so much more can be learned from studying Korean than just the written and spoken forms. In many ways, *han-cha* is the epitome of this fact. Listed below are 10 of some of the most thought-provoking examples of Chinese characters, and the meaning that can be derived from their radicals. I invite you to take a moment and consider how some of these words derived their meaning, and what they mean in English as a basis of comparison:[12]

Korean	Chinese	Roots	Meaning
지 (*gee*)	知	arrow/mouth	**knowledge**: those with knowledge have a mouth as sharp as an arrow (which kind of makes you wonder whether the ancient Chinese were thinking of intelligent scholars or cunning politicians).

[12] All of the meanings to the following Chinese roots come from James C. Whitlock Jr.'s *Chinese Characters in Korean.*

130

Korean	Chinese	Roots	Meaning
용 (*yong*)	冗	roof/legs	**useless**: the man that stays at home and has no work to do in the fields is useless.
산 (*san*)	算	abacus/bamboo/ hands	**calculation**: this is almost too easy to figure out from its roots. I think everyone gets the picture of how the Chinese used to count.
처 (*chaw*)	妻	hair/woman	**wife**: from the ancient custom of marrying a woman by dragging them by the hair.
망 (*mang*)	望	man/moon/ earth	**hope**: man staring at the moon on the surface of the earth represented hope. It was believed that someone looking up at the moon, or in the distance for that matter, carried with it the idea of hope.
성 (*sung*)	性	heart/innate	**nature**: funny enough, the Korean word for nature (성) is also the word for **sex**. This should be all the ammunition teenagers need when pleading with their parents that what they do with their partner is completely 'natural.' At the same time, parents can point to

Korean	Chinese	Roots	Meaning
			the root of this word when they say that has to be from the heart.
청 (*chung*)	廳	house/govern/ear/heart	**hall**: this is the character used with government halls, as in *shee-chung* (시청), city hall. Ideally, the notion of government was for the ruler to listen carefully to the concerns of the people with all of his heart (i.e. virtuously).
인 (*een*)	仁	man/two	**kindness**: the fundamental precept of Confucianism: to love each other is kindness.
억 (*awk*)	憶	thought/keep/	**remember/memory**: thoughts kept heart in the heart (often interchangeable with the word 'mind' in Korean) are remembered. In this case, I like to think of it in its literal meaning: ideas kept close to the heart are truly remembered.
신 (*sheen*)	娠	woman/clam shell	**pregnant**: the woman combined with the clamshells (which come in pairs or duplicates) are meant to signify the pregnant

Korean	**Chinese**	**Roots**	**Meaning**
			woman, or more aptly, the mother and her offspring.

Part 3

Everyday Usage:

Getting By In the Trenches

Even monkeys fall from trees
원숭이도 나무에서 떨어질 때가 있다

Chapter 12

Speaking Korean Day-to-Day
생활 한국어 말하기

Learning to speak Korean is a slow and laborious process. But where there's a will, there's a way, and with learning to speak Korean, if you have the will to practice day in and day out, in good times and in bad, you *will* learn this language. When going about your day with this new language in tow you'll find a whole world opening up to you. I've read a great deal about Korea, but nothing I've read *about* Korea comes close to capturing what it's like to *speak* Korean. As you become more fluent in Korean, you'll find speaking the language a fascinating window into the culture as it opens up before your very eyes.

HITS AND MISSES

Because most native English speakers learning Korean have no background in languages such as Chinese or Japanese (two languages that would be extremely useful in helping you learn Korean), Korean takes a good amount of time to learn. I liken learning Korean to a baby learning to walk. It takes months before a baby can even crawl, let alone walk. But over time, after watching others do the same thing over and over, a baby learns by instinct, by repetition, and by failure. With this in mind, learning Korean is entirely within your grasp.

The chapters preceding this one discuss how the language works on linguistic, grammatical, historical, and cultural levels, yet there is another side to the language that has to be kept in mind: the everyday side. As I've read in magazines like *National Geographic* countless times, language is one of the key conveyors of any culture. And it's not just the words themselves, but the mannerisms that go along with them: a flick of the hand, the arch of the back, the blink of an eye. It's not just in words that the language is expressed, but the tone, the hand movements, the eye contact, and a million other things that give meaning to the language as a whole.

SAME-SAME, BUT DIFFERENT

Koreans are exactly the same as people from other countries in too many ways to count; they have fears and desires and hopes and dreams and likes and dislikes and certain ways to communicate all these things. When you first venture out onto the streets of Seoul or Mokpo or Gangneung, it really doesn't matter where, you'll notice one thing right off the bat: Koreans speak very quickly. That's not to say that English speakers go slowly with each other, though. I'd guess it has more to do with the fact that Korean words have fewer syllables than their English counterparts, and so expressing thoughts in Korean can be done more quickly.

'Watch out for falling syllables' should be one of your first warning signs. Don't be scared to tell people to slow down. Most people will be very accommodating when they see you making an effort to speak the language, and slow down accordingly. Sometimes, however, people take this as a cue to switch into English. 'Sorry, would you mind saying that again,' or 'Sorry, would you mind, slowing down a little,' are two phrases occasionally understood by Koreans to mean, I'm sorry, I'm too embarrassed to say it, but would you mind switching into English so I can understand what on God's green earth you're saying? When this happens, simply stay in Korean and say something like this:

English	Wow, your English is amazing! But don't speak English on my account—you can speak Korean to me.
Korean	와! 영어 잘 하시네요. 근데요, 한국말로 하셔도 되요.
Phonetic Transliteration	*wa! yung-aw chal ha-shee-nae-yo. keun-dae-yo, han-goong-mal-lo ha-shaw-do dwae-yo.*

Why Learn Korean?

The first time a Korean asked me, 'But why are you learning Korean?' I thought she was joking. The woman was a friend of mine and knew I was living and working in Korea. Still, though, she was mystified as to why I was learning the language. As this began to happen more often, I became confused; the question seemed completely irrational and illogical.

Today, I think there are two major reasons why Koreans can't understand why a foreigner would learn Korean. The first reason is that many simply can't believe that a foreigner is speaking Korean to them. This has partly to do with the fact that some Koreans consider their language the most difficult language in the world, and so find it amazing that someone has learned it, and part to do with the fact that Korea really was a Hermit Kingdom for millennia upon millennia. Nowhere else in Asia have I seen the local population make such a big deal when a foreigner speaks the language. Although Korea's first contact with the West came in the 17th century, in truth, it didn't really come until the Korean War, that is, in the latter half of the 20th century. Most Koreans (though this is changing quickly) simply have no experience speaking Korean with someone of non-Korean decent, so the first time they do so they're quite taken aback.

The second reason has more to do with the non-native Korean population itself, though. Foreigners living in Korea, and here I should limit my scope to Westerners from Europe and North America, don't usually learn Korean.[1] It doesn't matter what walk of life they come from—teachers,

[1] In my own experiences, I've found that people from other parts of the world that live in Korea— Chinese, Japanese, Southeast Asians or Africans, for instance—speak Korean quite admirably.

138

diplomats, military personnel, business people—the fact is that most Westerners in Korea don't usually speak the language. As a result, you can't help but sympathize with Koreans' reaction to a Westerner speaking Korean when, in their experience, they have never seen, heard of, or met someone who actually spoke the language.

So the first time, or next time, a Korean asks you, 'Why in heaven's name are you learning Korean?' you can try my all-time favorite response and see what kind of reaction you get: because I live in Korea.

SMILE AND NOD

I think people do this in every language for one reason or another, but when you don't understand every single word being said—but you do get the gist—just smile and nod. Koreans have a tendency of asking if you understand what it is they just said. It's not meant as a test of how much you're picking up. It's simply a habit most people employ throughout the course of a dialogue. In situations where this happens, don't be shy to say yes and spare yourself the whole thing being done all over again. Obviously, if you have no idea what was said then it's important to say something, but don't be scared off by the repeated, 'Do you understand?' questions that will inevitably arise in a Korean conversation.

On another level, you'll notice that Koreans smile and nod a lot when they speak with other Koreans. There won't necessarily be an exchange of words, but merely a bow, a smile, and perhaps a nod of the head. This is especially true when older people see younger people on the street, in a hallway, or after they've finished talking with them and see them a moment later. In all these cases, a smile and a nod (or a bow) can mean as much as a whole sentence. I actually went over six months without hearing my landlady say a single word to me in public; every time she saw me on the streets around our apartment building she would simply smile quickly and nod. Did that mean she was angry with me or unwilling to acknowledge my existence? No. It was just her way of saying hello without any words and proof that there's more at play within this language (or should I say outside of the language) than meets the eye.

NEW NOTIONS OF DIALOGUE

When I first came to Korea, it would drive me crazy when students, rather than have a dialogue, would have two monologues with each other. The students would listen patiently until the other speaker was entirely finished, then go off on their own monologue and not be interrupted once. Initially, I was annoyed with this from a teaching perspective; students not *conversing* with each other defeated the notion of teaching English *conversation*. It was only after being here for some months and starting to speak a little Korean that I saw the cultural dimension at work.

When two people are close friends in Korea, they'll babble back and forth like good friends do in any culture. However, if the two people are not close, if there is a significant age gap, or if there is a hierarchical relationship at work, then the two people do not always converse on a dialogue basis. What they do instead is, like my students who are unfamiliar with their partner, sit and listen to an entire monologue before saying anything.

In this way, be prepared for monologue conversations when speaking Korean in certain situations. Although it's not the norm for English speakers from the West, for example, it can be the norm in Korea. I've actually had an entire conversation on the phone when I didn't say one word. I simply listened, said yes over and over, and then hung up. Was I rude? On the contrary, I think I was not only polite, but acting in accord with what was expected of me (it was a boss phoning me to let me know of work I had coming up). So the next time you're out for dinner or coffee or a few drinks and the person you're with wants to control the conversation, don't be offended and don't think they're being rude. It's simply a different way of conversing.

ASKING QUESTIONS

Asking questions is not done the same way in Korean for the same reason that verbs are conjugated for situation: it depends on the age and social relationship of the two people. Thus, for example, the first time I met my girlfriend's father, I knew better than to ask any questions. I let him do all the asking, while I took care of all the answers. Generally speaking, younger people do not ask questions to older people, or juniors of seniors, or employees of bosses. This is doubly so when the relationship is not developed, when there is no *jung*, so to speak, between the two speakers.

Some readers might be confused by what I'm saying about not asking questions, because in their experience Koreans have been nothing short of extroverted, friendly, warm, and inclusive in their conversations; Koreans have responded with a genuine smile when they were asked questions—even of a personal nature—by their non-native Korean friend. That is very likely true, but like I said earlier in this book, Koreans tend to transform themselves when speaking with non-native Koreans, especially when it's done in English. They shed a great deal of the linguistic weight on them from their own language and culture. Koreans who speak English have, it would appear, two personalities, one when speaking English and one when speaking Korean. The same freedom that English grants by its lack of hierarchy is not part of Korean and should be respected if you're to converse fluently and politely in the language.

A SENSE OF HUMOR

Despite what some people say, there is no word in the Korean language that means the exact same thing as 'sarcasm.' If you've watched any kind of comedy program in Korea, you're probably already familiar with the sense of humor—in your face, slapstick, over the top, funny. The fact that there's no word for sarcasm in the Korean language should be a pretty good indicator of the status of it for Koreans; I can't count the number of times I've told sarcastic jokes in Korean and been greeted by nothing more than a stone wall. That's not to say that Koreans can't be funny in English and that you can't be funny in Korean. Au contraire, all it takes is a little flexibility and a willingness to see things a different way for you to learn the rhythm of a new sense of humor. Part of what this requires is a decent knowledge of slang or everyday Korean. Although you won't know much of this when you begin your studies, indulging in the comedy aspect of the language is a fun way by which to increase and expand your knowledge of more commonly used words and phrases.

JOKE'S AT YOUR EXPENSE

Being laughed at is no fun in any culture. Learning to grin and bear it when Koreans laugh at your feeble attempt at speaking Korean (which is what inevitably happens to everybody) is an art, make no mistake about it. In my early days of learning Korean, I can't count the number of times people laughed at me in front of my face, told me what I was saying was completely wrong, and then proceeded to correct me in front of a crowd. As humbling an experience as it may be, it does take some time to get used to.

The first thing Koreans will tell you after having a laugh at your expense is that they're not used to hearing foreigners speak Korean. I don't think I was very different from many others early on when I would blush, laugh nervously, and then repeat the word or sentence once again in an attempt to correct my mistake. After a while I learned to take it with a grain of salt (perhaps a salt shaker is more accurate), but I've been witness to some foreigners that become visibly angry every time this occurs.

The key to understanding this laugh at your expense is that it is not done in malice. Koreans are genuinely surprised when they hear foreigners speak Korean and have no experience to balance it with when replying to an incorrect phrase or strangely pronounced word. Although you, the reader, may not do the same thing when Koreans try and speak English, it's important to remember that they are not out to get you, which you'll inevitably feel is being done when it happens your first time. In place of putting together a complex sentence to respond to this, something that will take a while to learn, I would suggest merely keeping your calm, smiling (as slight as it may be), and repeat what it is you just said. Getting angry and telling the person you're speaking with that it's absurdly rude to laugh at someone in their face will solve nothing and only create friction where it's not needed.

EVERYBODY'S FLUENT!

I mentioned in the preface to this book that people have been complimenting me on my Korean since the day I mastered *an-nyung-ha-sae-yo*

(안녕하세요), and I wasn't kidding. Koreans have told me over and over, 'You speak Korean really well,' since my first month in the country. In the beginning, this was naturally a big boost to my confidence and inspired me to learn even more. Yet after a while I realized the comments about my Korean weren't changing. After enrolling in my first course and completing a month's study at a *hagwon* (학원) in Seoul, people were still saying, 'You speak Korean really well.' Confusion quickly wore off and disappointment soon took its place.

Only when spending a significant amount of time with a friend who was truly fluent in Korean and seeing that she was told the same thing all the time did I realize that it was almost a knee-jerk reaction of Koreans. People just learning the language are told their Korean's wonderful and people who have learned Korean to near fluency are told their Korean's wonderful, I reasoned to myself. So how do Koreans differentiate between different levels of people learning the language? Simply put, they don't.

IS ANYBODY TRULY FLUENT?

I've personally never heard a Korean use the word fluent, *yoo-chang-ha-da* (유창하다), about anyone in my entire time in Korea. Without fail, a Korean will use the same phrase with you as they use for every non-native Korean learning the language, 'You speak Korean really well!' That being said, it's important to keep in mind that Koreans don't measure someone's ability with a second language the same way people do in the West. You might resent the fact that Koreans don't give genuine compliments about your language early on, but you should learn to accept it as nothing more than a cultural difference.

RIDING THE WAVES

On my good days I've bought stocks, rented a home, translated documents, conducted business, and won over my girlfriend after a fight. On my bad days I can't seem to understand anything. In the beginning I found the waves of highs and lows to come awfully close together, and this added to the difficulty in learning Korean. Over the years these waves *do* come less and less frequently, but I still *do* get them. And so will you. But that's all right because you're prepared. You're prepared for the ups and downs, the valleys and the troughs, the peaks and the canyons of this language.

If you stick with the language for years, anything is possible. But for those of you intent on only staying in Korea for a few months or a couple of years, be realistic. Korean is not Spanish, it's not French, and it's certainly not just another language. Don't get too down on yourself (like I tend to do), don't beat yourself when you make mistakes (as I love to do), and don't take everything so seriously when speaking the language (as I always do). This may seem like hypocritical advice considering I've just admitted to doing all of the above on a not-so-healthy regular basis, but it's the truth. Let the inner voice of reason take over when you just can't seem to make heads or tails of what the person you're speaking with is saying. As coaches of sports teams like to tell their athletes when the chips are down, 'Have fun out there.' And I would say the same thing to you: enjoy yourself out there with Korean, and don't kill yourself. Remember why you're out there in the first place—to learn a new language and to better understand a new culture. Whatever you do, though, don't ever take your frustrations of the language out on the closest person in your life (cough), especially if he or she happens to be a Korean boyfriend/girlfriend/spouse (cough cough). In my experiences, people in Korea are only too happy to lend a hand when you reach out in a (cough cough cough) soothing voice.

Chapter 13

Choosing the Right Word
바른 단어 선택하기

So, you've got conjugation down, you've memorized your first set of verbs and you're ready to take part in conversation, are you? Well, just one more thing I should point out: the words you're going to use to form sentences with may not be the right words. Oh, they're the correct words in meaning, don't worry about that. It has more to do with something loosely referred to as written vs. spoken, or, at other times, rude vs. polite. Basically, some words are used only in conversation and some words are used only on paper, while at other times it's not appropriate to use certain nouns in the company of older people. How do you know which ones go where and when? Practice. And a ton of hair pulling. Or chair throwing.

RULES OF ENGAGEMENT: DOUBLE MEANINGS

As mentioned in **Chapter 1**, a good portion of the Korean language is derived from Chinese. Now that's not to say that if there's a Chinese derivative there's not an equivalent in pure Korean. On the contrary, in some cases there are two words (one Korean, one *han-cha*) with the same meaning. Not a similar meaning, the *exact same meaning*.

This concept was particularly distressing for me when learning Korean early on because a teacher would teach me the word for 'future,' as an example, *mee-rae* (미래), and then five minutes later I would see the word *jang-nae* (장래) in a dialogue.[1] What's *jang-nae*? I would ask my teacher like an innocent schoolboy who's just had his lunch money stolen. *Jang-nae* means 'future' too, the teacher would respond. Okay, so not one word to learn, but two. That's all right. It just adds to the exotic flavor of Korean. Here's an example of other common words that come in pairs:

__Korean (1)__	__Phonetic Transliteration__	__Korean (2)__	__Phonetic Transliteration__	__English__
어떤	*aw-ddawn*	어느	*aw-ne*	which[2]
종이	*chong-ee*	용지	*yong-gee*	paper
여름	*yaw-reum*	하계	*ha-gae*	summer
겨울	*kyaw-ool*	동계	*dong-gae*	winter
부부	*boo-boo*	내외[3]	*nae-wae*	married couple
왼쪽	*waen-jjok*	좌	*jwa*	left
오른쪽	*o-reun-jjok*	우	*ooh*	right

POLITE/HONORIFIC NOUNS

Although you may not mean to, choosing the wrong noun in a given situation can lead to a misunderstanding. There are nouns in Korean that are formal just as there are nouns that are informal, similar to verb conjugations. Choosing the right noun can be a matter of strict importance. Koreans may be only too happy to give 'get out of jail free cards' to foreigners when speaking Korean, but there is a certain amount of responsibility on the person learning Korean. There was a time when I thought that the only word for 'person' was *sa-ram* (사람). However, unlike the example before with 'future,' where it was simply two words having the same meaning, what I learned with respect to *sa-ram* was that its identical meaning partner, *boon* (분), wasn't just a partner, but a more polite partner.

[1] This is a good example of how words differ from English and Korean. The words *mee-rae* (미래) and *jang-nae* (장래) are not exactly the same in Korean, but they are expressed the same way in English. Although some words are exactly the same in both languages, sometimes it's only the English that cannot distinguish between words.

[2] There's actually one more word that means 'which,' *moo-seun* (무슨). However, *moo-seun* is special because it's also used to denote the phrase, 'Which kind of.' Also, where *moo-seun* is only used with inanimate objects, *aw-ddawn* (어떤) can be used with people (i.e. which person), while *aw-ne* (어느) is the most infrequently used of the three words.

[3] Though the word *nae-wae* (내외) is not nearly as common as *boo-boo* (부부), the word *nae-wae* gives an interesting insight into Korean culture. The word is derived from Chinese characters, with the first character, *nae* (내), meaning 'inside,' and the second character, *wae* (외), meaning 'outside.' Traditionally, the man was expected to work outside, while the woman was expected to work inside, thus meaning that the home of the inside and outside worker was a married couple.

As if that were not enough, the split between pairs (or groups in some instances) of words is not always as easy as this one's polite and this one's everyday. Sometimes there are groups of words where several words are used in an everyday situation and several of them are polite. Whenever I've asked Korean friends and teachers in the past, 'Which word should I use then?' invariably the answer was, 'They're all fine. Just choose one.' Again, more practice is needed in this department to distinguish between them. Here are a few more examples of words that should be chosen carefully, depending on the situation:

Korean (common)	Phonetic Transliteration	Korean (honorific)	Phonetic Transliteration	English
이름	ee-reum	성함	sung-ham	name
나이 먹다	na-ee mawk-da	나이 드시다	na-ee de-shee-da	older person
나이	na-ee	연세	yun-sae	age
사람[4]	sa-ram	분	boon	person
밥	bap	진지	jeen-gee	rice[5]

1. Name: *ee-reum* (이름) & *sung-ham* (성함)

Most people are guilty of making this mistake for years on end because they think these two words mean the exact same thing. To be honest, though, schools and universities around the country are guilty of perpetuating this myth more than anyone. Every textbook that I have come into contact with translates name as *ee-reum* (이름) and leaves it at that. The thing is, though, when meeting people for the first time, and especially when they're older than you, *sung-ham* (성함) is used. No ands, if, or buts about it.

When talking to a close friend you can ask:

이름이 뭐지?   What's your/his/her/its name?
(*ee-reum-ee maw-jee?*)

[4] The words *sa-ram* (사람) and *een* (인) are used interchangeably in Korean. Therefore an American, for example, will sometimes be referred to as a *mee-gook-sa-ram* (미국사람) and sometimes as a *mee-gook-een* (미국인).

[5] For a complete list of words associated with 'rice,' please refer to **Ch. 22**

Yet when meeting a new co-worker, an elder friend, or someone you don't know, you should use the more polite form:

성함이 어떻게 되세요?   May I ask your name?
(*sung-ham-ee aw-ttaw-kae
dwae-sae-yo?*)

2. Older people: *na-ee mawk-daw* (나이 먹다) & *na-ee de-shee-da* (나이 드시다)

Because age is of such importance in Korea, the way age is expressed to or about older people is complicated and multifaceted. In Korean *na-ee mawk-da* (나이 먹다) is used commonly in everyday situations (in the abstract), whereas *na-ee de-shee-da* (나이 드시다) is used for older people when speaking to them directly, or when speaking about an older person that necessitates a polite conjugation, such as a paternal/maternal grandfather. These days in Korea, however, *na-ee man-ta* (나이 많다) is used very commonly in the abstract form in replacement of *na-ee mawk-da*. Also, when watching movies you'll often see *neuk-dda* (늙다)[6] used quite a lot as a translation from the English for 'old.' Finally, when referring to an old object, none of the aforementioned words are valid any longer. In situations like this, you switch to a completely different word, *o-rae dwaen* (오래 된) or *nal-dda* (낡다). Here are some examples using these words in sentences:

그 분 나이 드셨어요?   Is he/she old?
(*ke boon na-ee de-shaws-saw-yo?*)

우리는 둘 다 늙었어.   We're both old.
(*oo-ree-neun dool da neul-kaws-saw.*)

오래 된[7] 컴퓨터   An old computer.
(*o-rae dwaen kawm-pyu-taw*)

[6] This verb form is used very rarely in conversation, and is restricted in use, for the most part, to written Korean.

[7] The verb *nal-dda* (낡다) could be used in a situation like this as well, such as in the phrase *nal-geun kawm-pyu-taw* (낡은 컴퓨터).

그 사람은 나이를 얼마나 먹었어?　　　How old is he/she?
(*ke sa-ram-eun na-ee-reul awl-ma-na
mawg-aws-sau?*)

대통령 나이 많구나!　　　The president is (really) old!
(*dae-tong-nyung nai-ee man-koo-na!*)

3. Age: *sal* (살) & *nai-ee* (나이)

Just as talking about older people has its special situations, so too does asking someone's age. This is not to say that asking someone's age is rude in Korea; quite the opposite, asking someone's age is commonplace and more than acceptable when trying to determine where the other person falls on the cultural hierarchy ladder. However, just as some students only learn one form of asking someone's name at school, they also learn only one way to ask someone's age many times. In common situations like when you are with a friend or talking to someone younger, it's completely acceptable to ask:

몇 살이에요?　　　How old are you?/Can I ask your age?
(*myut sa-ree-ae-yo?*)

However, in situations when you're meeting an older person, or in a business situation where you want to maintain the harmony of the mood (politely), the correct question is:

나이가 어떻게 되세요?　　　May I ask how old you are?/May I ask
(*na-ee-ga aw-ttaw-kae　　　your age?
dwae-sae-yo?*)

Lastly, the honorific form of age is *yun-sae* (연세). As a question it can be substituted for *na-ee* (나이) in the previous example.

4. Person/People: *sa-ram* (사람) & *boon* (분)

Although *een* (인) is occasionally used when referring to a person, *sa-ram* (사람) is the more common choice for 'person' when speaking to friends, close relatives, and younger people. *Boon* (분) is used when speaking to older people, people you don't know, or simply when being polite about someone else (e.g. a friend's older brother). Thus, a general statement about people can come out as this:

한국 사람들은 영어 하는 걸 좀 창피해해요. (*han-gook sa-ram-de-reun young-aw ha-neun gul jom chang-pee-hae-hae-yo.*)	I think Koreans can be a little shy when speaking English.

If you want to use the word person in a more formal context, though, then the more polite *boon* should be used:

부인은 어떤 분이세요? (*boo-een-eun aw-ttawn boon ee-sae-yo?*)	What's your wife like? (i.e. what kind of person is she)

There's one more thing to know about the use of both *sa-ram* and *boon*: they can be pluralized. Though Koreans generally don't pluralize nouns, there are a few situations when they do, and *sa-ram* and *boon* is one such exception. Thus, a person is a *sa-ram* or *boon*, and a group of people is *sa-ram-deul* (사람들) or *boon-deul* (분들).

I Just (sniff, sniff) Wanted to Know (blow of the nose) How Old You Were (whimper, whimper) …

How important is it to know when to use the different words for age in

---

Korean? Important enough to avoid making a bad first impression like I feel I did with one of my girlfriend's cousins the first time I met him. Having shared a wonderful dinner, we were relaxing with some over-carbonated beer at a Beer Bank when I thought it appropriate to ask the cousin his age (so that I could firmly establish that always important relationship of who was older and who was younger). We had already been talking for some time when I asked him, '*myut sa-ree-ae-yo?*' (몇 살이에요?). Well, did that ever bring a chill to the Beer Bank. My girlfriend turned to me and said, 'Don't ask him like that. You have to ask him, *na-ee-ga aw-ttaw-kae dwae-sae-yo?*' (나이가 어떻게 되세요?).

'Don't use the Greek derivative, use the Latin one!' I wanted to scream at the time. But in the spirit of good taste, I turned to the cousin once again, smiled, and repeated the question with the right noun. I know the cousin forgave me for my linguistic slip up, but his reaction at the time was enough for me to never forget the important lesson that choosing the right noun can be just as important in Korean as verb conjugations.

SWEAR WORDS

I can't speak for an entire generation, nor can I speak for the entire English speaking population the world over, but I can say that swear words are so pervasive throughout English today that unless it's a formal situation (and not even then sometimes), swearing is as much a part of many people's vernacular as prepositions and verbs. That's not to say that everyone swears all the time. It's just that I, for one, do not bat an eyelash when someone intersperses their sentences with the occasional swear word (within reason).

Koreans are not quite as liberal with the use of swear words. In many ways, the use of swear words in Korean reminds me more of what it would have been like to swear in the 1950s or '60s in the West. Back then it was a still big deal to swear in public, to swear in front of your parents—to swear to anyone —save your closest friends. As a result, I don't encourage nor do I recommend learning how to swear in Korean. Not only is it useless in almost every situation, but the one time you might use a swear word in the wrong situation, you're bound to make yourself look like an uneducated boor.

Chapter 14

Numbers and Counting
숫자 세기

Learning to count is one of the most fundamental aspects of any language. With Korean, though, counting is a little more complicated than what you might expect. The counting dilemma can best be explained as follows: there are two counting systems, and everything that you count needs to be labeled with a specific title.

The truth is a little tougher than that last explanation, however. Native English speakers learning to count in Korean face several challenges:

- Which counting system to use and when (Chinese derivative numbers or pure Korean numbers)
- Counting itself (multiples in Korean are different from those in English, so that one hundred thousand in English, for example, is ten times ten thousand in Korean)
- Counting stems (everything is separated by category, both animate and inanimate objects)
- Counting money (because of the value of the Korean won, you're required to think in the hundreds of thousands and millions every day)
- Telling time (both counting systems are used in this instance)

TWO WAYS TO COUNT

The Korean language has two counting units, and though obvious to Koreans when to use each one, newcomers to Korean struggle with this for years. The two types of Korean numbers are Chinese derivatives (i.e. a number written in Korean with a Chinese character as its root) and pure Korean (i.e. numbers that have no Chinese root). With the exception of a few cases, Chinese derivative numbers are used for counting money, and pure Korean numbers are used for counting objects.

Here's a basic rundown of the two counting systems:

__Number__	__Chinese Derivative__	__Pure Korean__
1	*eel* (일)	*ha-na* (하나)
2	*ee* (이)	*dool* (둘)
3	*sam* (삼)	*saet* (셋)
4	*sa* (사)	*naet* (넷)
5	*o* (오)	*ta-sawt* (다섯)
6	*yook* (육)	*yaw-sawt* (여섯)
7	*cheel* (칠)	*eel-gope* (일곱)
8	*pal* (팔)	*yaw-dawl* (여덜)
9	*koo* (구)	*a-hope* (아홉)
10	*sheep* (십)	*yul* (열)
20	*ee-sheep* (이십)	*se-mool* (스물)
30	*sam-sheep* (삼십)	*saw-reun* (서른)
40	*sa-sheep* (사십)	*ma-heun* (마흔)
50	*o-sheep* (오십)	*shween* (쉰)
60	*yook-sheep* (육십)	*yae-soon* (예순)
70	*cheel-sheep* (칠십)	*eel-heun* (일흔)
80	*pal-sheep* (팔십)	*yaw-deun* (여든)
90	*koo-sheep* (구십)	*a-heun* (아흔)
100	*baek* (백)	*baek* (백)[1]
1000	*chun* (천)	

[1] From 100 on, the counting systems align, so that only the Chinese derivatives are used.

Number	Chinese Derivative
10,000	*man* (만)
100,000	*sheep-man* (십만)
1,000,000	*baeng-man* (백만)
10,000,000	*chun-man* (천만)
100,000,000	*awk* (억)
1,000,000,000	*sheep-awk* (십억)
10,000,000,000	*baek-awk* (백억)
100,000,000,000	*chun-awk* (천억)
1,000,000,000,000	*jo* (조)
1,000,000,000,000,000,000	*kyung* (경)
1,000,000,000,000,000,000,000	*hae* (해)

COUNTING/MULTIPLE SYSTEM

One thing you might have noticed is that the Chinese derivative numbers increase in multiples native English speakers are not familiar with. Thus, it's no longer twenty but 2 times 10; it's not one hundred thousand, but 10 times 10,000. This may seem like a real pain to those of you not quick at math, but I can assure you that with practice, the numbers will come to you just as easily as they do in English.

EXCEPTIONS TO PRONUNCIATION

You need to be careful when using the pure Korean counting system in spoken conversation because there are exceptions to the pronunciation of certain words. The exceptions include the pure Korean numbers one, two, three, and four:

- With the **number one**, *ha-na* (하나), the second half of the character is lopped off (i.e. the *na*) when counting things (i.e. 1, 11, 21, 31, 41), and a *nee-eun* (ㄴ) is added to the first character (i.e. the *ha*), so that people only say *han* (한) when it's followed by a noun. Examples of this include one person, *han myung* (한 명), eleven things, *yul-han gae* (열한 개), and 21 books, *se-mool-han gwawn* (스물한 권). However, when 'one' comes after a noun then you can use the original form of the number. Examples of this are one coke, *kol-la ha-na* (콜라 하나), and one pen, *bol-paen ha-na* (볼펜 하나).

- The **number two**, *dool* (둘), is also different in that it has its bottom root dropped when counting. Instead of saying *dool gae* (둘 개), for example, Koreans say *doo gae* (두 개), or *doo myung* (두 명), *saw-reun-do ma-ree* (서른두 마리), etc. However, the same rule applies for the number two when switching the position of the number and the noun as applies to the number one.

- The **number three** (셋) has its bottom character (i.e. the ㅅ) removed when counting people or objects. Therefore, three bottles is *sae-byung* (세병), not *saet byung* (셋 병), and three people is *sae myung* (세 명), not *saet myung* (셋 명). However, when attaching the number three to a vowel (only as a verb) right after it, the ㅅ character remains in place. Consequently, I'm 33 years old, comes out as *na saw-reun-sae-shee-ya* (나 서른셋이야).

- The same rules apply to the **number four** as apply to the number three. Consequently, four pencils is *yawn-peel nae ja-roo* (연필 네 자루), and not *yawn-peel naet ja-roo* (연필 넷 자루). But, I'm 24 is *se-mool-nae-shee-ae-yo* (스물넷이에요).

COUNTING STEMS, *soo-ryang-myung-sa* (수량명사)

Pretend you want to say that there are 'two pencils,' or 'three people,' or 'four roses,' or 'nine dogs.' This seems straightforward enough, doesn't it? Well, in Korean, every noun that you count needs to be qualified by a marker or a stem. What follows is a comprehensive list of the most common stems for counting in Korean and which situations they apply to. Keep in mind with counting units, though, that pure Korean numbers are used, that is *ha-na* (하나), *dool* (둘), *saet* (셋), etc.:[2]

English Stem	Korean Stem	Situation Used	Explanation
sal	살	**AGE**	attached to pure Korean numbers
ma-ree	마리	**ANIMALS/FISH**	every animal, fish, reptile, and bird
bul	벌	**ARTICLES OF CLOTHING**	suits, pants, dresses, shirts, skirts
gae	개[3]	**BASIC OBJECTS, NON-ELECTRICAL THINGS**	rocks, erasers lighters, etc.
gwawn	권	**BOOKS AND MAGAZINES**	as stated
byung	병	**BOTTLES**	glass bottles, beer bottles
gong-gi	공기	**BOWLS OF RICE**	at a restaurant
ke-reut	그릇	**BOWLS OF RICE**	at home, personal use; includes plates
jan	잔	**CANS, CUPS**	cups of water, coffee, tea, juice, milk, cans or cups of beer
cha-ryang	차량	**CARS**	individual subway and train cars only
kap	갑	**CIGARETTE PACKS**	this applies to any size cigarette pack
chae	채	**COMFORTERS**	*ee-bool* (이불), sheets
dae	대	**ELECTRONICS /AUTOMOBILES**	electronics of every kind, appliances, cars, buses, trucks
song-ee	송이	**FLOWERS**	single stem flowers (roses, carnations, tulips)
dan	단	**FLOWERS**	bunches of flowers
chae	채	**HOUSING**	apartments and houses

[2] There are a few exceptions to this. For a complete overview of the exceptions, please refer to the next sub-section, ***Exceptions***.

[3] This is probably the most useful counting stem in Korean. However, when unsure of which counting stem should be attached, it's best to use the number by itself. For example, 'one car' would simply be *cha ha-na* (차 하나).

English Stem	Korean Stem	Situation Used	Explanation
pyun	편	**MOVIES**	counted at theatres
jang	장	**PAPER AND PHOTOGRAPHS**	pieces of paper, tickets, ticket stubs, disks, pictures, photos
ja-roo	자루	**PENS AND PENCILS**	as stated
jawp-shee	접시	**PLATES**	plates, dishes, saucers
kan	칸	**ROOMS**	every room in the house
kyul-lae	켤레	**SHOES, SOCKS PANTYHOSE**	as stated
gok	곡	**SONGS**	a song play list will use this counting stem
ge-roo	그루	**TREES AND PLANTS**	as stated

Exceptions

The following exceptions exist with counting stems. With all of these exceptions, the Chinese derivative counting system is used to count (i.e. *eel* (일), *ee* (이), *sam* (삼)):

sae (세)   **AGE:** although people generally use the pure Korean counting system to refer to one's age, this method of using the Chinese derivative is sometimes used in its place.

bool (불)   **MONEY:** all Korean money is counted with the Chinese derivative counting system. The same goes for foreign money. The only thing that changes with foreign money is the currency stem. With dollars, *bool* (불) is used. Sometimes in its place, though, the pure Korean word *dal-law* (달러) is used. Implicitly understood is that that the dollar comes from the United States. To be completely clear, you could say *mee-hwa* (미화), which is literally American dollar, but this is usually not necessary.[4]

een (인) **PORTIONS/PEOPLE:** this stem is used when going out to eat a Korean restaurant (e.g. *kalbi* or *samkyupsal*) and is coupled with the character *boon* (분)—person—so that *ee-een boon* (이인 분) means 2 people worth, or 2 portions of something, and *sa-een boon* (사인 분) means 4 people worth, or 4 portions.

do (도) **TEMPERATURE:** *do* (도) means degrees. Korea uses the metric system, so Celsius is used unless otherwise stated. Temperatures above zero are referred to as *yung-sang* (영상), and temperatures below zero are referred to as *yung-ha* (영하). Thus, 10 degrees above zero is *yung-sang sheep-do* (영상 10도) and 10 degrees below zero is *yung-ha sheep-do* (영하 10도).[5]

ANOMALIES

There are only a couple of everyday anomalies to counting stems that can be remembered very quickly. These mostly have to do with **buying tickets** (e.g. for a concert, a movie, a play, etc.) and **ordering food and drinks** (e.g. at restaurants, bars, etc.).

In the first situation, for instance, you should theoretically use *jang* (장), for the pieces of paper, or *myung* (명), for the number of people. However, Koreans use *gae* (개) quite often when dealing with pieces of paper in this situation. So, if you were to go and buy four tickets for a movie, you could simply say the movie name and then, *nae gae joo-sae-yo* (네 개 주세요).

The second situation where there is a change in the counting stem is when ordering food and drinks. Instead of using the proper counting unit, most

[4] Although South Koreans use the Chinese derivative counting system for counting American dollars, North Koreans do not. Instead, they use the pure Korean counting system, and so say *han dal-law* (한 달러) *doo dal-law* (두 달러), etc.

[5] The words for Celsius and Fahrenheit are *sawp-sshee* (섭씨) and *hwa-sshee* (화씨), respectively.

people just substitute *gae* (개) for beverages. For example, instead of saying *byung* (병), most people just say *gae* (개). Thus, when ordering two bottles of *soju*, for example, you say, *soju doo gae joo-sae-yo* (소주 두 개 주세요). Also, when ordering cans of beer or soft drinks most people simply say *gae* (개) as opposed to *jan* (잔), bowls of rice are *gae* (개) instead of *ge-reut* (그릇), and cups are *gae* (개) instead of *jan* (잔) or *byung* (병).

TELLING TIME

Telling time in Korean is the real test of whether you have a full grasp of the two counting systems, because both are used at the same time. Hours, *shee* (시), are measured in pure Korean; minutes, *boon* (분), and seconds, *cho* (초) are measured in Chinese derivatives. So, for instance, **3:27** is expressed as follows:

Written	Korean Pronunciation	Phonetic Transliteration
3시27분	세시 이십칠분	*sae-shee ee-sheep-cheel-boon*

The following table looks at some more examples:

Time	English	Korean
12:00	twelve o'clock/noon	12시 / *yul-doo-shee* (열두시) / *jung-o* (정오)
1:00	one o'clock	1시 / *han-shee* (한시)
1:05	one oh five/	1시5분 / *han-shee o-boon* (한시 오분)
1:30	one thirty/half past one	1시 30분 / 1시 반 / *han-shee sam-sheep-boon* (한시 삼십분) / *han-shee ban* (한시 반)
1:45	one forty-five	1시45분 / *han-shee sa-sheep-o-boon* (한시 사십오분)
6:00	six o'clock	6시 / *yaw-saw-shee* (여섯시)

Time	English	Korean
12:00	twelve o'clock/midnight	12시 / *bam yul-doo-shee* (밤 열두 시)/*ja-jung* (자정)
1 p.m.	one p.m.	(오후) 1시/(*o-hoo*) *han-shee*(오후 한시)
9:30 p.m.	nine p.m.	(오후/밤) 9시 / *o-hoo/bam a-hope-shee* (오후/밤 아홉시)
3 a.m.	three a.m./ three in the morning	(새벽) 3시/ *sae-byuk sae-shee* (새벽 세시)
10:20 a.m.	ten twenty a.m.	(오전)10시20분/ *o-jun yul-shee ee-sheep-boon* (오전 열시 이십분)

OTHER USEFUL COUNTING UNITS

Understanding and discussing time in units bigger than minutes or hours can be just as perplexing because Koreans tend to mix both the Chinese derivative number system and pure Korean number system. Take a look at the following examples to see exactly what I mean.

English	Phonetic Transliteration	Korean
last century	*gee-nan sae-gi-ae*	지난 세기에
eight years ago	*pal nyun jun-ae*	8년 전에
the year before last	*jae-jang-nyun*	재작년
last year	*jang-nyun-ae*	작년에
three months ago	*sam-gae-wawl jun-ae*	3개월 전에
two weeks ago	*ee-joo jun-ae*	2주 전에
last week	*gee-nan joo-ae*	지난 주에
four days ago	*sa-eel jun-ae* (*na-heul jun-ae*)	4일 전에 (나흘 전에)
three days ago	*sam-eel jun-ae* (*sa-heul jun-ae*)	3일 전에 (사흘 전에)

English	**Phonetic Transliteration**	**Korean**
two days ago	*ee-eel jun-ae* (*ee-teul jun-ae*)	2일 전에 (이틀 전에)
yesterday	*aw-jae*	어제
today	*o-neul*	오늘
for the (entire) day	*ha-roo jong-eel*	하루 종일
this morning	*o-neul a-cheem-ae* (*o-jun-ae*)	오늘 아침에(오전에)
this afternoon	*o-neul o-hoo-ae (na-jae)*	오늘 오후에 (낮에)
this evening	*o-neul jaw-nyuk-ae*	오늘 저녁에
tonight	*o-neul bam-ae*	오늘 밤에
this week	*ee-bawn joo-ae*	이번 주에
these days	*yo-jeum*	요즘
recently/lately	*chae-geun-ae*	최근에
tomorrow	*nae-eel*	내일
tomorrow morning	*nae-eel a-cheem-ae*	내일 아침에
tomorrow afternoon	*nae-eel o-hoo-ae*	내일 오후에
tomorrow evening	*nae-eel jaw-nyuk-ae*	내일 저녁에
tomorrow night	*nae-eel bam*	내일 밤
in two days (2 days from now)	*ee-teul hoo-ae*	이틀 후에
in three days (3 days from now)	*sa-heul hoo-ae*	사흘 후에
in four days (4 days from now)	*na-heul hoo-ae*	나흘 후에
next week	*da-eum joo-ae*	다음 주에
the week after next	*da da-eum joo-ae*	다 다음 주에
this month	*ee-bawn dal-ae*	이번 달에
next month	*da-eum dal-ae*	다음 달에
in two months (2 months from now)	*ee-gae wawl hoo-ae* (*doo dal hoo-ae*)	2개월 후에/두달 후에 (이개월)

English	Phonetic Transliteration	Korean
this year	*ol-hae*	올해
next year	*nae-nyun*	내년
the year after next	*nae hoo-nyun*	내 후년
in two years (2 years from now)	*ee-nyun hoo-ae*	2년 후에
in four years (4 years from now)	*sa-nyun hoo-ae*	4년 후에
next century	*da-eum sae-gi-ae*	다음 세기에

18 Will Never Be the Same

One fine evening while waiting for my students to settle down in the classroom, I thought it a stroke of genius to announce to them, in Korean, the page number we would be starting on. Having been in Korea a little less than a month, I had only really learned to count, and though not significant in the grand scheme of things, I thought it impressive enough at the time to shower my students with my newfound wisdom. So, like the great orator I felt like at the time, I bellowed from the deepest part of my belly, '*sheep-pal*' (십팔), 18 in the Chinese derivative counting system.

All of a sudden a strained hush overcame the room as students stopped fidgeting and looked up at me. Fearing they had not really heard me clearly, I thought I would repeat my new bit of linguistic wonder. '*Sheep-pal*,' I repeated as my students broke into hysterics all of a sudden.

Naturally, I felt self-conscious and believed they were laughing at my accent, which at the time I knew was far from perfect. 'Teacher. Again! Again!' students yelled out to me.

Maybe it wasn't my accent after all, I considered. Maybe they were just so impressed that a non-Korean could utter Korean words that they wanted to see the magic show once more.

Okay, I responded. Gladly. '*Sheep-pal!*'

At that stage students started hollering at the top of their voices, begging me to do it again.

By then I was a little confused. Could students really go that crazy over one word of Korean? I asked myself. I changed subjects and began my lesson shortly thereafter, not forgetting to ask someone that same night why all the fame and attention over a seemingly simple word.

It was only a few hours later when, after being laughed at yet again from a good Korean friend, I was told that the way I pronounced *sheep-pal* was such that I didn't say the number eighteen, but rather an expletive too rude to be published here. In shock, I asked my friend how such a thing could happen. His response?

'Ha, ha, ha. Korean is difficult to pronunciate. You has to be careful.'

EVERYDAY COUNTING UNITS (WEIGHTS AND MEASUREMENTS)

Korea uses the metric system for the most part, but there are some variations. This is most apparent when you go to smaller fruit and vegetable stands and flea markets. It's at places like this that you'll see the traditional *chuk-kwan-bup* (척관법) system in use most. There was once a variety of traditional measurements used, yet today it's mostly *geun* (근), for fruits, and meat, and *pyung* (평), for measuring space in a home or office, that are used in the vernacular. With respect to the metric system, names have simply been transliterated into Korean, so they're easy to recognize and readily identifiable for weight. Look at the following examples for more precise information:[6]

[6] See Korea.com's website at *http://welcome.korea.com* for more information on traditional measurements and conversion scales.

Pure Korean Numbers Used

Korean	Phonetic Transliteration	Measurement
근	*geun*	1근=600 grams (meat), 1근=400 grams (fruit)
평	*pyung*	1평=3.3058 square meters

Chinese Derivative Numbers Used

Korean	Phonetic Transliteration	Measurement
킬로[7]	*keel-lo*	kilogram, 1 kilogram=2.2 pounds
리터	*lee-taw*	liter, 1 liter=0.22 gallons (U.K.) or 0.26 (U.S.)
센티(미터)	*saen-tee- (mee-taw)*	centimeter, 30 centimeters=1 foot
리	*lee*	ri, 1 ri=0.392 km

[7] *Keel-lo* (킬로) is also used in conversation to refer to 'kilometer,' so you have to pay careful attention to the situation.

Chapter 15

Foreign Words in Korean, Dialect and (the Phenomenon Called) Konglish

외래어 + 사투리 + 콩글리쉬

It's estimated that present-day Korean (in South Korea) contains over 10,000 words derived and adapted, in one form or another, from other languages.[1] And this astonishing number doesn't even include words derived from Chinese characters. Though the majority of foreign words in use in South Korea are overwhelmingly derived from English, there are some that are taken from other languages such as French and Japanese.

The same is not true of Korean in North Korea because the governments of North and South Korea have never pursued linguistic policies in alignment with one another for one fundamental reason: their political policies are reflected only too visibly in their linguistic standards. The North's government has always attempted to keep the Korean language as pure as possible, free from the corruption of other languages.

In fact North Korea went so far as to abolish the use of Chinese characters, *han-cha* (한자), in 1949, only reintroducing them in 1968 when Kim Il-sung emphasized, 'the necessity of such education for achievement of revolution in the South.'[2] However, although Chinese is now taught in North Korean schools, the education is so limited that defectors living in South Korea complain of having difficulty reading South Korean newspapers (where Chinese characters abound)

[1] See *www.transparent.com/languagepages/korean/overview.htm* for more information on current statistics with the Korean language.

[2] See the National Intelligence Service's (NIS) Website's North Korean Education and Sports page at *www.nis.go.kr*

and of being unable to write their name in Chinese (something the average South Korean can do).

READJUSTING TO THE NEW LANGUAGE

Since the end of the Korean War in 1953, North Korea has done its utmost to shun the outside world. This policy of isolation and self-reliance, or *joo-chae* (주체) as North Koreans call it, has included keeping the Korean language pure from the corruption of other languages. Ask South Koreans today if there is any difference between them and their brothers and sisters up in the North, and you're sure to get a resounding yes. The way each country's citizens speak Korean today is the clearest sign of this.

North Koreans who seek refuge in South Korea face a number of daunting challenges: understanding a capitalist economy, adjustment to a democratic society, the right to vote in pluralistic elections, the right to free speech, and the right to laugh at a picture of Dear Leader Kim Jong-il.

However, the one critical difference that is often overlooked is the readjustment to the version of Korean that South Koreans speak. Aside from having to contend with snide remarks and insults about their country accents, every single one of the refugees that seeks asylum in South Korea must also learn so much new vocabulary that it almost constitutes its own language. If the barrier between a generation of parents and children is sometimes unbridgeable due to a gaping chasm in vocabulary, then the plight of the North Koreans is more of a canyon. Foreign words permeate every facet of the (South) Korean language, so that North Koreans cannot get away with avoiding only one aspect of the language, like computer-related vocabulary for example. As you'll see, foreign words are now used everywhere, in every situation, both formal and informal, and between young and old in South Korea.

Unfortunately, it's not just the use of English words in (South) Korean today that makes it so hard for the average North Korean refugee. In the more than 50 years that the two countries have been separated politically, there have been twists and turns in each country's language. Examples of this range from the use of Japanese in South Korea today to the dialects and accents of the South

---

Korean countryside, *sa-too-ree* (사투리), to new words that have been integrated into the vernacular since the political separation of the two countries over half a century ago.

IS THERE ANY DIFFERENCE?

In the beginning North Korea's government may have tried to preserve the purity of the Korean language, but even they have relented a little over the years. Unlike South Korea, which chose to adopt most of its foreign words from English, North Korea chose to take many of its foreign words from Russian. In some instances, there is just one way of saying a Korean word in South Korea and one way of saying it in North Korea. The word bathroom, for example, is literally a 'make up room' in South Korea, *hwa-jang-sheel* (화장실). Yet in North Korea, they've chosen the more sterile and much more proletarian 'hygienic room,' *wee-saeng-sheel* (위생실). On the other hand, there are examples of differences that leave one wondering why there's a difference at all, like in the case of squid. In South Korea, squid and octopus are differentiated (as they should be), but in North Korea they are the same word. Here are some more examples of word differences between North and South Korea:

North Korean[3]	South Korean	English
어름보숭이 (*aw-reum-bo-soong-ee*)	아이스크림 (*a-ee-se-ke-reem*)	ice cream
조선말 (*cho-sun-mal*)	한국말 (*han-goong-mal*)	Korean (language)
남조선[3] (*nam-cho-sun*)	남한 (*nam-han*)	South Korea
북조선[4] (*book-cho-sun*)	북한 (*book-han*)	North Korea
가무이야기 (*ka-moo-ee-ya-gi*)	뮤지컬 (*myu-jee-kul*)	musical

[3] All of these words are taken from the South Korean government's KEDO official dictionary of North Korean words, *kyung-soo-ro saeng-hwal-soo-chup* (경수로 생활수첩).

[4] Although the North Korean word for South Korea is *nam-cho-sun* (남조선), 'South Joseon,' many people just say *nam-jjok* (남쪽), 'southern direction.' The same thing applies to the word for North Korea. Though officially called *book-cho-sun* (북조선), 'North Joseon,' many people just say *book-jjok* (북쪽), 'northern direction,' when referring to their own country.

168

North Korean	South Korean	English
간나 (*kan-na*)	처녀 (*chaw-nyaw*)	virgin
가슴띠 (*ka-seum-ddee*)	브래지어 (*be-rae-jee-aw*)	bra
고층살림집 (*ko-cheung-sal-lim-jeep*)	아파트 (*a-pa-te*)	apartment (building)
공민증 (*gong-meen-jeung*)	주민등록증 (*joo-meen-deung-nok jeung*)	citizen's card (ID Card)
과일단물 (*kwa-eel-dan-mool*)	쥬스 (*joo-se*)	juice
날맥주 (*nal-maek-joo*)	생맥주 (*saeng-maek-joo*)	draft beer

TWO KINDS OF FOREIGN WORDS: *WAE-RAE-AW* (외래어)

Of the foreign words that are now fully incorporated into the Korean language in South Korea, there are basically two categories of words. The first set of words is known as *wae-rae-aw* (외래어), and includes all those words that are direct transliterations from other languages into Korean characters. With words like these, the meaning is kept exactly the same as it is in the language it is borrowed from. Here are some examples:

Korean	Phonetic Transliteration	English
컴퓨터	*kawm-pyu-taw*	computer
아이스크림	*a-ee-se-ke-reem*	ice cream
버스	*bu-se*	bus
트렁크	*te-runk*	(car) trunk
가스	*ga-se*	gas

Korean	Phonetic Transliteration	English
인터넷	*een-taw-naet*	Internet
뷔페	*bwee-pae*	buffet (all you can eat)
소파	*so-pa*	sofa/couch
앨범	*ael-bum*	album (i.e. music and photo albums)
(이) 메일	*(ee) mae-il*	(e)-mail
유머	*yoo-maw*	humor

TWO KINDS OF FOREIGN WORDS: KONGLISH (콩글리쉬)

On the other hand (and unfortunately to the pain and agony of Korean language students), the majority of foreign words in Korean are what are better known as konglish (콩리쉬). Konglish is a combination of Korean and English, a hybrid cousin of janglish, singlish, and chinglish. Today, konglish is an entity unto itself. Konglish, in essence, means words, and sometimes phrases, that are borrowed from English and then strangled, mutilated, and sometimes beaten to death in their transformation into Korean. Examples of konglish range from those that are **close in meaning** to the original, (*kun-ning* (컨닝) refers to someone who cheats) **to the strange** (a *haen-deul* (핸들) is a car steering wheel) **to the funny** (a *gol sae-rae-mo-nee* (골 세레모니) refers to a person celebrating after a goal or touchdown).

Konglish is not inherently difficult to learn, especially for native English speakers, but it does take some time, as there are quite a few words to re-learn. Here are some examples of konglish in use today:

Korean	Phonetic Transliteration	Direct Translation	Proper Translation
오디오	*o-dee-o*	audio	stereo
포켓볼	*po-kaet-bol*	pocket ball	pool/billiards

Korean	Phonetic Transliteration	Direct Translation	Proper Translation
백미러	*baeng-mee-raw*	back mirror	rear view mirror
카센터	*ka-saen-taw*	car center	car garage
게임	*gae-eem*	game	computer/video game
게임룸	*gae-eem-loom*	game room	arcade
에어콘	*ae-aw-kon*	air con	air conditioner
하드	*ha-de*	hard	Popsicle
누드핫도그	*noo-de-hat-do-ge*	nude hot dog	plain hot dog (without a bun)

A LANGUAGE WITHIN A LANGUAGE

At work within the different echelons of Korean society today is a fad to use English words even when a Korean counterpart exists. Of course in sectors like information technology, computer science, and biogenetics, many languages adopt the same word as everyone else does; the Internet is the Internet no matter where you go in the world; a PC is a PC.

At first, I thought the reason why so many people were using these English words when they spoke to me had to do with my skin color and nationality. That was until I saw Koreans doing the same thing with other Koreans. I began asking students and friends why this was, why people were calling a car in Korean a *ka* (카)? Why people were calling South Africa *sa-oo-se a-pe-ree-ka* (사우스 아프리카)? It was one thing when non-native Korean speakers who were just learning the language stealthily slipped in English words here and there if they didn't know the Korean equivalent. Yet Koreans born and raised in Korea were doing this with other Koreans more often as each year passed.

The most common answer I got was that it's vanity that leads most people to use English words when there is a clear Korean equivalent. It's a means by which people can show off and let every one around them bask in their intelligence and linguistic prowess. Yet I don't think this answers my question to a sufficient degree because it's not just the intelligentsia or the foreign-educated that do this; salespeople in department stores do it as much as the next professor.

THE CULT OF ENGLISH AND ENGLISH EDUCATION IN KOREA

The most convincing argument I've heard to do with this use of English in Korean's place has to do with the craze for learning English, speaking English, and showing off in English. The English language has undoubtedly reached a cult-like status in South Korea. Today, people from all walks of life can be seen using English words and phrases with other Koreans. That's not where the obsession with English in South Korea stops, though. Parents from every financial background are educating their children in English as much as possible. Some parents do it themselves, others use mediums like television and the Internet to help them. Still others send their children to privately-run cram schools, called *hagwon* (학원), in a bid to have their children attain the highest level of English, especially before writing the country's university entrance exam, the *soo-neung* (수능).

Learning English is not a bad thing, nor is speaking English necessarily a bad thing. The danger arises when the reason for learning becomes not the learning process itself, nor even the end goal of speaking English fluently, but a twisted sense of keeping up with the Kims. Those who speak English in Korea are venerated and celebrated; English teachers are usually more respected than other foreign language teachers. English is not only seen as the global language of the 21st century, but a path by which to draw awe and respect from others.

As a result, Koreans who use any amount of English interspersed with their Korean when speaking or writing are regarded as just that much more intelligent or well-educated. And this fad or trend or whatever it's called of replacing Korean words with English ones is not going away anytime soon. English is here to stay in South Korea.

Listed here are but a few examples of English-Korean word pairs where the English word is sometimes/usually/always used instead of the Korean:

Korean	English Word Transliterated into Korean	English
권력누수현상 (kwul-lyuk-noo-soo hyun-sang)	레임덕 (lae-eem-duk)	lame duck (political)
지지하다 (jee-jee-ha-da)	서포트하다 (saw-po-te-ha-da)	to support (people)
빵 (bbang)	브레드 (be-rae-de)	bread
표 (pyo)	티켓 (tee-kaet)	ticket
포도주 (po-do-joo)	와인 (wa-een)	wine
성관계[5] (sung-gwan-gae)	섹스 (saek-se)	sex

English Words Coming Back to Haunt Me

One would think that the easiest words to understand in a foreign language would be the words from one's native tongue. However, quite the opposite of this assumption, the only words that continue to stump me time after time while speaking Korean are English words transliterated into Korean. It's not the meaning that stumps me—I can't even understand the word that Koreans are using with me most of the time. What inevitably ends up happening in a situation like this is the Korean looks at me like they can't believe I wouldn't know the meaning of a particular word, and I look at the Korean like they've just said something from an African tribal language.

'You don't know what *ja-pa-ne* means?' a Korean will ask me, for instance.

'No, I have no idea what you're saying. What's a *ja-pa-ne*?' I ask back.

Ja-pa-ne, Ja-pa-ne.

'I'm sorry, but can you explain what that is?'

[5] I rarely hear Koreans use *sung-gwan-gae* (성관계) when referring to the act of lovemaking. Although I've had conversations about sex, both in private and in public, Koreans invariably use the borrowed word from English, *saek-se* (섹스), especially younger people.

This causes the person I'm speaking with to look at me with great amazement and then declare, 'But you speak English, don't you?'

'I do.'

'How can you not know what a *ja-pa-ne* is then?'

At this point in the conversation I then think through every possible pronunciation of the word in question and, if I'm lucky, stumble upon the word.

'You mean Japan?'

'Of course I mean Japan. What did you think I was talking about?'

'Why didn't you just use the Korean word, *eel-bon* (일본), and save us the confusion?'

However, this is where I tend to lose the attention of the person I'm speaking with. They look at me and fail to understand why I couldn't understand the word *ja-pa-ne*, and I look at them and fail to understand why they couldn't use the Korean word in the first place. It just teaches me that the more I improve my Korean, and the more vocabulary I pick up, the more my own language comes back to haunt me in Korean.

SA-TOO-REE

Sa-too-ree (사투리) is usually translated as 'accent' or 'dialect.' In South Korea, the government recognizes six official dialects today: Central, Northwest, Northeast, Southeast, Southwest, and Jeju-do.[6] All of these dialects are very similar, with the exception of the Jeju-do accent, which even Koreans say is hard to understand sometimes unless you're from Jeju. Also, the term Central, which the government uses to denote one of the six accents, is often called Seoul-*mal* (서울말) by Koreans. Seoul-*mal* means Seoul Talk if translated directly, and is now the most common accent that people speak, some because they are living in Seoul, others because they do not wish to be discriminated against by other Koreans who sometimes see regional accents as provincial and backwards.

[6] See the Ministry of Culture and Tourism's (MCT) website at www.mct.go.kr

A RICH VOCABUALRY

Unlike accents in the West that do not as a matter of principle necessitate a new vocabulary, *sa-too-ree* is almost defined by this very fact; the accent itself is almost the embodiment of the new formation of words (both written and spoken). For example, a Southern accent may be different in sound from a Californian one, but it's not the words from the two accents that distinguish them so much as it is the fact that they sound so completely different when spoken.

Learning *sa-too-ree* can be a fun way of learning different ways of expressing yourself, especially among friends when you have much more free reign to say whatever it is you want (some *sa-too-ree* is considered a little rude at times, depending on the word or phrase). What I've listed here in this book is just a taste of the many words and phrases that people use these days in different parts of Korea. Though *sa-too-ree* is quickly becoming streamlined, so it's not as common to find one using it in Seoul today as it was even ten years ago. Here are some examples:

Sa-too-ree	Seoul-*mal*	English
뭐라카노? (*maw-ra-ka-no?*)	뭐라고? (*maw-ra-go?*)	What's that?
와이라노? (*wa-ee-ra-no?*)	왜 그래요? (*way ke-rae-yo?*)	What are you doing?/What the heck?
미친나? (*mee-cheen-na?*)	미쳤어? (*mee-chees-sau?*)	Are you crazy?
퍼뜩 (*paw-ddeuk*)	빨리 (*bbal-lee*)	quickly
토깽이 (*to-kkaeng-ee*)	토끼 (*to-kkee*)	rabbit
얼라 (*aul-la*)	아기 (*a-gi*)	baby
할배(할부지) (*hal-bae*)	할아버지 (*ha-ra-baw-gee*)	grandfather, older man

175

Sa-too-ree	*Seoul-mal*	English
할매(할무이) (*hal-mae*)	할머니 (*hal-maw-nee*)	grandmother, older woman

Chapter 16

The Family Tree
가족

If Korean verbs are the hardest part of the language on a technical level, then the family tree is easily the most difficult part from a memorization point of view. Learning all the family titles is next to impossible (I have yet to meet a Korean that knows every one of them), so what's more important is to learn the ones that apply to you and your situation, and, if none of them apply to you, to understand them from a social perspective; just looking at the family tree at the end of this chapter should be enough for anyone to comprehend how important family titles are for Koreans.

MAKING SENSE OF WHO GOES WHERE

Family titles, like most everything in this linguistic maze, require deft maneuvering and split second timing. Anyone who has spent even a few short weeks in this country could probably tell you that Koreans value family above everything else. This, of course, is a good thing. But where Korean customs are to be admired on this point, the fact that names are not usually used when addressing family members means that titles must be learned. What was Uncle Mike in English, now becomes a big father or perhaps a little father on the paternal side, or another title altogether if on the maternal side, for example. People's titles in the family change depending on a variety of factors, such as:

- whether you are a man or a woman
- whether the person in question is from the maternal or paternal side of the family
- whether you are older or younger than the person you're talking to/about
- whether the spouse of the person is older or younger in comparison to the speaker
- whether you're married to a Korean or just courting him/her
- whether you're trying to get the person's attention or talking about the person, referred to as *ho-cheong* (호칭) and *gee-cheong* (지칭), respectively

---

And You Would Be ...

I know I'm not the only one that has faced a crisis of names or titles when speaking with a member of a Korean family, but it doesn't take anything away from the fact that it's still powerfully etched in my mind. I've wanted to have conversations with a person, wanted to ask for something from the other side of the table, wanted to just say something to someone standing nearby on numerous occasions, but I couldn't think of what I was supposed to call that person. In the case of children, the answer is usually pretty simple—Hey you, or *ya*! (야) as you can say in Korean. However, with adults, and especially with older adults who pull rank in the family, I've been too scared to say anything. In English, as I pointed out in **Chapter 10**, that wonderfully ubiquitous pronoun of 'you' is so useful in English. With Korean, however, I've had my hands tied on too many occasions as to what to say, and so, like many others, I did the polite thing and said nothing. For all those out there that have gone through that energy-draining process of meeting a loved one's family, the family tree in this chapter is for you. No more staying quiet at the dinner table anymore!

FAMILY NAMES

I'll never forget the first time I met a Korean with only two names. I looked at the name on my class list, looked up, looked down, looked back up, looked back down, and then scratched my head. Korean family names are *traditionally* three names, the family name coming first, followed by two given names (e.g. Lee In-ju · 이인주). Korean given names are also *traditionally* drawn from the roots of Chinese characters, so that many Koreans today have names by which they write in Korean and Chinese (e.g. 박은주 · 朴恩珠).

However, three characters from pure Korean or Chinese is not always the case anymore. It's more than plausible today that you'll run into a Korean with one family name and one given name, such as Kim Yong (김용), that you'll meet a Korean with two family names and two given names, or that (even occasionally) you'll encounter a Korean with a five-character name—three family names (all put together, much like a hyphenated name would be in the West), and two given names. The rules governing Korean names today are not as clear as one thinks from the average person you meet.

These days, in another twist to family names, some Koreans bear the name of famous Biblical figures, so that their names look exceptionally strange in Korean, but completely normal in English, like in the case of Joseph Kim, Kim Yo-saep (김요셉).

THE WRITING OF PEOPLE'S NAMES

The way Korean names are written in English has changed over the years. Reading books published before the 1990s, one was sure to come across names that were spelled with the family name, followed by the given name, which would be separated by a hyphen, such as in the case of **Jung Dae-sung** (정대성). This still remains one of the standard methods of writing names in English, but it is not the only way. These days, it's just as common to see the hyphen dropped between first names, such as in **Jung Dae sung**, as it is the first names combined, like in the case of **Jung Daesung**. Once in a while, I now see the names separated without a hyphen and both capitalized, for example **Jung Dae**

Sung, as well as all three names capitalized and separated with a hyphen in the given name, such as **Jung Dae-Sung**.[1] The newest fad, however, is to write the family name, follow that by a comma, and then write the two given names together, like **Jung, Daesung**

MARRIED WOMEN

One of the most common mistakes people coming to Korea make with respect to names has to do with married women. Many assume that women in Korea take on their husband's family name upon getting married as do most women in the West. This is not the case, however. Korean women do not change their name when married, but at the same time, their children adopt the family name of the father.

THE FAMILY TREE

The following family trees should make it somewhat less complicated (I stress *somewhat*) to get a grip on the fundamentals of family titles. When unsure what someone's title is, the safe thing to do is simply make the sentence respectful so that the person you're speaking with knows who the subject of the sentence is or is not. If you're talking to a child and can't remember his or her name, however, you're in a little more trouble. I'd like to be positive and say, when in doubt just ask, but I've been here too long to know that asking a question is never as easy it looks. That being said, here's a look at the basic Korean family trees:

<u>The Basic Family Tree</u>

ha-ra-baw-jee (할아버지)-*hal-maw-nee* (할머니) (**grandfather-grandmother**)
|
a-baw-jee (아버지)-*aw-maw-nee* (어머니) (**father-mother**)
|
a-deul (아들)-*ddal* (딸) (**son-daughter**)

[1] With respect to non-native Koreans writing their names in Korean, most Koreans still write a person's first name followed by his or her family name, both names clearly separated (e.g. Richard Harris, 리차드 해리스).

180

Grandfathers and grandmothers are almost always called nothing more than *ha-ra-baw-jee* (할아버지) and *hal-maw-nee* (할머니), but occasionally for the purposes of being honorific, a person will call their grandfather *ha-ra-baw-neem* (할아버님), and their grandmother *hal-maw-neem* (할머님). Parental titles are a little more varied. When wanting to be more polite, Koreans say *a-baw-jee* (아버지) for father, and *aw-maw-nee* (어머니) for mother. The more everyday words for these last two titles are *awm-ma* (엄마), mom, and *a-ppa* (아빠), dad.[2]

With respect to the children themselves, there are different titles used for siblings. Although we only have brother and sister in English, Koreans change the title depending on age and sex. For males addressing older sisters, the title is *noo-na* (누나), and for younger sisters *yaw-tong-saeng* (여동생). For women addressing their older brother, *o-ppa* (오빠) is used. When addressing a younger brother, they say *nam-dong-saeng* (남동생). Men talking to their older brothers say *hyung* (형), but say *nam-dong-saeng* (남동생) for their younger brothers. Lastly, for women addressing older sisters the title is *awn-nee* (언니), and for a younger sister it's *yaw-dong-saeng* (여동생). However, it's useful to keep in mind that when just speaking in the rapid course of conversation, Koreans usually drop the sex marker so that all younger siblings are simply *dong-saeng* (동생).

To make matters a bit more complicated, the titles *awn-nee*, *noo-na*, and *hyung* can be used outside of the family between friends. *Hyung* is used between men when there is an older friend involved. Therefore my older best male friend, speaking as a male, will be referred to as *hyung*. However, I should point out that the title *hyung* is further complicated by the fact that women can use *hyung-neem* with sisters-in-law in certain situations.

Men who happen to have an older female friend that they are quite close with will call her *noo-na*. However, the friend has to be close, and under no circumstances will a younger man refer to his older girlfriend (romantically involved) as *noo-na*.

With regards to women talking to women who are close in age, the term *awn-nee* is often used. This title is described in great detail in **Chapter 17**.

[2] Depending on the situation, these Korean titles can be translated as 'mommy' and 'daddy,' respectively.

PATERNAL AND MATERNAL FAMILY TREES

The following family trees should make it easier to address family members when looking at it from a child's point of view. Because family titles change from a child's perspective depending on if the family member is connected with the mother or father's side of the family, it's necessary to keep in mind who exactly is being discussed or addressed in the course of conversation:

The Paternal Family Tree
(from the child's point of view)

keun-a-baw-jee (큰아버지) **(uncle)** — *keun-aw-maw-nee* (큰어머니) **(aunt)**
|
sam-chon (삼촌) **(uncle)** — *ko-mo* (고모) **(aunt)**
|
(go-jong) sa-chon (고종사촌) **(cousin)**

cha-geun a-baw-jee (작은아버지) — *cha-geun aw-maw-nee* (작은어머니)
(uncle) | **(aunt)**
sa-chon (사촌) **(cousin)**

In this family tree, you can see that the father's older brother is referred to as a 'big father' and his wife as a 'big mother.' A father's younger brother is referred to as the 'little father' and his wife as the 'little mother.' A father's sisters can all be referred to simply as *ko-mo* (고모). 'Uncle,' as a generic term, is simply *sam-chon* (삼촌).

The Maternal Family Tree
(from the child's point of view)

sam-chon ((외)삼촌) **(uncle)**/*ee-mo* (이모) **(aunt)**
| |
sa-chon (사촌) **(cousin)**　　　*sa-chon* (이종)사촌 **(cousin)**

The maternal side of the family is made easier by the fact that traditionally women and their families are not as prominent as the man's family. Although this is not a good thing for the equality of the sexes, it's certainly welcome relief for the student of the Korean language.

THE MARRIAGE TREES

For people of other nationalities that marry into Korean families, remembering everyone's title can be a serious headache. There are so many titles to keep in mind that all you want to do is escape to the next room where you can watch TV. The next two family trees keep this fact in mind from the perspective of a person marrying a Korean man/woman and what titles should be used in accordance with the fact that you are a male or a female.

The Marriage Tree
(when a woman marries a Korean man)

shee-a-baw-jee (시아버지) — *shee-aw-maw-nee* (시어머니)
(father-in-law) | **(mother-in-law)**

shee-a-joo-baw-nee (시아주버니) **(older brother)**

shee-noo-ee (시누이) **(older sister)**

woman marries Korean man: *nam-pyun* (남편)

shee-dong-saeng (시동생) **(younger brother)**

shee-noo-ee (시누이) **(younger sister)**

No one that I know has ever denied that Korean is a patriarchal language. This means that when a woman marries into a Korean family (foreigners included), the respect that must be given to the husband's parents-in-law is more than that of the man to the wife's in-laws. The best example of this is the fact that on a traditional Korean marriage day, the bride and groom will exchange vows and then sneak away so that the two of them can change into traditional *hanbok* clothing before going to a private room where they bow on their knees to the father and mother of the husband. Is this ever done for the wife's parents? Not that I've ever heard.

<u>The Marriage Tree</u>
(when a man marries a Korean woman)

jang-een (장인) **(father)** — *jang-mo* (장모) **(mother)**
|
chaw-nam (처남) **(older brother)**

chaw-hyung (처형) **(older sister)**

man marries Korean woman: *a-nae* (아내)

chaw-nam (처남) **(younger brother)**

chaw-jae (처제) **(younger sister)**

There are several names used to denote one's wife. The one used above, *a-nae* (아내), is the most commonly taught word for wife, but not necessarily the most commonly used by Koreans day to day. Some people use the title *a-nae* quite naturally, but there are other titles you should be aware of. One common title used for the word wife when being respectful is *boo-een* (부인). With the use of English so widespread in Korean, though, the term *wa-ee-pe* (와이프) is used as well sometimes. When speaking among friends, however, the word *jeep-sa-ram* (집사람) is also used to refer to one's wife, while yet another title that is used to refer to one's wife when being extremely respectful (when talking to a president's wife, for example) is *sa-mo-neem* (사모님).

A ROUGH GUIDE TO THE FAMILY TREE

I'm the first to admit that the family trees and titles I've just thrown at you are confusing. First and foremost, there are a ton of titles. Second, the titles are so dependent on so many factors that it's hard to make sense of it all. That's why the following list is intended to make it a little easier. But before I go any further, let me stress the rough in **A ROUGH GUIDE TO THE FAMILY TREE**. The family tree warrants its own book, and since I am writing a book on the Korean language from a general point of view, I can't detail every title with a thorough description that each needs (and deserves). Koreans that have helped me edit this book have been adamant about pointing this fact out, and to be fair, I must then point this out to you, the reader. Thus, the best way to approach this family tree is to use it as a guide and nothing more. If you are marrying into a Korean family, or are simply interested in the Korean family, then I urge you to look at the following titles and then **ask a Korean how and when each title is used properly**. This is the only way to ensure the title you are using is not only polite (which is critical in this situation), but appropriate.

Also, the following things should be kept in mind while reading this summary. **First**, titles are listed as their basic title. When using some of these titles the neem (님) suffix is attached. So, for instance, in certain circumstances, *hyung* (형) becomes *hyung-neem* (형님), and *hyung-soo* (형수) becomes *hyung-soo-neem* (형수님). **Second**, when I write 'from the man' or 'from the woman,' I'm writing that with the speaker (or the topic of conversation) as the subject. Also, when I say things like 'through the older sister' or 'through the wife,' what I mean to say is that you gain in-laws through many ways, and though in English the words and titles may be irrespective of the link, in Korean they matter a great deal. Thus, a brother-in-law through a younger sister, an older brother, or through the husband or wife will all have different titles in Korean. With that, I invite you to look at a basic summary of the family tree:

Korean Word	Phonetic Transliteration	Relationship/Meaning

Grandparents/Grandchildren

Korean Word	Phonetic Transliteration	Relationship/Meaning
할아버님	*ha-ra-baw-neem*	**grandfather**, honorific
할아버지	*ha-ra-baw-jee*	**grandfather** (generic), common
조부	*jo-boo*	**grandfather** (paternal)
할머님	*hal-maw-neem*	**grandmother**, honorific
할머니	*hal-maw-nee*	**grandmother** (generic), common
손녀	*son-nyaw*	**granddaughter**
손자	*son-ja*	**grandson**
손주	*son-joo*	**grandchildren**

Parents/Parents-in-law

Korean Word	Phonetic Transliteration	Relationship/Meaning
부모	*boo-mo*	**parents** (from the Chinese characters 'father' and 'mother')
아버님	*a-baw-neem*	**father**, honorific
아버지	*a-baw-gee*	**father**, common
아빠	*a-ppa*	**dad**, common
아범	*a-bawm*	**dad** (from wife, in front of in-laws)
애비	*ae-bee*	**dad** (from wife, in front of in-laws)
시아버지	*shee-ah-baw-jee*	**father-in-law** (from woman, through husband)
장인	*jang-een*	**father-in-law** (from man, through wife)
어머니	*aw-maw-nee*	**mother**, honorific
엄마	*awm-ma*	**mom**
어멈	*aw-mawm*	**mom** (from husband, in front of in-laws)
시어머니	*shee-aw-maw-nee*	**mother-in-law** (from woman, through husband)
장모	*jang-mo*	**mother-in-law** (from man, through wife)

Korean Word	Phonetic Transliteration	Relationship/Meaning

Children/Siblings/Brothers- and Sisters-in-law

Korean Word	Phonetic Transliteration	Relationship/Meaning
형제	*hyung-jae*	**brothers**[3]
자매	*ja-mae*	**sisters**
남매	*nam-mae*	**brother and sister**
오누이	*o-noo-ee*	**brother and sister**
동생[4]	*dong-saeng*	**younger brother** or **younger sister**
외아들	*wae-a-deul*	(only) **son**
외동딸	*wae-dong-ddal*	(only) **daughter**
장남	*jang-nam*	**eldest son**
장녀	*jang-nyaw*	**eldest daughter**
오빠[5]	*o-ppa*	**older brother** (from woman)
형[6]	*hyung*	**older brother** (from man)
처남	*chaw-nam*	**older brother-in-law** (from man, through wife)
시아주버니	*shee-a-joo-baw-nee*	**older brother-in-law** (from woman, through husband)
형부	*hyung-boo*	**older brother-in-law** (from woman, through older sister)
매형	*mae-hyung*	**older brother-in-law** (from man, through older sister)
자형	*ja-hyung*	**older brother-in-law** (from man, through older sister)
누나[7]	*noo-na*	**older sister** (from man)
언니[8]	*awn-nee*	**older sister** (from woman)
손윗 누이	*son-wee noo-ee*	**older sister** (from young boy)
새 언니	*sae awn-nee*	**older sister-in-law** (from woman, through older brother)
형수	*hyung-soo*	**older sister-in-law** (from man, through older brother)
처형	*chaw-hyung*	**older sister-in-law** (from man, through wife)

[3] Though *hyung-jae* (형제) literally means 'brothers,' it's also used to speak loosely of one's siblings. Also, this word is sometimes coupled with *ja-mae* (자매) when referring to one's siblings.

[4] This title is also used with younger friends who are close to the speaker.

[5] This title is also used by a woman referring to an older male friend, as well as when talking to/about her older boyfriend.

[6] This title is also used by men referring to an older male friend, but in cases where *hyung* (형) is used, the friend should be a close friend. See the **The Basic Family Tree** for more information.

[7] This title is also used by men referring to an older female friend who is close to them. Also, the honorific title for *noo-na* (누나) is special. The respectful term for older sister becomes *noo-neem* (누님).

[8] This title, though it means 'older sister' from a woman's point of view, is also used by women to address other women sometimes. (See **Ch. 17** for more information)

Korean Word	Phonetic Transliteration	Relationship/Meaning

Children/Siblings/Brothers- and Sisters-in-law

Korean Word	Phonetic Transliteration	Relationship/Meaning
여동생	*yaw-dong-saeng*	**younger sister** (from man or woman)
누이동생	*noo-ee-dong-saeng*	**younger sister** (from old boy)
처제	*chaw-jae*	**younger sister-in-law** (from man, through wife)
제수	*jae-soo*	**younger sister-in-law** (from man, through younger brother)
시누이	*shee-noo-ee*	**younger sister-in-law** (from woman, through husband)
올케	*ol-kae*	**older or younger sister-in-law** (from woman, through brother)
동서	*dong-saw*	**younger sister-in-law** (from man, through husband)
형님	*hyung-neem*	**older sister-in-law** (from woman, through husband)
아가씨	*a-ga-sshee*	**unmarried younger sister** (from woman, through husband)
남동생	*nam-dong-saeng*	**younger brother** (from man or woman)
처남	*chaw-nam*	**older or younger brother-in-law** (from man, through wife)
시동생	*shee-dong-saeng*	**younger brother-in-law** (from woman)
도련님	*do-ryun-neem*	**younger brother-in-law** (from woman, through husband)
처형	*chaw-hyung*	**older sister-in-law** (from woman, through sister)
제부	*jae-boo*	**younger brother-in-law** (from man, through wife)
매부	*mae-boo*	**younger brother-in-law** (from woman, through younger sister)

Korean Word	Phonetic Transliteration	Relationship/Meaning
매제	*mae-jae*	**younger brother-in-law** (from man, through younger sister)

Extended Family

Korean Word	Phonetic Transliteration	Relationship/Meaning
삼촌	*sam-chon*	**uncle** (generic)
외삼촌	*wae-sam-chon*	**uncle** (maternal)
큰아버님	*keun-a-baw-neem*	**uncle** (paternal, older than father), honorific, married
큰아버지	*keun-a-baw-gee*	**uncle** (paternal, older than father), married
작은아버님	*cha-geun-a-baw-neem*	**uncle** (paternal, younger than father), honorific, married
작은아버지	*cha-geun-a-baw-gee*	**uncle** (paternal, younger than father), married
고모	*ko-mo*	**aunt** (paternal), father's sister
외숙모	*wae-soong-mo*	**aunt** (maternal), mother's brother's wife
숙모	*soong-mo*	**aunt** (paternal), father's brother's wife
이모	*ee-mo*	**aunt** (maternal), mother's sister
큰어머니	*keun-aw-maw-nee*	**aunt** (paternal, father's elder brother's wife), married
작은어머니	*cha-geun-aw-maw-nee*	**aunt** (paternal, father's younger brother's wife), married
사촌	*sa-chon*	**cousin** (generic)
이종사촌	*ee-jong-sa-chon*	**cousin** (maternal)
고종사촌	*go-jong-sa-chon*	**cousin** (paternal)

Chapter 17

Titles: For Everyday Use and Business

직함:[1] 일상생활 + 회사

Using one's given name is not nearly as common in Korean as it is in English. For the most part, when Koreans interact with each other on the street or in the office, at home or at work, they use titles and titles only: a young girl asking an older man a question, a receptionist talking with her boss, one teacher discussing something with another teacher, a man looking for directions from an elderly woman. In all of these situations there's no use of a name to distinguish one person from the other. Even when talking directly to a man or a woman, a title is often used so that it feels like you're speaking in the third person when face to face with someone.

EVERYDAY TITLES

When interacting with Koreans on the street, in and around town, or just about anywhere day to day, there are a few titles which are essential to know. Except in office settings, schools, and the military—when someone's title from the corporate ladder or chain of command will be used—there are several generic titles that people use all the time.

First of all, children are not usually referred to as anything (which may give

---

[1] The word *jeek-ham* (직함) is only used for business titles.

you a sense of their worth linguistically), so that when addressing a young child, an adult may simply say *Ya!* (야!), which is roughly 'Hey, you!' in English. When it comes to young students, no other title except **hak-saeng** (학생), student, is generally used. For young male adults, most men get lumped into the **a-jaw-sshee** (아저씨) category,[2] but if the person is noticeably young, then you may from time to time hear an older woman (sometimes an older man) call him a **chong-gak** (총각). For men of advanced age (anyone of a grandfather's age), the term **ha-ra-baw-jee** (할아버지) is used.

Although the titles for young children and students are exactly the same for girls as they are for boys, from their early twenties, women are addressed by different titles than men. The title **a-ga-sshee** (아가씨), a young unmarried woman, is often used to refer to university aged women and young business ladies. This title carries with it an implication that the woman is unmarried. For women in their thirties on, or married women as the case may be, the title **a-joom-ma** (아줌마) is used. Finally, for women in their golden years, the term **hal-maw-nee** (할머니) is used.

MR., MRS. AND MS.

So, you're meeting someone whose name you know, but whose occupation you don't. What are you supposed to address them by? A common dilemma that fortunately has a simple answer most of the time. In formal situations, or should I say when you're not familiar with the person or close enough to switch into *ban-mal*, the title *sshee* (씨) is used after addressing someone by their given name. If you want to say something to Kim Young-bum (김영범), for instance, then you say Young-bum *sshee* (영범씨).

Now this all seems fine and dandy if you think of *sshee* as Mr., Mrs. or Ms., but the problem is that it just doesn't work out that way in Korean all the time. If those translations (Mr., Mrs., Ms.) are in fact true down to the letter of the law, then I've been calling some of my friends Mr. and Ms. for years. It's hard to describe what *sshee* is in English exactly without giving some background.

The Korean character for *sshee* is derived from the Chinese characters *sshee* (씨 · 氏) and *jok* (족 · 族), with the definition being listed under the word **'clan'**

[2] This word technically refers to a married man, but is sometimes translated as 'uncle.'

or '**tribe**' in an English dictionary. The character is derived from the radicals meaning 'floating plant,' and 'without roots,' which 'proliferates and wanders.'[3] According to this meaning then, the *sshee* character symbolizes a wandering group of people. That's why today when you ask someone for their genealogy,[4] they say the place name followed by their family name followed by the title *sshee*. Therefore, a person with the family name Park that's from the village of Miryang says that they are Miryang Park *sshee* (밀양박씨). As an extension of all this, people refer to each other as so-and-so *sshee* when addressing a stranger and wanting to be polite. However, this title can also be used with someone you know well, and wanting to be polite. The *sshee* title can be especially useful in business relationships or when sending e-mail.

THE COMPLICATION SURROUNDING *NEEM* (님)

With most other titles, especially in a work environment or when you don't know the person well, the suffix ***neem*** (님) is attached to the title to make it more polite. The suffix *neem* is said to mean everything in English from honorable to distinguished to esteemed. The truth, however, is that the Korean suffix *neem* cannot be translated naturally into English.

Neem is attached to professional titles (e.g. in the workforce) and family titles when talking to a person. Examples of this range from *sa-jang-neem* (사장님), president, to *hyung-soo-neem* (형수님), older sister-in-law. The *neem* suffix is also used with titles when wanting to be respectful and talking about someone who is not present, though. That's not to say that it's always used when talking about someone who is not present, however. For instance, when talking about someone's title in an abstract form (such as, Being a teacher would be great), the suffix *neem* can be dropped. Thus, when talking about the role of a teacher in the abstract, it would simply be *sun-saeng* (선생), yet when talking to Mr. Kim the teacher, it would be Kim *sun-saeng-neem* (김 선생님).

ONE OF THE MOST USEFUL TITLES

Undoubtedly, one of the most common and most useful titles in Korean

[3] See James C. Whitlock Jr.'s *Chinese Characters in Korean*.

[4] The word for 'genealogy' in Korean is *bo* (보), which comes from the Chinese character [譜].

society is *sun-saeng-neem* (선생님). This title, which *does* mean **teacher**, is special in that it's not only confined to situations whereby a person is a certified instructor or teacher. *Sun-saeng-neem* can also be used to show respect to people in other professional fields, so that an administrator or a boss or someone of higher authority can be called *sun-saeng-neem* as well. In cases like this, the title *sun-saeng-neem* means something closer to a respectful form of **Mr**. or **Ms**.[5]

For university students and professors of English in Korea, the term *kyo-soo-neem* (교수님), **professor**, is used quite a bit. Although for many of the English teachers working at universities in Korea, they are more used to using the title *kang-sa* (강사), **lecturer**, as their official title. In schools from the elementary level to the secondary level, though, the title *sun-saeng-neem* (선생님), **teacher**, is as common as any other word in a student's vocabulary.

THE ALL-ENCOMPASSING TITLE OF *AWN-NEE* (언니)

In **Chapter 16** I defined the title *awn-nee* (언니) as an older sister from a woman's point of view. While that's true, the term *awn-nee* has another use in Korean society which makes it one of the most common titles used by women. When one woman wants to get the attention of another woman, the term *awn-nee* can be used (the woman being addressed can be younger or older in a situation where the two women don't know each other). Between friends, the term *aw-nee* is also used, but in these cases the younger woman uses it when addressing the older woman, not the other way around.[6]

The Difficulty of Speaking with Parents

This is a lesson I really, really wish I knew years before I made myself look like an ignoramus with parents on too many occasions to count.

When I first started teaching children in Korea, I inevitably met the mothers of these children. At these times, I would take the opportunity to strike up a conversation. Being the guy I was then, I would always ask the

---

[5] In point of fact, the term *sun-saeng-neem* cannot be translated properly when outside the realm of education. When used in offices (or in society) to address people of authority, it's better to think of this title as nothing more than a polite title with no proper English equivalent.

[6] From a dictionary point of view, the term *awn-nee* (언니) means 'older sister', from a man's and woman's perspective. In reality, though, usually women use this title. Although older men occasionally use the title *awn-nee* to address a woman, it's usually reserved for woman-to-woman situations.

woman for her name (thinking names were more common than titles, of course). Invariably, the mother would tell me her name was so-and-so's mother, to which I smiled and said, 'No, I mean *your* name.' At this, the mother would become slightly embarrassed and laugh softly as she fiddled with her hair and looked away from me. I struggled to understand what the problem was. This whole time I figured it had something to do with me before the day that a friend of mine explained this custom to me. When my friend explained that it was natural for mothers to assume the name of their child (with the title mother right after it), I was bewildered.

'Is it impossible to call a mother by her name in Korea?' I asked my friend.

'Not impossible,' my friend replied. 'Just uncommon, and well, to be frankly, rude.'

In the end, I finally figured out that mothers (and sometimes fathers, too) were not called by their given names or even by their social titles at home or at school, but by the name of their eldest child. I've never fully adjusted to calling a woman or man so-and-so's mother or father when talking directly to them, but I do it nonetheless. As they say, when in Rome...

CHILDREN

One would think that because children fall at the absolute bottom of the Confucian social ladder that they'd be one of the easiest groups of people to identify linguistically in Korean, but such is not the case. Quite the opposite, children are a real pain in the butt because they are so complicated to refer to in Korean both directly and indirectly. For what it's worth, children still make me cringe to this day when I have to speak to them if only because I'm not sure which title I should be using.

Look up the word 'child' in your handy English-Korean dictionary and you'll find the words *dong-ja* (동자),[7] *so-een* (소인), *a-ee* (아이), *a-dong* (아동), and *aw-reen-ee* (어린이). Follow that up by looking for the words under 'children'

[7] This title is only used with child (Buddhist) monks.

194

and you'll find *a-ee-deul* (아이들), *aw-reen-ae-deul* (어린애들), *ja-sheek* (자식), *ja-nyaw-boon* (자녀분), and *ja-nyaw-bun-deul* (자녀분들). Talking to or about children in Korean depends on a range of variables, but to make things easier, let me say this: the most honorific way to refer to children (in the third person, such as when you're asking your boss about his/her kid(s)) is to use *ja-jae-boon-(deul)* (자제분(들)). A common way to refer to kids in a casual situation is with *aw-reen-ae-(deul)* (어린애(들)), and when referring to children in an academic way, *a-dong,*[8] such as *a-dong-hak* (아동학), children's studies. One last thing you'll hear quite a lot when hanging around large groups of kids is *yae-deu-ra* (애들아), which is something adults say when addressing a group of children.[9] Finally, two more titles that you see written a fair bit concerning children are *so-nyaw* (소녀), girl, and *so-nyun* (소년), boy.

BUSINESS TITLES

Like the family tree, the business tree is an intricate system of titles and positions that requires no less studying than a list of verbs when learning Korean. I find it useless to translate most business titles into English because it's not simply the words you are translating, but the business culture itself. Except for positions of public importance (e.g. presidents of companies, government officials), there is no need to remember an English equivalent for each and every business title, I believe. What's more important is to remember what order the titles fall in. Remembering the order of the business ladder allows you to form a mental image of the hierarchy which exists in the Korean corporate world, and thus, better understand the picture.

THE OFFICE TREE

As mentioned, learning this system of titles is done easiest and most effectively by remembering nothing more than the hierarchy attached to all these titles. Trying to think of each one with an English equivalent will compound the learning process and lead to nothing but confusion and a greater stockpiling of Tylenol, as some titles are translated differently depending on the

[8] This title is also used in stores with clothing, so that children's clothing is referred to as *a-dong-bok* (아동복).

[9] The word *yae-de-ra* (애들아) is a more natural way for many Koreans to say *a-ee-de-ra* (아이들아). However, it's use is not restricted to only children. Sometimes, you'll hear adults use this when trying to get the attention of a large group of people.

dictionary, and depending on the person using the title.

It's also relevant to point out that there can be variations to this office tree. Just as titles and positions are changing and evolving in the West, so too are they changing and evolving in Korea. This office tree is only an overview of the standard office in Korea:

Phonetic Transliteration	**Korean Title**	**English** (in rough terms)
hwae-jang	회장	CEO[10]/founder
sa-jang	사장	CEO/president/owner
boo-sa-jang	부사장	vice-president
jun-moo	전무	executive director/ managing director
sang-moo	상무	managing director
ee-sa	이사	area head/director
sheel-jang	실장	executive manager
boo-jang	부장	manager
cha-jang	차장	assistant director/deputy-chief
teem-jang	팀장	team/department head
kwa-jang	과장	section director
dae-ree	대리	assistant section manager
kae-jang	계장	chief clerk
joo-eem	주임	employee/clerk

SMALL BUSINESS OWNERS AND THE *SA-JANG-NEEM* (사장님)

One more useful piece of knowledge to know from the office tree has to do with the title *sa-jang* (사장). An article I read years ago taught me that using the title *sa-jang-neem* (사장님), which is conjugated for respect with the suffix *neem* (님) when used in conversation, to your everyday small business owner is a great way to look respectful in the eyes of the owner. Using this title at the right moment not only demonstrates an ability to use the language naturally, but an ability to kiss just the right amount of butt. People who are small business

[10] The term *hwae-jang* (회장) would be used to denote a CEO in the case of a multinational corporation, or a CEO of a Korean conglomerate, known as *chae-bawl* (재벌).

196

owners in Korea generally love to be called *sa-jang-neem*, and in situations when you're trying to request something (like a discount or a speedy delivery, for example), this title is really useful to throw in.

Part 4

Studying Korean Formally:

Navigating Your Way Through Shark-Infested Waters

Like the dog that learns by waiting outside the schoolhouse for
three long years
서당 개 삼 년에 풍월을 읊는다

Chapter 18

Learning Strategies
학습 전략

   I would be lying if I said that learning Korean is unlike pulling teeth—it's not exactly a barrel of laughs the whole way through. There are an assortment of hills and valleys the likes of which deter people to the point of quitting the study of this language altogether. But that doesn't mean that learning Korean is impossible. Quite the opposite, Korean is an exhilarating challenge. I like to think of it as something akin to scaling Everest: you have to go through a ton of learning and practice before you actually ascend the mountain itself, and even then you're not guaranteed a chance to stand on the peak and marvel at your accomplishment. People die climbing Everest (this part may be a bit extreme for learning a language, but bear with me), and in the end only a handful of people from around the world can say that they've climbed Everest. It's a daunting goal and a lofty dream, but not impossible enough to discourage thousands of people from trying to reach the acme every year. In that round about fashion, Korean is the same way; learning the language to near fluency is the pinnacle of the linguistic world, and an aim worthy of the effort.

DON'T GIVE UP HOPE!

But there's hope! There are ways in which to learn Korean that make things go smoother, methods of studying that allow you to soak up more information quicker. There are ways, in short, that minimize hair pulling (and thus preserve your hairline) and maximize learning. The following are ten ways in which I believe you can learn the Korean language more expeditiously, more effectively, and more intelligently. Alongside these strategies are six things to be careful of when learning Korean. Taken together, I believe they will help the present or future student of Korean learn the language more enjoyably and in a shorter amount of time.

1. LEARN NEW VOCABULARY BASED ON CHINESE ROOTS

This learning strategy is not as difficult as it might appear. Unlike English, which has roots in a plethora of languages (and thus makes studying roots harder), Korean is mostly derived from one language—Chinese. As such, many words are related to one another in ways that make a lot of sense. Learning one root and building on that root is a quick way to increase your vocabulary. Look at the following examples:

Korean	Phonetic Transliteration	Chinese Roots	English
학교	*hak*-kyo	study/school	school
학생	*hak*-saeng	study/person	student
학원	*hag* won	study/building	academy/cram school
대학교	dae-*hak*-kyo	big/study/school	university
대학원	dae-*hag* won	big/study/building	graduate school
대학생	dae-*hak*-saeng	big/study/person	graduate school school
휴학	hyu-*hak*	rest/study	semester/year off (from school)
전학생	jun-*hak*-saeng	transfer/study/person	transfer student (until high school)

Not only do the Chinese roots make sense, but they allow you to remember the words in Korean more easily. This is not to say that every time you see or hear the *hak* (학) character in Korean it's going to mean 'study.' Chances are, though, if the conversation has something to do with school or students, it's a safe bet that the *hak* character is going to mean 'study.'

Look at one more example:

Korean	**Phonetic Transliteration**	**Chinese Roots**	**English**
전쟁	*jun*-jaeng	war/dispute	war
전장	*jun*-jang	war/place	battlefield
휴전	*hyu***jun**	rest/war	armistice/peace agreement
전투	*jun*-too	war/fight	battle
참전용사	*cham***jun**-yong-sa	participate/war/brave/person	(war) veteran

Not only is this a good way by which to increase your vocabulary, but it gives you insight into ancient culture, both Chinese and Korean. As corny as this sounds, I sometimes open up my Chinese-English-Korean dictionary and sift through it looking for something interesting. On one such random look-through, I saw the following words with their Chinese roots: **dissatisfaction, ambition, greed,** and **passion** (sexual). Do they share anything in common? Consider the derivation of each word's meaning from its Chinese roots and you decide:

dissatisfaction: *yok-goo-bool-man* (욕구불만)
欲求不滿 → desire creates demand, which goes unfulfilled.

ambition: *yong-mang* (욕망)
欲望 → desire and hope mold together to give one ambition in life.

passion (sexual)**:** *yok-jung* (욕정)

欲情 → desire (sexually) that is stroked by the fans of feeling, *jung* (정), and closeness.

greed: *yok-sheem* (욕심)
欲心 → desire that is kept too close to one's heart manifests itself into greed.

2. LISTEN TO KOREANS SPEAK ENGLISH

After more than five years in a Korean classroom, I've learned that even the best Korean speakers (near fluent in fact) translate almost word for word from Korean. Whether that's because of awful translations in archaic dictionaries or simply an incorrect thought process is up for debate, but the point is that listening carefully to Koreans speak English will teach you a lot about speaking Korean.

It's not that Koreans are necessarily wrong most of the time, it's more that they tend to choose the verbs and nouns and adjectives that native English speakers wouldn't nine times out of ten. This means that if you keep a sharp ear about you, you're bound to pick up on translations that Koreans are making when speaking English.

For example, Koreans speaking English almost always use the verb **to meet** when talking about plans with friends. In English, other verbs are used in the same instance, like **get together**, **see**, **hang out**, and **go out**, depending on the situation. This is a quick lesson that the verb **to meet**, *man-na-da* (만나다), is very versatile in Korean and used in all of the above situations.

As well, Koreans often use the noun **promise** or **appointment** when talking about plans with friends. They don't distinguish between a professional appointment and a social appointment. Hence, when you learn the noun *yak-sok* (약속) in Korean, you know it's a pretty safe bet that it's a common word, one that you can use in both social and professional situations.

3. ASK KOREANS WHAT THE WORD OR PHRASE IS

Koreans like to show off their English even while speaking Korean, but that's not of any benefit to you, the student of Korean. The next time a Korean uses an English word or phrase while speaking Korean, politely ask the person what the word or phrase they just mumbled in English was and whether it's common or not among Korean speakers. In some cases, the Korean is only using English with you because he/she assumes that you don't know the Korean word. However, in other cases, Koreans use the English word or phrase with other Koreans as well. For example, even though Koreans have a word for brown bread, *bo-ree bbang* (보리빵), many people simply say the Koreanized word instead, *be-ra-oon be-rae-de* (브라운 브레드).

4. READ THE NEWSPAPER

This has the obvious effect of not only increasing your vocabulary, but also of learning Chinese. Korean teachers the world over will preach to you about how beneficial it is to study *han-cha* (한자), but the truth of the matter is that most students lack the time, energy, and willpower for such an endeavor. The compromise lies somewhere in the middle. By reading the newspaper, even occasionally, you'll begin to recognize certain Chinese characters that appear frequently, and thus increase your knowledge of *han-cha* almost inadvertently while keeping up with current events.

5. FIND AN E-MAIL PARTNER

Writing in Korean is helpful for several reasons. With the advent of the Internet there's no easier way to practice the art of writing than with someone you know through e-mail. Korean is unique in the written form and in some ways is a completely different language than the spoken version. Having a friend who is close to you and feels comfortable writing in *ban-mal* (반말) is especially useful, as you'll be able to learn things from them that you wouldn't any other way. Keeping up a friendship through e-mail is one sure way to make sure you don't get lost with a new generation of Korean.

Also, carrying out a friendship through e-mail improves your typing, and if you ever have any aspirations to do something serious with the Korean language (like get a job), you'll need to be able to type faster than five words a minute.

Yet one more thing that having an e-mail partner does is increase your vocabulary in areas that you might not otherwise increase. For instance, by working on a computer and using different programs, you'll learn words such as **tool(s)**, *do-goo* (도구), **edit**, *pyun-jeep* (편집), **footnote**, *kak-joo* (각주), and **delete**, *sak-jae* (삭제), to name but a few.

6. BE AWARE OF THE WORLD AROUND YOU

Look at words on signs, billboards, and advertisements, and ask yourself whether you know the meaning of the word or phrase. At first, this will probably include almost everything you see, but you'll be amazed at how quickly you see words reappearing and how well you remember them. For me, being able to read and then understand most of what I saw around me was like that scene in the movie *Pleasantville* when everything goes from black and white to color. It's an incredible feeling.

7. DON'T BE SCARED TO SPEAK KOREAN

I have many friends that have studied Korean, some for a few months, others for a few years. Yet one disappointing aspect to many of these same people is that they rarely use the Korean they've learned except in survival situations when they're forced to speak the language. Most of the time it's because people are nervous or simply downright scared to speak Korean in public. It's the oldest saying in the world for languages, but it's a fact nonetheless: if you don't speak it, you won't learn it.

8. STUDY KOREAN FORMALLY

I don't care who you are, no one (no matter what some people may claim) learns this language by just listening and hanging out with Koreans. It's a sham; a lie. Don't believe any of it. It's not necessary to learn Korean formally through a school for your whole life, but in the beginning it's imperative to learn from someone who's qualified so that your pronunciation is on the right track, your grammar is working, your mistakes are corrected, your verbs are conjugated properly, your word choice is natural, and on and on and on. **Chapter 19** lists several places you can study Korean, but you should attend a school at some point in your studies if you're really serious about the language. I have friends that routinely go back over the course of years to brush up and learn new things and I think that's a brilliant idea. Don't fall prey to the megalomaniac I'm-smart-enough-to-be-an-auto-didact syndrome. It won't get you very far at all.

9. ASK QUESTIONS ALL THE TIME

I tell this to my own students all the time. It sounds so obvious that most people forget to do it, though. Korean is an extremely interesting language steeped in thousands of years of history. Often times when you have a question, you'll be surprised how cool or mind blowing the answer is. Instead of just taking everything in around you in a sort of mute daze, write it down, ask your friend, pester your husband/wife, inquire with someone who knows-just ask. Personally, I've had more fights with my girlfriend than I care to remember over asking questions, but I also know that it's because of this last point that we now converse in Korean more than we do in English.

10. FIND AN AREA OF INTEREST

Almost everyone has something that they're interested in learning about. That should be a great impetus for you to learn about your interest in Korean. Whether that means studying history or literature, collecting stamps, drinking wine, or playing video games, it should provide an outlet by which you engage yourself in Korean thoroughly.

And for those party animals out there whose greatest hobbies lie in the nightclub and bar, meeting lots of new men/women should be the single greatest reason you study Korean fast and furiously.

Ask Me After Class

How different is the teaching methodology in Korea from that in the West? About as different as they come. Teachers are God-like figures in many of the classrooms that I've been a part of, and so the student is not always made to feel like it is a real learning environment. The best example of this for me was a teacher I once had at university. She and I got along famously before I enrolled in her course. We had even gone out drinking on one occasion, so I thought all signs pointed to it being a really fun class.

On my first day in the class, however, I asked her to explain a question to do with conjugations. She gave me the evil eye before responding to my question, 'You can ask me questions like that after class, Richard.' Having never been so frustrated for asking a question, I told her so after class. She stuck to her guns, though. 'Questions like that are not to take up class time,' she told me matter-of-factly. The reality that verb conjugations are the most important part of Korean grammar didn't seem to faze her. The fact was I had disrupted her teaching plan and did something not commonly done in Korean classrooms: I had asked the teacher a question she was not necessarily prepared to deal with.

Things to Be Careful of

1. ARCHAIC DICTIONARIES

I'm convinced that every dictionary written for people learning Korean was written in the 16th century. Just a cursory glance through any reputable dictionary leads one to believe that Koreans speak much like Shakespeare did hundreds of years ago. Phrases and words are often translated in ways that not even my parents would recognize. This makes using a dictionary frustrating for two reasons: first, when searching for a word that is common vernacular today, you're bound to find nothing in its place in a modern English-Korean dictionary, *yung-han sa-jun* (영한 사전). Moreover, when searching for a word in a Korean-English dictionary, *han-yung sa-jun* (한영 사전), you sometimes find a translation that makes you wonder what kind of priest translated it. Added to this is the fact that most dictionaries do not provide ample explanations as to how and when the term is used.

2. SUBTITLES

There is little doubt that subtitles to Korean movies and television are getting better every year. But be cautious with the best of them. Remember that native Korean speakers translate every movie and show and that their linguistic abilities in English are limited, so when seeing sentences pop up on the screen that may seem awkward in English, remember that it's coming from a Korean speaker.

Moreover, when watching English movies be wary. As explored in **Chapter 9**, there are many examples of words and phrases that are common in written Korean, but not in spoken Korean (e.g. *ke-dae* (그대) and *tang-sheen* (당신)).

3. NATIVE KOREAN SPEAKERS

Don't gasp. The same can be said for Koreans learning English—asking native English speakers will not always yield the correct answer. On many occasions I've asked intelligent Koreans a question about grammar that I found confusing, only to have the person look at me with a blank stare and a shift of the head. Sometimes Koreans, just like native English speakers, overextend their knowledge and provide an answer that may seem satisfactory to them, but proves useless or more confusing to you, the student of Korean. To be fair, ask the average person in Buffalo, Victoria or Edinburgh the difference between the past perfect and present perfect tenses and see what kind of answer you get from them. Not everyone is a linguist, which is why it's important to ask several people the same question when it's a matter of great difficulty.

4. TEXTBOOKS

Korean textbooks tend to be geared toward teaching proper and formal Korean. This makes many of them somewhat useless for teaching colloquial Korean words and expressions. As well, although there are some good textbooks out there that can help you understand the basic mechanics of Korean grammar, most of them serve no great function for teaching *ban-mal* (반말), which is just as essential as *jon-dae-mal* (존대말) for getting by in Korea (despite what Korean teachers might tell you).

5. CORRECTIONS

People are usually happy enough that you're making an effort in Korean to not correct you, even when making the most egregious of mistakes. I've been witness to non-native Korean speakers using rude Korean expressions in public, using the wrong choice of words, killing conjugations, and generally making errors which in most cases they are not aware of. Obviously in public, nobody wants to embarrass the speaker in front of others. However, when in a more causal or laid-back situation where there is room for giving a suggestion or helping with improvement, don't be shy to ask the person you're speaking with if what you have said is actually correct (and natural for that matter). For those of you that have been living in Korea a long time, you'll be surprised (or shocked) as to how much of what you say is not actually used by Koreans or, worse yet, incorrect grammatically.

6. LEARNING FROM STRANGERS

I've been burned by learning from strangers a great deal, especially in my early days of studying the language. Learning from people while taking the bus or subway has always been a favorite past time of mine in Korea. I just sort of lend my ear to the conversation and see how much I understand, pick up a couple of words, maybe a phrase or two, and then feel as if I've made progress for the day. This method came back to bite me in the butt early on, though.

One time while talking with a producer at a TV station, I kept repeating that I understood by saying, '응, 응.' Now, even though that literally means, Yes, yes, it's the rude way by which to say it in a formal situation. What I should have been saying was either *nae, nae* (네, 네) or *yea, yea* (예, 예). The problem, of course, was that I had learned 응, 응 from people speaking on the bus and subway millions of times, so when I was first learning the language, I didn't think there was a difference between the different ways to say yes. From that embarrassing episode with the producer, I learned to always verify what I learned from strangers with someone I could trust.

Chapter 19

Learning Korean in Korea and Through the Internet
한국에서, 그리고 인터넷으로 한국말 배우기

There are a number of places at which you can study the Korean language. They range from Internet sites where you can learn at your own speed, to places staffed with volunteers helping non-native Korean speakers learn Korean, to *hagwon* (학원) with credible teachers, to universities with certified programs. The extensive list of schools on the pages following should allow you to find the place just suited for you.[1]

Like Trying to Find a Needle in a Haystack

You'd think that finding a school to study Korean in Korea would be an easy task, but truth be told, it's not. First, almost every school and university in Korea is located in Seoul, which means if you live elsewhere you might be out of luck. Although there are some *hagwon* (학원) and universities that offer Korean language programs outside of Seoul, they are few and far between. When I was living in Mokpo, there were no formal programs offered, and so I did what most everyone else did that wanted to learn Korean: I hired a private tutor. Speaking from experience, a private tutor is

[1] In the interest of helping others, I'd like to suggest that anyone who has information about schools or programs not listed in this book to please let me know so that in subsequent editions of this book, this section can be updated.

certainly easier than enrolling in a program, but it's harder to learn as much and will cost you more in the long run.

The second problem with trying to find a school to study Korean in Korea is that search engines aren't as useful as you might imagine. Try typing 'Learning Korean' as your keyword on any major search engine, and see how many sites you come up with (6), 'Learning Korean in Korea' (136,000), or 'Studying Korean' (128,000). It seemed that with every search one of two things inevitably happened to me: one was that there were too few resources (6), or the other was that there were way too many (128,000), with schools and programs not organized in any decipherable way. Thus, what I initially assumed would be one of the easier sections of this book to write turned out to be one of the more time-consuming, challenging and frustrating research projects.

LISTING THE SCHOOLS

You'll notice quite quickly that the spelling of place names and school names is wildly erratic. I don't wish to be held responsible if someone reading this book can't get in touch with one of these schools because of one of my translations, so I've kept the names exactly as I found them through my research.

With respect to Internet studies, I've listed them in alphabetical order, and with schools in Korea, I've listed them by city (alphabetically), and then by school name (alphabetically).

Internet Studies

1. **Internet Public Library:** *www.ipl.org.ar/youth/hello/korean.html*
2. **An Introduction to Korean, by J. David Eisenberg:** *www.langintro.com/kintro/*
3. **Korean Ministry of Culture and Tourism's Korean language website:** *http://www.mct.go.kr*
4. **Life in Korea:** *www.lifeinkorea.com/Language/korean.cfm*

5. **Mr. Oh's Learn Korea.com:** *www.learnkorean.com*
6. **Seogang University's on-line study website:** *http://korean.sogang.ac.kr*

Studying at a School

ANDONG (안동)

Andong National University Language Center (안동대학교 어학원)
388, Songcheon-dong, Andong-si, Gyeongsangbuk-do 760-749, Korea
Tel: 82-54-820-5696
Website: http://korea.andong.ac.kr/en

BUSAN (부산)

Dong-Eui University (동의대학교)
Foreign Language Education Center
San 24, Gaya-dong, Pusanjin-gu, Busan-si 614-714, Korea
Tel: 82-51-890-1770
Fax: 82-51-894-6211
E-mail: language@hyomin.dongeui.ac.kr
Website: www.deu.ac.kr

Pusan National University (부산대학교)
Language Education Center
Pusan National University
San 30, Jangjeon-dong Geumjeong-gu, Busan-si 609-735, Korea
Tel: 82-51-510-1984
Fax: 82-51-514-3944
E-mail: sing@bnu.edu
Website: http://pnuls.pusan.ac.kr/pnuls/html

Sungsim College of Foreign Studies (성심외국어대학교)
The Korean Language School

249, Bansong 3-dong, Haeundae-gu, Busan-si 612-743, Korea
Tel: 82-51-540-7104
E-mail: shlee@sungsim.ac.kr

CHEONAN (천안)

Sunmoon University Korean Language Institute (선문대학교 한국어교육원)
381-7, Samyong-dong, Cheonan-si, Chungcheongnam-do 330-150, Korea
Tel: 82-41-559-1338
Fax: 82-41-559-1339
Website: www.sunmoon.ac.kr

CHEONGJU (청주)

YMCA Korean Language Center (YMCA 한국어학당)
119-5, Seomun-dong, Sangdang-gu, Cheongju-si,
Chungcheongbuk-do 360-130, Korea
Tel: 82-43-259-6104
E-mail: sejonghangeul@hotmail.com

DAEGU (대구)

Kyungpook National University (경북대학교)
1370, Sangyeok-dong, Buk-gu, Daegu-si 702-701, Korea
Tel: 82-53-950-6091~2
Fax: 82-53-950-6093
E-mail: interknu@knu.ac.kr
Website: www.knu.ac.kr

DAEJUN (대전)

Paichai University (배재대학교)
Paichai Korean Language Institute

214

439-6, Doma-dong, Seo-gu, Daejeon 302-735, Korea
Tel: 82-42
E-mail: ickwhan@mail.pcu.ac.kr
Website: http://www.pcu.ac.kr/~kli/eng/

GWANGJU (광주)

Korean Language Institute of Chosun University (조선대학교)
375, Seoseok-dong, Dong-gu, Gwangju-si 501-759, Korea
Tel: 82-62-230-6667.6674,7329
Fax: 82-62-234-6769
Website: http://lei.chosun.ac.kr

SEOUL (서울)

Dankook University (단국대학교)
Dankook University Language School
Room 818 Seokwan Building
San 8, Yongsan-gu, Hannam-dong, Seoul 140-714, Korea
Tel: 82-2-709-2217
Fax: 82-2-709-2064
E-mail: pencil58@yahoo.com
Website: www.dankook.ac.kr

Ehwa Womans University (이화여자대학교)
Institute of Language Education
Ehwa Womans University
11-1, Daehyeon-dong, Seodaemun-gu, Seoul 120-750, Korea
Tel: 82-2-3277-318
Fax: 82-2-3277-2855
E-mail: korean@lu.ewha.ac.kr
Website: http://ile.ewha.ac.kr/english/

Ganada Korea Language Institute (가나다 한국어 학원)

568-51, Yongnam-dong, Mapo-gu, Seoul 121-240, Korea
Tel: 82-2-332-6003
Fax: 82-2-332-6004
Website: http://www.gkli.co.kr

Hankuk University of Foreign Studies (한국외국어대학교)

270, Imun-dong, Dongdaemun-gu, Seoul 130-790, Korea
Tel: 82-2-961-4174
Fax: 82-2-962-0575
E-mail: flttc@maincc.hufs.ac.kr

Hanyang University (한양대학교)

Hanyang International Language Institute
Hanyang University
17, Haengdang-dong, Seongdong-gu, Seoul 133-791, Korea
Tel: 82-2-2290-1663
Fax: 82-2-2290-1664
E-mail: annep@email.hanyang.ac.kr
Website: http://www.hviliuf.hanyang.ac.kr

Korea University (고려대학교)

Korea University Institute of Foreign Language Studies
Korean Language & Culture Center
5-1, Anam-dong, Seongbuk-gu, Seoul 136-701, Korea
Tel: 82-2-3290-1455 or (82)-(2)-927-3690
Fax: 82-2-921-0534
Website: http://langtopia.korea.ac.kr

Kyung Hee University (경희대학교)

Seoul Institute of International Education (IIE)
Seoul Campus IIE Building, First Floor
1, Heogi-dong, Dongdaemun-gu, Seoul 130-701, Korea

Tel: 82-2-961-0081-2
Fax: 82-2-959-9018
E-mail: iie@khu.ac.kr
Website: http://korea.iie.ac.kr

Seogang University (서강대학교)

Korean Language Center
1, Shinsu-dong, Mapo-gu, Seoul 121-742, Korea
Tel: 82-2-705-8088
Fax: 82-2-701-6692 / 713-8005
Website: http://sgedu.sogang.ac.kr/korean

Seoul Korean Language Academy (서울한국어아카데미)

4F Jichoun Bldg.
818-1, Yeoksam-dong, Gangnam-gu, Seoul 135-080, Korea
Tel: 82-2-563-3226
Fax: 82-2-563-3227
Website: http://www.seoul-kla.com

Seoul National University (서울대학교)

Korean Language Program, Language Research Institute
san 56-1, Sillim-dong, Gwanak-gu, Seoul 151-742, Korea
Tel: 82-2-880-5488
Fax: 82-2-871-6907
E-mail: korlang@email.com or salri001@snu.ac.kr
Website: www.snu.ac.kr

Sookmyung University (숙명여자대학교)

Korean as a Foreign Language Education Program
53-12, Cheongpa-dong 2-ga, Yongsan-gu, Seoul 140-742, Korea
Tel: 82-2--710-9165
Fax: 82-2--710-9278
E-mail: juhik@sookmyung.ac.kr

Website: www.lingua-express.com

Sungkyunkwan University (성균관대학교)

Humanities and Social Sciences Campus
53, Jongno-gu, Myeongnyun-dong 3-ga, Seoul 110-745, Korea
Tel: 82-2-760-0114
Fax: 82-2-744-2453
Website: http://www.skku.ac.kr

Yonsei University (연세대학교)

Korean Language Institute
The Institute of Language Research and Education, Yonsei University
134, Sincheon-dong, Seodaemun-gu, Seoul 120-749, Korea
Tel: 82-2-2123-3464
Fax: 82-2-393-4599
E-mail: yskli@yonsei.ac.kr
Website: http://www.yonsei.ac.kr/~kli/

YBM/Sisa/ELS

Korea Language Institute
48-1, Jongno 2-ga, Jongno-gu, Seoul 110-122, Korea
Tel: 82-2-2278-0509
Fax: 82-2-2269-0275
E-mail: sisakli@ybmsisa.co.kr
Website: www.ybmedu.com

SUWON (수원)

Kyung Hee University (경희대학교)

Suwon Institute of Continuing Education (ICE)
Suwon Campus Institute of Continuing Education
Kyung Hee University

1, Seocheon-ri, Giheung-eup, Yongin-si, Gyeonggi-do 449-701, Korea
Tel: 82-31-201-2155~8
E-mail: khwd8319@khu.ac.kr

YONGIN (용인)

Myongji University (명지대학교)
E-mail: renai@mju.ac.kr
Professor Hahn, Sang-Dae
San 38-2, Nam-dong, Yongin-si, Gyeonggi-do 449-728, Korea
Tel: 82-31-330-6113(7)
Fax: 82-31-330-6617
Website: www.mju.ac.kr

Studying Korean Outside of Korea

For a complete overview of schools and universities in countries outside Korea, please see the following websites:

1. **The Korea Foundation:** *www.kf.or.kr/english/index.html*

2. **National Institute for International Education Development of the Republic of Korea:** *www.interedu.go.kr*

Part 5

Language in Motion, Cultural Extensions:

A World of Knowledge Unraveled

Books hold a house of gold

책은 집채만한 금을 안고 있다

Chapter 20

The Calendar: Seasonal Divisions, Public Holidays, Special Times of Year and Memorial Days

달력: 절기+ 공휴일 + 명절 + 기념일

The history and use of the calendar in both China and Korea is a fascinating story. The word calendar, *dal-lyuk* (달력), is derived from one pure Korean character, *dal* (달), meaning **moon**, and one Chinese root, *ryuk* (력 · 曆), from the character **calendar** or **calculate**. Although it's not something that most people consider throughout the course of their lives, the creation of a calendar is a remarkable event, and a great feat that different cultures the world over take great pride in commemorating. Korea adopted the traditional lunar calendar from the Chinese centuries ago, and though lunar calendar events are still remembered to this day in Korea, the Gregorian calendar became the official calendar when the Republic of Korea was founded in 1948.

THE OLDEST CALENDARS

The first known calendars to have been excavated in China date back to the 14th century B.C.[1] In the late second century B.C., a Bureau of Astronomy was established in China whose job it was to maintain the calendar, predict astrological anomalies, and calculate astronomical events such as eclipses.[2]

1 See the State University of New Mexico's (NMSU) College of Arts and Science's website at *http://astro.nmsu.edu*

2 See NMSU's website at *http://astro.nmsu.edu*

From the time of the first dynasties in China over two millennia ago, the calendar became one of the most important objects in every emperor's reign (and future kings in Korea as well). Dynasties in China and Korea both relied on what is commonly referred to as the Mandate of Heaven,[3] which implied that the emperor (or king) was heaven's representative on earth, and that all those under him were to obey his every word and action as if it were a directive from heaven itself. The calendar played a critical role in maintaining the harmony between heaven and earth. A correct calendar, it was believed, was the **key to successful harvests** (when to plant and when to reap), to **increased safety** (in predicting when exactly the rainy season would begin, for example), and to maintaining the principle that the **emperor was heaven's representative on earth** (thus, he should be able to predict events like eclipses of the sun and of the moon).

IN THE BEGINNING…

There's no specific initial epoch for counting years in the Chinese/Korean calendar like there is in the West with the Gregorian calendar (i.e. the birth of Christ). Historically, dates were specified by counts of days and years in sexagenarian cycles (i.e. cycles of sixty) and by counts of years from a succession of eras established by reigning monarchs. (Please see **Chapter 21** for a more detailed explanation of sexagenarian cycles). That's why, even today, when you visit palaces in Seoul and other important shrines and monuments around the country you see something written about a place's history as, 'In the such-and-such year of King so-and-so.'

SEASONAL DIVISIONS, *CHUL-GI* (절기)

In Korea, the 24 cycles of the lunar calendar, or *eum-nyuk* (음력), were the primary way in which a year was broken up in the past; 24 events that roughly corresponded to two-week intervals marking the progression of phases of the moon. Some of these seasonal divisions have an English equivalent from Western astrology, but not all do. So, for lack of a simple romanized word in

[3] This was referred to as 'tian ming' in Chinese. According to Arthur Cotterell, 'the Mandate of Heaven was a democratic theory, a kind of safety valve in the Chinese constitution, derived from Mencius' belief that ultimate sovereignty lay with the people — Heaven granted a throne but succession depended on the people's voluntary acceptance of the new ruler.' See Arthur Cotterell's *China: A Cultural History*, p. 73.

Korean, I've attempted to translate the divisions as best I can. The following is a brief summary of each of the traditional seasonal divisions:

Korean	Phonetic Transliteration	Meaning	Time of Year-Solar Calendar (approx.)
입춘	*eep-choon*	onset of spring	Feb 4
우수	*oo-soo*	rainwater	Feb 19
경칩	*kyung-cheep*	waking of frogs	Mar 6
춘분	*choon-boon*	spring equinox	Mar 21
청명	*chung-myung*	pure brightness	Apr 5
곡우	*ko-goo*	planting of rice	Apr 20
입하	*eep-ha*	onset of summer	May 5
소만	*so-man*	greening of fields	May 21
망종	*mang-jong*	grain in ear	June 6
하지	*ha-jee*	summer solstice	June 22
소서	*so-saw*	slight heat (of summer)	July 7
대서	*dae-saw*	great heat (of summer)	July 23
입추	*eep-choo*	beginning of autumn	August 8
처서	*chaw-saw*	limit of heat	August 23
백로	*baeng-no*	white dew	September 8
추분	*choo-boon*	autumnal equinox	September 23
한로	*hal-lo*	cold dew	October 8
상강	*sang-gang*	descent of frost	October 24
입동	*eep-dong*	onset of winter	November 8
소설	*so-sul*	slight snow	November 22
대설	*dae-sul*	great snow	December 7
동지	*dong-gee*	winter solstice	December 22
소한	*so-han*	slight cold (of winter)	January 6
대한	*dae-han*	great cold (of winter)	January 20

PUBLIC HOLIDAYS, *GONG-HYU-EEL* (공휴일)

People living in Korea are most familiar with public holidays because these are the days that everybody gets off from work and school. There are 12 of these holidays scattered throughout the year, at least one in every month, save November. All of the following holidays' dates fall on days set out according to the solar calendar, *yang-nyuk* (양력), except for *Chusok* (추석), *Sollal* (설날), and Buddha's Birthday (석가탄신일):

Holiday (English)	**Holiday** (Korean)	**Date**
New Year's Day	신정	**January 1**
Chinese New Year/*Sollal*/ Lunar New year	설날	**Late January/Early February**
Samil-jul	삼일절	**March 1**
Arbor Day	식목일	**April 5**
Children's Day	어린이날	**May 5**
Buddha's Birthday	석가탄신일	**Middle of May**
Memorial Day	현충일	**June 6**
Constitution Day	제헌절	**July 17**
Independence Day	광복절	**August 15**
Korean Thanksgiving/ *Chusok*	추석	**Late September/Early October**
National Foundation Day	개천절	**October 3**
Christmas	성탄절	**December 25**

REASONS BEHIND THE HOLIDAYS

New Year's Day, *sheen-jung* (신정)
Like Christmas, this a holiday that means more in the West than it does in Korea, but because the Republic of Korea adopted the solar Gregorian Calendar, New Year's is a public holiday.

Sollal, (설날)
Please see SPECIAL TIMES OF YEAR for more information.

Samil-jul (삼일절)
Samil-jul (삼일절) is derived from the Korean characters meaning three, *sam* (삼), or, in this case, March, one, *eel* (일), or, in this case, the first day of the month, and *jul* (절), or day. On March 1, 1919 there was a large uprising against the Japanese, the colonial rulers of the Korean peninsula at the time. Many Korean historians point to this day as a grave example of how tight a reign the Japanese kept over their colonial subjects in Korea. Thousands of Koreans marched from Jongno, a busy center in the north of Seoul, after signing a proclamation of independence, only to be brutally rounded up and tortured, some even being killed at the notorious Seodaemun Prison, *Seodaemun hyung-moo-so* (서대문 형무소). Many people died either directly as a result of the brutality at the hands of the Japanese that day or soon thereafter. This is why *Samil-jul* can be a very emotional day for many Koreans, especially for older people who were alive during Japan's occupation.

Arbor Day, *sheeng-mok-eel* (식목일)
Arbor day in Korean is derived from the Chinese characters meaning plant-tree-day respectively. This day marks the entrance of spring and the planting of trees.

Children's Day, *aw-ree-nee-nal* (어린이날)
Part of a busy May lineup in Korea, Children's Day is still recognized as an official holiday, although Parent's Day is not. This is the day that children are to be celebrated by people all over the country.

Buddha's Birthday, *sawk-ka-tan-sheen-eel* (석가탄신일)
Buddha's birthday, is derived from the characters Buddha, *sawk-ka* (석가), birthday—of someone important like a deity or royal figure, *tan-sheen* (탄신)—and the word day, *eel* (일). However, it's also referred to as *boo-chaw-neem-o-sheen-nal* (부처님오신날), which means, The day Lord Buddha arrived. It's

occasionally referred to as *sa-wawl-cho-pa-eel* (4월초파일), which means the event at the beginning of April (this name referring to April according to the lunar calendar). An event that is obviously paramount in the Buddhist world, the day is fun for people of any faith, though. For weeks before and after the event, people can see beautiful traditional lanterns adorning the streets and temples in every corner of the country, lanterns being where Buddhist monks place a wish before hanging it. This is a wonderful time of year to visit Buddhist temples and see them at their splendid best.

Memorial Day, *hyun-choong-eel* (현충일)
Just as in many other countries around the world, Memorial Day in Korea is a day for people to pay their respects to those that have fallen in the course of war defending the nation. This day is also translated in English as 'Veterans Day' sometimes.

Constitution Day, *jae-hun-jul* (제헌절)
An important holiday for the young democracy that the Republic of Korea is, this holiday commemorates the day when, on July 17, 1948, the constitution of this country was promulgated.

Independence Day, *kwang-bok-jul* (광복절)
This is a proud day for Koreans to wave the national flag, *tae-geuk-gi* (태극기), while remembering that on August 15, 1945 the Japanese surrendered and Korea gained its independence.

Chusok (추석)
Please see **SPECIAL TIMES OF YEAR** for more information.

National Foundation Day, *kae-chun-jul* (개천절)
Sometimes referred to by Koreans in English as, 'The Day the Sky Opened,' *kae-chun-jul* (개천절)—which literally means opening-sky-day—is not thought of much by young people today as anything more than a day off work and school. Historically, however, the day has great importance as it marks the day

that Dangun came down from heaven to found the nation that is now Korea. (For more information on the myth of Dangun, please see **Chapter 21.**)

Christmas, *sung-tan-jul* (성탄절)

Although it's technically called *sung-tan-jul* (성탄절)—the day of the saint's birth—most Koreans don't actually use this word. Instead, you'll hear *ke-ree-se-ma-se* (크리스마스) in its place.

Like almost every other nation on earth, Koreans celebrate the day that marks the birth of Christ. Unlike the West, though, Koreans don't make a big deal of the day and often times do not give presents to each other. The only people that seem to benefit from this day in some regard are children and bar owners, as everyone tends to go out and celebrate with a round (or four) at the local pub on the eve of this holiday.

SPECIAL TIMES OF YEAR, *MYUNG-JUL* (명절)

Myung-jul are the most important holidays in Korea. Anyone that has had an opportunity to spend *Chusok* or *Sollal* with a Korean family will tell you that it's very different from most people's idea of a typical Christmas or Thanksgiving in the West. The five special holidays are as follows:

Korean	**Phonetic Transliteration**	**Date** (lunar calendar)
설날	*Sollal*	1st day of first lunar month
대보름	*dae-bo-reum*	15th day of first lunar month
한식	*han-sheek*	105th day after winter solstice
단오	*dan-o*	5th day of fifth lunar month
추석	*Chusok*	15th day of eighth lunar month

Sollal (설날)

Also known as **Lunar New Year** and **Chinese New Year**, *Sollal* is one of the two biggest holidays of the year for Koreans. Family members get together at this time no matter how far away they live from each other. And though Korea may be a small country in geographic terms, traffic jams at this time of year rival the worst ones anywhere in the world. Everyone has horror stories of spending 12 hours going from Busan to Seoul, 8 hours from Daegu to Seoul, 9 hours from Sokcho to Seoul, trips that would regularly take no more than half this time in the worst of traffic. As almost everybody is heading for the *keun-jeep* (큰집)—the house where the eldest brother lives (literally translated as the 'big house')—highways, airports, train stations, and bus terminals are overflowing beyond capacity. If you ever want to travel during this time, think twice.

The holiday itself is very pleasant, however. On the morning of *Sollal*, women and children often don traditional *hanbok* (한복), or sometimes the new age *hanbok* called *kae-ryang hanbok* (개량한복). The ceremony of *cha-rae* (차례) is what's held first thing in the morning, a ceremony where family members pay their respects to their ancestors. A great deal of food is prepared and eaten before the dishes are cleared away and everyone performs their New Year bows to their elders, called *sae-bae* (세배) in Korean. This is the part of the day that is most like Christmas morning for kids in the West because after the young ones perform their *sae-bae* bows, they're presented with money, a little if they are extremely young, usually much more when they're older. This money is called *sae-baet-don* (세뱃돈).

After this, families eat *ddawk-gook* (떡국), a traditional rice cake soup served with dumplings. Kids and adults alike then usually play traditional games for the better part of the day, one of the most popular of these traditional games is *yoon-no-ree* (윷놀이), but for many nowadays, *Sollal* means marathon TV-watching sessions.

dae-bo-reum (대보름)

Dae-bo-reum is not as important as it once was in Korea. Nonetheless, people both young and old remember it if only for historical and health reasons. *Dae-bo-reum*'s meaning is derived from the Chinese character for great, *dae* (대 · 大), and the pure Korean characters *bo-reum* (보름), meaning fifteen days (*dae-bo-reum* falls on the fifteenth day of the first lunar month). On this holiday, families are supposed to stay together and eat nuts in the morning, with the belief that eating these nuts will provide warmth for the coming winter. People pray to the moon and make wishes, while farmers traditionally pray to the moon for a successful harvest.

han-sheek (한식 · 寒食)

Han-sheek is a very solemn holiday that's still respected by many families across Korea. The name of the holiday literally means 'cold food' in English from its two Chinese roots [寒] and [食]. On this day farmers plant and sow throughout the fields, while others use the day as a chance by which to pay their respects to their ancestors and take care of the gravesites that hold their remains. Families go to the gravesites after making a special meal to be left in front of the grave. The meal is often elaborately prepared and includes meat, vegetables, fruit, rice cakes, and alcohol. Unlike *Chusok* or *Sollal* where people are happy and boisterous, though, *han-sheek* is a time to remember one's ancestors and reflect on the past.

dan-o (단오 · 端午)

Dan-o is arguably the least remembered *myung-jul* of the year for Koreans. Many hundreds of years ago a Chinese man by the name of Kulwon committed suicide by drowning himself in a river in order to stay faithful to his principles and prove a point.[4] Chinese (and thereafter Koreans) who wanted to praise the actions of this brave man held a festival in his name and called it *dan-o*. Originally, people celebrated this event to commemorate a martyr, but over time the holiday changed, so that many years after, people took to washing their hair (to ward off evil spirits) and exchanging fans (to ward off diseases) instead. Also, people traditionally played many types of games, most popular among these was *ke-nae-ddwee-gi* (그네뛰기) and the Korean version of sumo wrestling, *sshee-reum* (씨름). Although most Koreans don't pay much heed to this holiday anymore, there's still a popular festival held in the coastal city of Kangneung every year to re-enact traditional parts of this ancient festival.

Chusok (추석 · 秋夕)

The name *Chusok* is derived from the Chinese characters *chu* [秋], meaning

[4] See AtticWorld Company, Limited's website at *http://english.attic.co.kr/infor/basic-sollal.htm*

230

autumn, and *sok* [夕], meaning dusk. This is why *Chusok* is occasionally translated in English as Harvest Moon Festival, the day when the moon looks orange in the sky above. Tied for the biggest holiday of the year in Korea, *Chusok* is like *Sollal* in that transportation is a mess, so it's best to avoid going anywhere unless you absolutely must. Commonly referred to as **Korean Thanksgiving**, *Chusok* is also called *han-ka-wee* (한가위) in Korean.

Like Thanksgiving in North America, it's a time for families to get together to give thanks for the harvest. On the morning of *Chusok*, people put on new clothes and perform a ceremony to pay their respects to their ancestors before settling down to eat breakfast. Instead of *ddawk-gok* (떡국), which is served for *Sollal*, another dish called *song-pyun* (송편), a variety of stuffed rice cake, is served for *Chusok*. There is then a special dinner where people eat, drink, and are merry. Like *Sollal*, many games are played, with *hwa-too* (화투), a traditional Korean card game, being very popular.

The Fusing of Tradition and the Television

Spending my first *Sollal* with a Korean family was an interesting experience that I don't think I'll ever forget. Many of the women at the *keun-jeep* (큰집) were wearing *hanbok*, while the men were dressed smartly in suits and ties. After performing *sae-bae* (세배) to my girlfriend's parents, everyone adjourned to the living room where we sat down on the floor and exchanged stories. Lunch was later served and just as tradition requires, it was a feast of the greatest order. All sorts of traditional food coupled with everyday things like *kimchi* and other *ban-chan* (반찬) made it a food-lover's dream.

However, it wasn't until after lunch that I learned another new custom associated with special holidays in Korea: TV-watching. It's not just TV-watching for an hour or two, though. The sessions can last hours upon hours, and if you're not a fan of watching TV, then the day can pass painfully slow. The other fact that makes this unique for many foreigners living in Korea is that the size of the TV room is usually fairly small relative to the number of people watching TV. In my case there were five of us in a tiny little room staring at a television almost as big as the wall. Only the next day when talking about it with friends that have spent holidays at Korean homes did I realize that my experience wasn't so special, and indeed, a new trend among modern families. The almighty TV has now penetrated the oldest and most special of Korean holidays, *Sollal.*

MEMORIAL DAYS, *KEE-NYUM-EEL* (기념일)

This is the final set of special days in Korea, and includes days that are neither fully recognized by the government as statutory holidays, nor days that in the past divided the calendar up into different parts of the year. These days range from the celebration of the creation of *Hangeul* to the outbreak of the Korean War to the anniversary of the birth of one of the most famous Koreans in history, Yi Sun-shin. They are as follows:

Korean	Phonetic Transliteration	English Name	Date (Solar Calendar)
납세자의날	*nap-sae-ja-ae-nal*	Taxpayers Day	March 3
상공의날	*sang-gong-ae-nal*	Commerce and Industry Day	March 19
세계물의날	*sae-gae-moo-rae-nal*	World Water Day	March 22
향토예비군의날	*hyang-to-yea-bee-koon-ae-nal*	Reserve Forces Day	April 5
보건의날	*bo-gun-ae-nal*	Health Day	April 7
임시정부수립기념일[5]	*eem-shee-jung-boo-soo-reep-kee-nyum-eel*	Establishment of Provisional Gov't Memorial Day	April 13
혁명기념일[6]	*hyung-myung-kee-nyum-eel*	Revolution Memorial Day	April 1

[5] This marks the day when the provisional government opposed to Japanese occupation of the Korean peninsula was established in Shanghai, China in 1919.

[6] This day marks the anniversary of the student movement that helped topple the government of Syngman Rhee in 1960.

Korean	Phonetic Transliteration	English Name	Date (Solar Calendar)
장애인의날	jang-ae-een-ae-nal	Day for the Physically Challenged	April 20
과학의날	gwa-hak-ae-nal	Science Day	April 21
정보통신의날	jung-bo-tong-sheen-ae-nal	Telecommunications Day	April 22
충무공탄신일	choong-moo-gong-tan-sheen-eel	Anniversary of Yi Sun-shin's Birth	April 28
법의날	bup-ae-nal	Law Day	May 1
근로자의날[7]	geul-lo-ja-ae nal	May Day	May 1
어버이날	aw-baw-ae nal	Parents Day	May 8
스승의날	se-seung-ae nal	Teachers Day	May 15
5.18민주화운동기념일[8]	meen-joo-hwa-oon-dong-kee-nyum-eel	May 18 Democratic Movement Memorial Day	May 18
성년의날	sung-nyun-ae-nal	Coming of Age Day[9]	Third Monday of May
발명의날	pal-myung-ae-nal	Inventors Day	May 19
방재의날	bang-jae-ae-nal	Disaster Prevention Day	May 25
바다의날	pa-da-ae-nal	Ocean Day	May 31
환경의날	hwan-kyung-ae-nal	Environment Day	June 5
6.25사변일[10]	yoo-gi-o-sa-byun-eel	Outbreak of Korean War Day	June 25
사회복지의날	sa-hwae-bok-jee-ae-nal	Social Welfare Day	September 7
철도의날	chul-do-ae-nal	National Railway Day	September 18
국군의날	gook-goon-ae-nal	Armed Forces Day	October 1
노인의날	no-een-ae-nal	Senior Citizens Day	October 2
재향군인의날	jae-hyang-goon-een-ae-nal	Reservists Day	October 8
한글날	Hangeul-nal	Hangeul Day	October 9

[7] This day was formerly known as no-dong-ja-ae nal (노동자의날).

[8] This day commemorates the democracy movement that came to a tragic end on May 18, 1980 in Gwangju. On that day, police and military forces cracked down on protesters that left hundreds dead. Many Koreans today refer to it as simply 5-1-8, o-eel-pal (오일팔).

[9] This day celebrates someone's 21st birthday (Korean age).

[10] This day is usually written as a number and is pronounced 6-2-5 in Korean, yoo-gi-o (육이오).

233

Korean	Phonetic Transliteration	English Name	Date (Solar Calendar)
체육의날	*chae-yook-ae-nal*	Physical Fitness Day	October 15
문화의날	*moon-hwa-ae-nal*	Culture Day	October 20
경찰의날	*kyung-chal-ae-nal*	Police Officers' Day	October 21
국제연합일	*kook-jae-yun-hap-eel*	United Nations Day	October 24
저축의날	*jaw-chook-ae-nal*	Savings Day	October 28
학생의날	*hak-saeng-ae-nal*	Students' Day	November 3
소방의날	*so-bang-ae-nal*	Fire Fighters Day	November 9
농업인의날	*no-aup-een-ae-nal*	Farmers Day	November 11
순국선열의날	*soon-gook-sun-yul-ae-nal*	Patriots Day	November 17
무역의날	*moo-yawk-ae-nal*	Trading Day	November 30
소비자보호의날	*so-bee-ja-bo-ho-ae-nal*	Consumer Protection Day	December 3
국민교육헌장선포기념일	*koong-meen-kyo-yook hun-jang-sun-po-kee-nyum-eel*	Constitution of National Charter of Education Day	December 5
세계인권선언기념일	*sae-gae-een-gwawn-sun-un-kee-nyum-eel*	World Human Rights Day	December 10

Chapter 21

Korean Mythology, Chinese Zodiac and Oriental Fortune-Telling

한국의 신화 + 띠 + 사주

Korean mythology, intimately tied with that of Chinese mythology, has played an important role in the history of the Korean peninsula. Mythology has helped Koreans understand their role in the universe for centuries upon centuries and it has continued to exercise a sizeable influence on them in a number of facets from the time of the very first myth. Tied up as inextricably within the myths, however, is the role that animals play and have played in life. In the beginning there were only two important animals according to Korean mythology, but that number grew over time to include the twelve animals of the Chinese zodiac.

THE FIRST KOREAN MYTH[1]

A long time ago in a galaxy far, far away lived a king by the name of **Hwan-een** (환인). He in turn had a son named **Hwan-oong** (환웅), or Hwan-hoong as he is sometimes referred to in English, who worried a great deal about the state of affairs on earth. He saw the way people behaved towards each other and it upset him greatly. Wanting to try and do away with such human acts as hatred and deceit, Hwan-oong asked for his father's permission to go and live among the people on earth so that he could help them. Although his father was

[1] I received a great deal of my information on the myth of Dangun from Seo Dae-seok and Peter H. Lee's *Myths of Korea*. I also found helpful information in the *Korea Herald*, Friday October 4, 2002, p. 10.

235

sad at first that this would lead to their separation, he realized the good his son was trying to impart on mankind and so let him go.

Hwan-oong descended down to earth and brought with him the Earl of Wind, the Master of Rain, and the Master of Clouds, along with 3000 servants that were to serve under him. Hwan-oong's father had given his son the legitimacy to rule by granting Hwan-oong The Mandate of Heaven, the same legitimacy tool that emperors in China would use for millennia up until the establishment of the Republic of China in 1912, and the same tool that Korean kings would use until the annexation of the country at the hands of the Japanese in 1910.

Hwan-oong made his capital near Chindansu and called it the City of Shin, *shin-shee* (신시). From the moment he landed on earth, things did in fact become better; people became kinder with one another, animals were more obedient to their masters, and the land was ruled over with benevolence and fairness.

One day, out of the blue, a tiger and a bear came to Hwan-oong requesting that he change them into humans. Hwan-oong was taken aback at the request, doubting the will of the animals. The tiger and the bear were determined, however, and said that they would endure anything for the chance to become human. Hwan-oong thought about this for some time before replying that the road to becoming human was an arduous one that would require great strength of character. The tiger and the bear excitedly replied that they were ready for this test of character. They would give anything for the chance to become human, they said. Hwan-oong accepted the request and went on to explain that if they truly wanted to become humans they would have to take 20 cloves of garlic and sacred mugwort, *ssook* (쑥), go to a cave, and 'shun sunlight for one hundred days, [at which point] you will assume human form.'[2]

Happy at being given the chance to fulfill their dream, the tiger and the bear accepted the king's conditions and set off to a cave nearby with the garlic and the mugwort. Day after day passed as the two animals prayed and prayed while suffering horribly with hunger and loneliness.

After some time, though, the tiger could no longer endure such horrific conditions. Too many dark, lonely nights forced the tiger to bid good-bye to the bear. The bear was sad to see his friend leave, but was more resilient. In the end, the bear hung on and walked out of the cave a woman. Upon exiting the

[2] See *Myths of Korea*, p. 3.

cave, Hwan-oong immediately named the bear **Oong-nyaw** (웅녀), or Woong-nyo as she is sometimes referred to in English translations, her name meaning 'beautiful bear' from the Korean characters. So taken aback with Oong-nyaw's beauty was Hwan-oong, in fact, that he decided to marry her upon her leaving the cave and the two were as happy as could be.

Years later good fortune visited Hwan-oong and Oong-nyaw when Oong-nyaw became pregnant. They named their first son **Dangun** (단군), and though he didn't know it at the time, Dangun was to be the first ancestor of the Korean people. Dangun grew and grew and one day succeeded his father as ruler of the City of Shin. However, upon taking over from his father, Dangun sought to move the capital to Baekak-san (백악산), a mountain near modern day Pyeongyang, and renamed the country *Ko*-Joseon (고조선), or Old Joseon.[3] This was done in the year 2333 B.C.

From that day forward, Dangun promised to rule the nation as a king devoted to the welfare of his people, helping to shine the warmth of heaven's rays upon the land and its citizens so that everyone could live in harmony and prosperity. Dangun followed through with this promise and ended up ruling benevolently hundreds of years longer. Finally, at the age of 1908, Dangun retired to the mountains around Baekak-san.

And so 2333 B.C. marks the first year in the Korean mythological calendar. Even though people use the Gregorian calendar today, Koreans still claim ancestry back to this myth, so that they say Korea is five millennia old. It's interesting to note that, like the written language of *Hangeul*, Koreans have an exact year in which they believe they can trace their lineage back to.

HISTORY OF THE ZODIAC

Koreans have a special relationship with the Chinese zodiac, or *ddee* (띠) as it's known in Korean. Like the myth of Dangun, Korean *ddee* is closely tied with certain animals. This is still true today for two important reasons: first, the role of animals has always been important in Korean folklore, health, and language. Second, Koreans have been a spiritual people for time immemorial. When the Chinese zodiac arrived on the Korean peninsula, no one is exactly sure. Rumors

[3] *Ko*-Joseon (고조선) is derived from the Chinese characters 'old' [古], 'morning' [朝], and 'calm' [鮮]. These same Chinese characters for 'morning' and 'calm' were used in the name of the last Korean dynasty, Joseon dynasty (조선시대).

differ depending upon who you ask, but my favorite story goes like this...

Legend has it that one day the Jade King, jade being the most precious of all gemstones in ancient China, was so bored that he sent for twelve animals to keep him company.[4] The king was bored all by himself and thought the animals might help pass the time more interestingly. His servants, not wanting to disappoint the Great King, ran off right away and issued invitations to the **rat** and the **cat** to appear before the Jade King. The rat, being sly and cunning, decided not to tell the cat about the invitation, and instead went up to see the king alone. Further invitations were then issued to the ox, the tiger, the rabbit, the dragon, the snake, the horse, the sheep, the monkey, the rooster, and the sheep to appear before the king the following day.

Only when all the animals were lined up before the Jade King did the servants realize that there were not 12, but only 11 animals (the rat having deceived the cat). Embarrassed at the miscount, the servants rushed back to earth to retrieve another animal as quickly as possible. The first animal they passed along their way down on earth was a pig. The servants grabbed the pig and delivered it to the king right away.

The twelve animals then stood in front of the king. The rat, always on the uptake, leapt onto the back of the ox and proceeded to play the flute. It was a bid, no doubt, to win over the king, and it succeeded because the **rat** was awarded first place after his performance. The **ox**, having showed good sportsmanship, was allotted second place among the animals, with the **tiger**, which appeared the most courageous, being awarded third place. The **rabbit** was then given fourth, the **dragon** fifth, the **snake** sixth, the **horse** seventh, the **sheep** eighth, the **monkey** ninth, the **rooster** tenth, and the **dog** eleventh. Though the cat later came up to the Heavens above begging for a place among the other animals, the Jade King turned its request down and gave the **pig** twelfth place.

IT'S NOT ALL AN OLD WIVES' TALE

Though a fantastic tale, the myth behind the creation of the Chinese zodiac does not exactly inspire confidence in its ability to predict events and help people solve problems. Yet there's much more to this age-old system than

[4] This story was adapted from a website with a great deal of information on the Chinese Zodiac. Please refer to *http://chinese.astrology.com/history.html* for more information.

meets the eye. The first interesting fact with the Chinese zodiac has to do with the numbers **12** and **5**. There are **5** basic elements in the Chinese universe (and consequently in the Korean one as well), which are metal, water, wood, fire, and earth. With these five elements, it takes 60 years to assign each element to the **12** animals. It's known that ancient Chinese astrologers favored a 60-year cycle, with each cycle representing a third of the Great Solar Cycle of 180 years. Thus, the five elements worked in tandem with the twelve animals, which were then in turn in synchronicity with the cycles of the universe. Like much of ancient Chinese and Korean science, the Chinese zodiac is no different from anything else in that it's history is colorful and interesting.

MODERN LEGACIES

Regardless of whether there's any semblance of truth to the myth of the zodiac's roots or not, the fact remains that Koreans have been influenced by this myth for centuries. As a form of divination related to astrology, the animal cycle is also related to the two counting systems that Koreans used to measure time up until the end of the Joseon dynasty. These twelve earthy branches, *kan-jee* (간지), had two solstices and two equinoxes, two snowfalls and two rains, and other events that worked in pairs like this. Together, these divisions represented the 24 parts of the year that Koreans measured time with and called *chul-gi* (절기), as explained in **Chapter 20**. Five 12-year cycles of this sort were then known as *yook-kap* (육갑), a marker of sixty years. When someone celebrated his or her 60th birthday, a tradition that's still alive and strong in Korea today, it was an important event because it represented the human completion of the same cycle that's linked with measuring time, and the twelve animals that originally started this whole thing in the first place.

Yet it's not just the *hwan-kap* (환갑) that has survived the test of time. Koreans may not adhere to the Chinese zodiac like they once did, but today every Korean still knows their animal (or their *ddee* as they say), and many still believe that the characteristics associated with one animal or another live on through them. People consult these animal guides upon the birth of a child, upon marriage, or when seeking information about the fate of a friend or loved one with regard to everything from work to love to money.

But it's more than just personalities that are measured up against the animals of the Chinese zodiac. The fact that the five ancient elements were tied up with the twelve animals meant that they had influence upon one's character as well. Thus, when looking upon the Chinese zodiac, it's helpful to not only look upon the chart that coincides with your animal, but to look at the element that most closely corresponds to your personality. Listed below is a basic breakdown of the five elements as they apply to people's characters:[5]

Water

These people are creative, captivating, diplomatic, and intuitive. Water people have a special talent for making people trust them and follow them no matter how far they go in life. Their confidence is like the fluidness of a river and goes where it wills itself. However, this same self-assurance can lead to passiveness and indecisiveness so that water people sometimes let themselves be bent to others' opinions or beliefs.

Fire

Fire people have, not surprisingly, a fierce charm about them. They are born leaders that can be restless with their emotions and impulsive with their enthusiasm. They rely a great deal on their instincts and draw people to them through their charisma. They love as fiercely as they work, and will not be driven from what it is they set their sights on.

Metal

People born under the influence of metal tend to be enjoyers of the good life, while being self-reliant and forceful. As much as they like being congratulated for what they have done (and done well), they like to work on their own much of the time. Other people look to them for help and inspiration. They demand a great deal of themselves and of others and, in this way, make a dedicated lover and partner.

[5] I've adapted the description of these five elements from a Chinese astrology website: http://chinese.astrology.com/history.html

Earth

People born under the earth sign are moral and responsible people. Like the earth itself, they have their feet planted firmly on the ground most of the time. They work more with their head than with their heart; logic comes much easier to them than emotion. They are disciplined and earn the respect of other people through their actions. They can be too controlling at times, though. Sometimes they don't share enough of themselves with those that need them, and consequently suffer as a result.

Wood

Wood people grow and become wiser with each passing year like their elemental counterpart. They are open-minded and fun to be around and for this reason people like to be with them. They see the value of the small things in life and therefore do not get easily caught up in the race for money and possessions. However, this makes them a little too passive at times, so that friends occasionally take advantage of them.

FINDING YOUR BIRTH ANIMAL

Although you need your exact time of birth (or the closest approximation), along with the year, month and day (according to the lunar calendar—see the sub-section **ORIENTAL FORTUNE-TELLING** in this chapter for more information) to discover intimate information about your own personality, many people still find it fun and interesting to search through the traditional characteristics associated with their birth animal. For general observations, the chart following gives you information about which animals are associated with which birth years. There's one thing to keep in mind, however. The Chinese zodiac is based on the lunar calendar, and the lunar New Year (*Sollal*) usually falls somewhere in late January or early February according to the solar calendar. Therefore, people born in January or early February should consult years both attached to their solar birth year and the one before it to see which personality description more closely matches them.

Years and Animals Associated with the Chinese Zodiac

Rat	1900	1912	1924	1936	1948	1960	1972	1984	1996	2008
Ox	1901	1913	1925	1937	1949	1961	1973	1985	1997	2009
Tiger	1902	1914	1926	1938	1950	1962	1974	1986	1998	2010
Rabbit	1903	1915	1927	1939	1951	1963	1975	1987	1999	2011
Dragon	1904	1916	1928	1940	1952	1964	1976	1988	2000	2012
Snake	1905	1917	1929	1941	1953	1965	1977	1989	2001	2013
Horse	1906	1918	1930	1942	1954	1966	1978	1990	2002	2014
Sheep	1907	1919	1931	1943	1955	1967	1979	1991	2003	2015
Monkey	1908	1920	1932	1944	1956	1968	1980	1992	2004	2016
Rooster	1909	1921	1933	1945	1957	1969	1981	1993	2005	2017
Dog	1910	1922	1934	1946	1958	1970	1982	1994	2006	2018
Pig	1911	1923	1935	1947	1959	1971	1983	1995	2007	2019

A BRIEF EXPLANATION

What follows is a brief outline of certain personality characteristics that are said to be related to each animal. Accompanying each animal's name in bold is the next year that is the year of that specific animal, along with the name of the animal in Korean.[6]

Rat (2008), *jwee* (쥐)

Winter is your season while December is your month. You enjoy life's great pleasures. You're crafty and a wonderful opportunist. You love your friends and family when in their presence, but once separated you are very independent and self-oriented. You navigate well through the world of politics and business with your cunning sense of deal making. You are extreme with money, saving like no one else or spending like there is no tomorrow. You seem egotistical on the outside, but those that know your inner side know how thoughtful and sensitive you are. You can be very emotional and only ask that your partner

[6] See *http://astrology.yahoo.com/us/astrology/divination/chinese* for more information on this.

accept you for who you really are.

Ox (2009), *so* (소)

Winter is your season while January is your month. You go through life at a slower pace than others. You love nature and working outdoors. You respect traditions and customs and can be extremely stubborn once you've set your mind to something. Just as the mountain does not scare you when climbing, so too does a load of difficult work not frighten you or cause you to run away. You simply accept such challenges. You are one of the most reasonable people with money, saving when needed, spending a reasonable amount on the things that are necessary. You are slow, but prudent when it comes to love. You never rush into anything, but make the good things last a long, long time.

Tiger (2010), *bawm* (범)

Winter is your season while February is your month. You're extremely energetic and a ferocious leader. Nothing stands in your way when it comes to adventure. You move as much by impulse as by cold, calculated thoughts. You're a charismatic person who is always the leader. You're extremely independent and crave the attention of others. You don't like saving money at all; it's all about the here and now. Money is only a means to an end. You fear nothing when it comes to love and will do whatever it takes to win over the love of your life. However, you are easily bored and can run out on commitments before seeing them through.

Rabbit (2011), *to-kkee* (토끼)

Spring is your season while March is your month. You're lively, yet peaceful. Tranquility is important to you. You're an excellent listener and have the ability to circulate in the most urbane of crowds. Your open-mindedness is a wonderful skill for work and valued by those around you. You feel things more intuitively than think of them logically. You're neither rich nor poor, never too far from the happy medium, which allows you to live a comfortable, but not elaborate, lifestyle. People count on you all the time, but when it comes to love interests, you like to bring out the sentimental side of your partner. You're a romantic who likes to see others express themselves honestly and openly.

Dragon (2012), *yong* (용)

Spring is your season while April is your month. You're an exceptional person and love being King/Queen of your own castle. You take defeat better than others and learn from your mistakes much quicker than the average person. You're not afraid to take on big projects no matter how large in scope they may be. You love living large. For you, there is no such thing as saving your pennies for a rainy day. However, you're equally as generous with yourself as you are with your friends. You find that love is something owed to you, that you expect it from those around you. You are, indeed, the mighty, all-powerful dragon.

Snake (2013), *baem* (뱀)

Spring is your season while May is your month. You're refined, funny and gifted when it comes to getting other people do what you want them to do. The snake is admired for its wisdom and you definitely show this attribute. You like solving problems on your own and do not depend on the advice of others as much as your friends do. You like money, but more for the medium it is than the end it might provide in false hope; a good trip or a nice piece of art is more important than any material value to be found in assets. You're a sensual and passionate lover, but can be over-demanding of your partners.

Horse (2014), *mal* (말)

Summer is your season while June is your month. Horses have traditionally represented happiness so you have a natural vivacity about you that others lack. You're worldly and enjoy good conversation, as your intelligence and sociability shine through in times like this. Independence is very important to you and your work has to reflect this; being cooped up in an office all day won't do for you. You live for today with regards to money and are not very good at saving money for the future. You are always in love and thrive on riding the vicissitudes of emotion that love often brings with it. At the first sign of repetitiveness, you leave and look for more exciting times.

Sheep (2003), *yang* (양)

Summer is your season while July is your month. You are an eternal artist. Regular work bores you and you're constantly dreaming of being in a better place. You love working with your hands and excel in the creative fields. You have no problem spending money on others and will pay for something no matter how much it costs if your heart is set on it. You live for the feeling that love brings with it and so seek it out regularly. You constantly need a companion, but have no problem being faithful to one person once you've met that special someone you want to be with.

Monkey (2004), *wawn-soong-ee* (원숭이)

Summer is your season while August is your month. You are the most intelligent of the animals in the Chinese zodiac. You can be charming, clever, and witty. However, you have trouble committing to anything for a significant length of time. You like branching out from one place to the next, from one person to the next. You are very ambitious at work and incredibly resourceful. This is due in some small way to your love of money and the lengths you will go to attain it. Your relationships are often just as exciting and crazy. You prefer passion to stability and strive for the perfect love. Though your standards can be high, you're successful in the game of love nonetheless.

Rooster (2005), *dak* (닭)

Autumn is your season while September is your month. According to ancient Chinese tradition, the red combs on a rooster's body scare evil spirits away.[7] You seek gratitude and respect from others and feel that appearances are very important. You're realistic when it comes to work and manage your money well. You're not one to take risks financially, though, so you invest prudently and slowly. You prefer stable relationships to wild flings and can be brutally honesty when it comes to looks, including your own.

Dog (2006), *gae* (개)

Autumn is your season while October is your best month. You're a good friend to people and because of that others trust you much more than they

[7] Red is also the color used to scare away ghosts and evil spirits in Korea.

might ordinary friends. You're an honest and conscientious worker and don't mind helping others around the office or in matters associated with the workplace. You're scared of being poor, but do not excel at making money. You're not the kind of person who plays the field. You like serious commitment and when you fall in love it's for one person and one person only.

Pig (2007), *twae-jee* (돼지)

Autumn is the best season for you while November is the best month. You are honest and upright as a person and rarely lack money, as the pig symbolized wealth in ancient times. You enjoy working, but have a limit. Entities like love are more important to you, for example. You hate lies and people that spread them and seek to avoid stormy times and stormy relationships, choosing rather to wait such times out than deal with them directly.

WHAT'S YOUR SIGN, BABE?

For you romantics out there that give a lot of credence to these heavenly predictions, the following is a chart of the Chinese zodiac animals that are most- and least-compatible with one another.[8]

Compatibility of Chinese Zodiac Animals
1= Least Compatible, 10= Most Compatible

Animal Name	Rat	Ox	Tiger	Rabbit	Dragon	Snake	Horse	Sheep	Monkey	Rooster	Dog	Pig
Rat	9	6	4	7	10	7	3	4	10	6	8	8
Ox	6	8	4	8	7	9	5	2	4	9	7	7
Tiger	4	4	5	5	6	3	9	4	2	4	9	7
Rabbit	7	8	5	8	7	7	5	9	4	2	8	9
Dragon	10	7	6	7	9	8	8	7	10	9	2	8
Snake	7	9	3	7	8	8	4	7	4	9	8	4
Horse	3	5	9	5	8	4	8	8	5	6	9	6
Sheep	4	2	4	9	7	7	8	9	5	5	4	9

[8] See http://chinese.astrology.com/history.html

246

Animal Name	Rat	Ox	Tiger	Rabbit	Dragon	Snake	Horse	Sheep	Monkey	Rooster	Dog	Pig
Monkey	10	4	2	4	10	4	5	5	9	4	8	7
Rooster	6	9	4	2	9	9	6	5	4	4	5	5
Dog	8	7	9	8	2	8	9	4	8	5	7	7
Pig	8	7	7	9	8	v	6	9	7	5	7	8

ORIENTAL FORTUNE-TELLING, *SA-JOO* (사주) AND *JUM-SOOL* (점술)[9]

Sa-joo (사주) literally means four pillars, *sa* (사) meaning 'four,' and *joo* (주) meaning 'foundation' or 'pillar.' These characters are derived from the Chinese characters [四] and [柱]. Actually, on a technical level, *sa-joo* is part of a process called *jum-sool* (점술),[10] which refers to one's fortune as predicted through the four pillars, but for the sake of convenience, I'll refer to **fortune-telling** in this section as simply *sa-joo*.

The four pillars of fortune-telling are the **year, month, day** and **hour** of one's birth. With this information, the flow of energy from in an individual, called *ki* (기 · 氣) in Korean, along with the energy in the rest of the universe is determined. A fortune-teller then performs an analysis of how the flow, or harmony, of this energy is maintained. This flow, known commonly in the West as yin and yang, or *eum* (음) and *yang* (양) respectively in Korean, is what fortune-tellers measure. The harmony of this yin and yang is then balanced against the **wood, water, fire, metal** and **earth** inherent in *sa-joo* to make predictions and insights into one's character and future. In Korea, *sa-joo* doesn't relate quite as much to the occult as you might think; a link to science and an ability to read the heavens above is about as wild and crazy as *sa-joo* gets.

BACKING IT UP WITH SCIENCE

A person's *sa-joo* is read by a complex, but mathematically sound process of character divination. *Sa-joo* is comprised of **8 Chinese characters** which, along with a set of **10 heavenly characters**, known as *chun-gan* (천간), and a set of **12 earthly characters,** known as *gee-gee* (지지), are combined to

[9] The bulk of the information in this section is taken from the Korea Herald's Weekender section, February 15, 2002, p.9.

[10] Or simply *jum* (점), as it's commonly referred to in spoken Korean.

create **60 character pairs**, called *yook-sheep kap-ja* (육십 갑자) in Korean. These character pairs are then assigned to represent each year, month, day, and hour that passes. In essence, this makes *sa-joo* a representation of four character-pairs, totaling eight characters in all. The word *pal-ja* (팔자) is derived from this fact (*pal-ja* meaning eight characters in Korean). What's interesting is that the word *pal-ja* also has another meaning in everyday Korean: 'fate' or 'fortune.' When a fortune-teller ascertains the necessary information about your birth, he or she then refers to a book known as *man-sae-ryuk* (만세력) to discover the eight characters (*pal-ja*) needed to make the necessary predictions about your future.

Although not as important as it once was in the decision making process of Koreans, fortune-telling is still popular for many people wanting to know more about the future, especially when it comes to finding out about the compatibility of two people before getting married.

Death and Her Twenty-Six Accomplices

In **Chapter 10**, I talked about the fact that Korean words (those derived from Chinese) have so many meanings that often times it's hard to keep track. The word *sa* (사) is no different in this respect. *Sa* is only one character long (and thus one syllable when spoken), yet take a moment and look at its meanings, as derived from Chinese characters originally: **moment, vicious, company, history, examine, shoot, gratitude, affair, think, incite, sand, gravel, teacher (militarily), word (part of speech), control, snake, write, private, temple, thread, serve, lion, bestow, slant, forgive**. And you wonder why it's hard to make out what Koreans are saying all the time! However, there's one more meaning to *sa* that I didn't list, and that's **death**, from the Chinese character [死].

Some people believe that the notion of death from this last character is derived from the chip radical, which is the symbol for death. Other scholars, however, have pointed out that the character has a picture of a man kneeling over a pile of bones. Now, even though the word *sa* has 26

---

other meanings, Koreans are superstitious about *sa*'s use because it's connected to death; 26 meanings out-muscled by one. That's why if you ever come to Korea you'll rarely, if ever, see the number four listed in an elevator (it's usually listed as a capital F). Just like the West's superstition with the number 13, Koreans don't like using the number four, especially in places where they live or work.

Yet one more interesting thing to note is that *sa* is not the only Chinese character for 'death.' *Saw* (서), for example, also means 'death' when looked at from Chinese roots [逝]. However, *saw* also means 'west,' from the Chinese character [西]. Do Koreans have any superstition with using the word 'west,' then? No, the superstition only lies with the number four.

STILL FUN AND EXCITING

One of the most popular ways of using *sa-joo* to discover other kinds of interesting information is to perform *goong-hap* (궁합). A fortune-teller performs *goong-hap* when someone wants to know the compatibility of two people because they are dating or thinking about getting married. *Goong-hap* requires the fortune-teller to examine the *sa-joo* of two different people and then work out the harmony—or discord as the case may be—that lies in store. Although this method of ascertaining two people's compatibility was once used by the majority of Koreans when arranging marriages (the parents taking charge of the entire process), today it's more common for younger people to go and consult with a fortune-teller as a matter of fun. Going in and around the Apgujeong (압구정) area in the south of Seoul, for instance, will show you just how popular some of these fortune-telling places still are among the general population. But it's not only Apgujeong that abounds with fortune-telling houses; there are fortune-tellers in every city in South Korea. So popular is *sa-joo*, in fact, that the Internet has also become a bastion of money-making potential for many of the business savvy fortune-tellers out there.

Chapter 22

All About Rice
밥에 대한 모든 것

Rice holds a special place in Korea's culture and language, as it does throughout many other countries in the world. So important is rice in Korea, in fact, that there's an honorific word for rice, different words for different grains of rice, and slang used commonly throughout Korea today that are all connected to the word 'rice.'

SHOW ME THE RICE!

People coming to Korea learn the most generic, most common and simplest form of the word rice upon arrival here: *bap* (밥). And though it's true that *bap* indeed means rice, it does have another meaning.

As mentioned, rice has an honorific word in Korean but is seldom used in conversation. Only when talking with much older people (or about deceased relatives, for instance), will the honorific word for rice, *jeen-jee* (진지), be used. As you'll see in the appendix entitled **Important Phrases**, the use of rice in questions isn't always related to the act of eating the grain so commonly served with meals in Korea. Consider the following example:

bam maw-gaws-saw-yo? (밥 먹었어요?)

This question can be conjugated a host of other ways, but for the sake of convenience, let's just look at the example listed above. Although the question means 'Did you eat rice?' if translated word for word, it is more naturally translated into English as 'Have you eaten (yet)?' In this sense the question seems to make a lot of sense. Upon closer inspection, however, the meaning changes.

I have a hard time explaining to Korean students studying English what exactly 'How are you?' means, because there really isn't a perfect translation of it in Korean. Many students often say, 'Yes,' as a reply to, 'How are you?' which baffled me for years until my Korean got to a point where I understood what it was I had to say in Korean, and so could draw a parallel.

In English, people often use 'How are you?' or some other related greeting when seeing people they know, and sometimes people they don't know. Though native English speakers know how to answer the question naturally, Koreans often don't because they're thinking of it in Korean, and in Korean one of the most common greetings is Have you eaten? (thus making a pre-programmed answer of Yes totally acceptable). Whether you're seeing a friend on the street, talking to a colleague on the phone, or simply meeting someone you know, there's a good chance that the Korean will greet you with an *an-nyung-ha-sae-yo* (안녕하세요), followed by a, 'Have you eaten?'

A WHOLE LOTTA RICE

As helpful as the last explanation may be in better understanding this language and culture, the situation with rice only gets more diverse from there. As soon as you venture out of the greeting stage and want to use the word 'rice' in another situation, for example, things get a little crazy. When buying rice at a rice shop (these kinds of stores actually exist in Korea), for instance, you don't say *bap*, but rather *ssal* (쌀). If you look in a dictionary under *ssal*, you'll see that it says both cooked and uncooked rice. This can lead to confusion because the English language doesn't separate between the word rice that is cooked or uncooked. It's all still rice.[1]

However, if you go to your local corner store and buy a pack of pre-cooked rice, which is popular among students and travelers, you'd better not say that you're looking for *ssal* or *bap* to the store clerk, or else he might look at you like you've just asked for directions in Polish. In this case, you have to use yet another word, *haet-ban* (햇반).

RICE, RICE AND MORE RICE

So, we eat *bap* at home, we buy *ssal* at a rice dealer, and purchase *haet-ban* at the corner store. Now we're off to the restaurant and we hear people continually using the term *gong-gi-bap* (공기밥) when ordering their side portions of rice. At a restaurant, rice is generally ordered by the silver bowlful, so rice changes form yet again like the chameleon that it is. But that's not the end of it. No, siree, there's more rice where that came from.

As you might remember from the tale about the history of the word America in Korean, the original meaning for *mee* (미) from Japan, as in the reference to America, was rice [米].[2] Therefore, you may hear *mee-gok* (미곡) spoken here or there by a Korean when referring to rice. As an extension of this, the rice stores that sell nothing but rice are called *mee-gok-sang* (미곡상). And if that weren't enough, there are different kinds of rice with different color shades. Up until the Korean War, the majority of Koreans were too poor to afford nice, clean white rice (the kind you see all over Korea today). So, destitute as they were, and not able to find anything else, many people ate what is sometimes referred to in English as black rice or in dictionaries as a dark, unpolished grain rice, *heung-mee* (흑미). As Koreans became more affluent, however, the quality of their rice improved too; by the time Korea hosted the 1988 Summer Olympics, white rice, *baeng-mee* (백미), was in restaurants everywhere. In yet another linguistic turn of events, though, a type of dark rice is still served at many restaurants around Korea to this day. This rice is called *bo-ree-bap* (보리밥), and because it's considered to be better for you than regular white rice, some restaurants will

[1] It's not fair to say that 'grains of rice' distinguishes these two stages of rice in English because that's a phrase and not a word. Also, if only the word 'grain' were used, it would lead to confusion.

[2] Actually, the Chinese character for rice, *mee* (미 · 米) comes from a Chinese pictogram of a rice paddy.

serve *bo-ree-bap* without offering *baeng-mee*.[3]

That's not the last grain of rice with this issue, though. When you go out to the countryside and marvel at the beautiful shades of green that adorn the horizon, it shouldn't surprise you to know that the word for rice changes once again. When looking at a rice paddy (notice the word rice is still used for this in English), you say *byaw* (벼) when referring to the rice paddy itself, and *non* (논) when referring to the rice plant from which it is grown.

Opening Up to Rice

When I first arrived in Korea, I was ignorant about much to do with Korean culture. Some things I could learn quickly about the new home I was living in, but other things took a longer amount of time. Rice was actually one of the first things that helped open up my mind to a new world.

Early in my stay, a friend's mother made me breakfast one morning before school. Not thinking about it before the food came, I assumed it would be something I was used to from back home: juice, cereal, pastries. After all, I had seen those things in Korea, so it would have made perfect sense if people ate them for breakfast. I received quite the surprise, however, when the mother placed some beef, rice, *kimchi*, broth, and other assorted vegetables in front of me on the table. So conditioned was I to believe that rice was only served with lunch or dinner that it genuinely shocked me when I had it for breakfast. Not wanting to be rude, but not used to rice and vegetables (especially at the crack of dawn), I ate a little and then made my way to work.

Thinking about it later that day, though, I realized there was nothing odd or strange about having rice and vegetables for breakfast. Not only was it healthy, but it made a lot of sense—Koreans love their rice. It was a small step, but a step in the right direction when I opened up to rice that morning years ago, because as I learned further down the road, it was all about opening your mind to new possibilities while living in a new and fascinating land such as Korea, rice and all.

[3] Though clear to the naked eye that *baeng-me* (백미) and *bo-ree-bap* (보리밥) are different, the two are just usually referred to as *bap* (밥) at most restaurants.

253

MEASUREMENTS OF RICE

In **Chapter 14** I included a chart separating the different units of weights and measures used commonly in Korean. I didn't include the terms used for rice because they are a unique entity in and of themselves. When ordering rice at a restaurant, say, the rice comes by the silver bowl full, each bowl called *gong-gi* (공기). However, when serving bowls of rice at home, the counting unit changes to *ke-reut* (그릇). When buying rice at a *mee-gok-sang*, on the other hand, bags are usually sold by the *ka-ma-nee* (가마니). Yet when exporting or donating rice in huge quantities, Koreans measure rice by the *sok* (속). Finally, when measuring rice paddies in terms of the space they occupy in the fields, the term *ha* (하) is used.

RICE IN KOREANS' VERNACULAR

찬밥: *chan-bap*
Koreans have always served rice hot, either from a black cauldron, called a *ka-ma-sot* (가마솥), as was done traditionally, or more recently from rice cookers, called *bap-sot* (밥솥). This type of rice is referred to as *dde-gaw-oon bap* (뜨거운 밥) and unless someone leaves their rice sitting for any length of time, the rice will always be eaten as it's still steaming. If, however, someone serves you cold rice, it is as clear an indication as a Korean can give that you are not welcome, that your presence is *persona non grata,* and that you should vacate the premises immediately. This is how the term *chan-bap* came to mean excluding others, or, in the lingo of Korean, to make someone feel like they are a *wang-dda* (왕따), completely ostracized from the group.

떡밥: *ddawk-bap*
If you're at all familiar with Korean cuisine, you'll recognize the first character of this rice-related term. *Ddawk* (떡) is a flat white rice cake that is usually served in broths and soups. Funny enough, though, instead of using what the typical fisherman from the West would use if out of money and resources—a worm at the end of the line—Koreans use *ddawk*. Thus, as humorous as it

sounds when translated directly into English, 'rice cake rice,' is what lures the fish for some fishermen.

콩밥: *kong-bap*

Kong-bap is yet another type of rice that is made from bean sprouts. As it's a low-end rice, it has traditionally been the rice of choice in prisons throughout Korea. As a result of this fact, Koreans began using the term *kong-bap* to refer to criminals.

말밥: *mal-bap*

In the old days, Koreans fed their horses carrots when they had nothing else to feed them. From this tradition grew a phrase that meant, 'It's a carrot,' or translated a little more naturally as, 'You better believe it!' From this then came the story of the horse's food (literally translated from *mal-bap*—horse rice) so that today, *mal-bap-ee-chi* is a very slangy way of saying, 'Damn right!' or, 'For sure!' However, even Koreans get a kick out of hearing this phrase used so that every time I use it (which, I should point out, is not that often as it is seen as very low-brow), the phrase 'damn straight horse rice,' is followed by a cacophony of laughter.

MAKING SENSE OF ALL THE RICE

Okay, this is a little much for me, I hear you saying to yourself. Is it humanly possible for one word to be so complicated, to have so many meanings, so many innuendos, and still be remembered by one human being? It is, but more than that, it's necessary. That's why I've come up with the following chart for you to try and remember all the words and phrases associated with rice. This way you can use it as a quick reference and not have to keep flipping through different parts of the dictionary to find the term you're looking for:

Korean	**Phonetic Transliteration**	**Meaning**
밥	*bap*	rice (cooked, pure Korean)
진지	*jeen-jee*	rice (cooked), honorific

Korean	Phonetic Transliteration	Meaning
미곡	*mee-gok*	rice (uncooked, from *han-cha*)
쌀	*ssal*	rice (uncooked)
찹쌀	*chap-ssal*	rice (sweet, sticky)
백미	*baeng-mee*	rice (white)
흑미	*heung-mee*	rice (dark, black rice)
보리밥	*bo-ree-bap*	rice (mixed with barley that you eat)
현미	*hyun-mee*	rice (brown, unpolished)
공기밥	*gong-gi-bap*	rice (served in a bowl at a restaurant)
햇반	*haet-ban*	pre-cooked rice (sold at stores)
미곡상	*mee-gok-sang*	rice dealer
밥솥	*bap-sot*	rice cooker (electric)
밥 하다	*bap ha-da*	to make rice (i.e. in a rice cooker)
가마솥	*ka-ma-sot*	rice cauldron
벼	*byaw*	rice plant
논	*non*	rice paddy
벼를 심다	*byaw-reul sheem-da*	to plant rice/to grow rice
벼를 베다	*byaw-reul bae-da*	to harvest rice
체	*chae*	rice strainer (colander)
햅쌀	*haep-ssal*	first harvested rice after *Chusok*
찬밥	*chan-bap*	cold rice, shun someone (*wang-dda* (왕따))
콩밥	*kong-bap*	rice mixed with soy beans, a prisoner
말밥이지	*mal-bap-ee-chi*	damn straight! (for sure!)
떡밥	*ddawk-bap*	fishing bait
그릇	*ke-reut*	one bowl (counting unit for rice bowls at home)
공기	*gong-gi*	one bowl (counting unit for rice bowls)
가마니	*ka-ma-nee*	(one 가마니 equals 10 kg of packaged rice)
하	*ha*	(1 *ha* equals 2.47 acres of land)
속	*sok*	(one *sok* equals 144 kg of packaged rice)

ROADMAP TO RICE REDEMPTION

When all is said and done, doesn't it all come back to Korean? There are so many links and subterranean levels to this language that navigating your way around it is, hmm...what's the word? Ah, yes: difficult. As I'm reminded every single day of my life in Korea, learning the language here is difficult. Amen.

In the end, however, I like to think that all that's been written in this book can be summed up in one last explanation. (Enough, the reader, says, enough). After all the chapters on the history of Korean, its cultural influences, the beast called grammar, the role of Chinese characters, the role the language plays in the lives of Koreans today—after everything, in short—I like to think that one last example, more than any other, captures the spirit and the feeling of this book.

You might remember that in **Chapter 3** I discussed how some dictionaries define *jung* (정 · 情) as 'feeling,' but that my favorite dictionary defines it as 'sincerity, affection, and devotion, coupled with a sense of love and friendliness.' This concept, I wrote, is a particularly important one for Koreans, as it defines the kindness and warmth they show friends, loved ones, and strangers; a concept that drives the wheels of society here as much as anything else.

What I neglected to tell you, though, was the root of the Chinese character for *jung*. The character is composed of two roots, 'heart' and 'blue.' However, the color blue is also associated with purity in Korean, much like the color white is in English, thus making the meaning of 'feeling' a pure heart. What's more is that the word for 'spirit' in Korean is also expressed as *jung* (정), through a different Chinese character [精]. This character for *jung* is composed of two roots as well, 'rice' and 'blue.' As a result, if the character for spirit is to be understood literally, its meaning is pure rice, which, in a fitting way, brings us right back to the beginning. By being able to read and decipher the Chinese characters, by understanding the connotations of the radicals, by relating them to the culture and its ancient history, we increase our knowledge of this language and of the people who speak it, thereby enriching our own lives; the spirit and feeling of Koreans is encapsulated in a **pure heart** and **pure rice**, two things I'm reminded of every day I'm in Korea, and two things which bring us all one step closer to understanding this enigmatic, mysterious and truly unique nation.

Appendices

Jade is useless until polished; a man is good-for-nothing until he is
educated

구슬이 서말이라도 꿰어야 보배다

Appendices

Proverbs

속담

On a personal note, proverbs are one of my favorite parts of the Korean language. Proverbs are not only a wonderful insight into the language of a culture, but a new way to think about things. Whether a student of Korean or a simple bystander interested in learning about Korea, proverbs are an invaluable way to gain new knowledge about this nation's long history.

As mentioned in **Chapter 21**, Koreans have long had a tendency to use animals not just in their astrology and spirituality, but in their vernacular as well. This is reflected in Korean proverbs, too. Another interesting theme which is almost impossible to miss when going through these proverbs is the role that food plays in expressing Koreans' feelings. Although this enters the most common speech in most people's vocabulary by the universal question, 'Have you eaten?' the role that food plays in other expressions and idioms is thought provoking if nothing else.

Do Koreans still use proverbs? Definitely not as much as they once did. Other ways to express knowledge have eclipsed this (e.g. the use of English, the expansion of colloquial Korean, the role of Internet Korean), but there is still the occasional proverb which will be thrown at the student of Korean that, armed with this knowledge, only makes the experience all that much better.

As I said, it doesn't matter whether you're studying Korean or not in this section—these proverbs are all fascinating. Some of the expressions are self-explanatory, but others are thoroughly complex and require a knowledge of the language as well as the history associated with it, which is why I've provided brief explanations after each and every one of the them. Also, for convenience's sake, I've organized the proverbs into groups that have common themes. These themes include proverbs dealing with **animals**, **culture**, **family, food, nature**, and **relationships**.

With that, I bid you enjoy my 50 favorite proverbs and philosophical maxims:

<u>Animals</u>

고래 싸움에 새우 등 터진다
(ko-rae ssa-oom-ae sae-oo deung taw-geen-da)
In a fight between whales, it's the shrimp's back that breaks

When giants fight, the little people get hurt worst. This applies to individuals as much as it applies to countries. Historically, Korea has been the shrimp between the whales (being bordered by Japan, China and Russia), so this proverb has special significance.

그림 속 호랑이
(ke-reem sok ho-rang-ee)
Like a picture of a tiger

Some people may be more familiar with the proverb, 'Like paper tigers,' but this has the same meaning. Someone or something might look frightening or daunting from afar, but in reality the opposite is true.

호랑이를 잡으려면 호랑이굴로 들어가라
(ho-rang-ee-reul ja-be-ryaw-myun ho-rang-ee-gool-lo deu-raw-ka-ra)
If you want to catch a tiger you have to venture into a tiger's cave

Nothing ventured, nothing gained. You have to try and try again in life no matter what kind of adversity you may face.

소 잃고 외양간 고친다
(so eel-ko wae-yang-gan ko-cheen-da)
Like fixing the barn after the cow is lost

Once the cow is lost there isn't much use in fixing the barn; it should have been done while the cow was there. Things may appear 20/20 in hindsight, but that doesn't do much toward fixing what's already transpired.

개천에서 용난다
(kae-chun-ae-saw yong-nan-da)
Like a dragon rising from the ditch

Dragons traditionally came from the sea in ancient folklore, so the fact that a dragon is rising from a ditch in this proverb leads one to believe that anything can happen; the impossible is possible. It is especially used in situations with reference to poor people making it big, the veritable rags to riches story.

호랑이도 제 말 하면 온다
(ho-rang-ee-do jae mal ha-myun on-da)
Speak of the tiger and henceforth it appears

This has the same meaning as 'Speak of the devil.' It is commonly said with a loud laugh as the object of the previous conversation comes into sight.

미꾸라지 한 마리가 온 웅덩이를 흐려 놓는다
(meek-koo-ra-gee han ma-ree-ga on oong-dung-ee-reul he-ryaw no-neun-da)
One mudfish clouds the whole pond

The meaning of this proverb is just as you'd presume: one rotten egg spoils the lot.

쥐구멍에도 볕 들 날 있다
(jwee-goo-mung-ae-do byut deul nal eet-dda)
Sunlight has even the possibility of entering a rat hole

A rat hole is small and out of the way, which makes it difficult for sunlight to get to. Just as those in dire straits sometimes believe nothing good can come of life, there are times when fortune visits the meek and most disadvantaged in society.

서당 개 삼 년에 풍월을 읊는다
(saw-dang gae sam nyun-ae poong-waw-reul eum-neun-da)
Like the dog that learns by waiting outside the schoolhouse for three long years

People who try to learn by osmosis have a disappointing end lying in wait. Learning is a long and arduous task, which must be done fastidiously if it is to be retained at all.

지렁이도 밟으면 꿈틀한다
(gee-rung-ee-do pal-pe-myun ggoom-teu-ran-da)
Even an earth worm wiggles if trodden upon

Everyone has their threshold for how much they can take.

원숭이도 나무에서 떨어질 때가 있다
(wawn-soong-ee-do na-moo-ae-saw ddaw-raw-geel ddae-ga eet-da)
Even monkeys fall from trees

Though it may be hard to believe, even monkeys can tumble down from the branches up above occasionally. Even the best of us are fallible.

Cultural

가다말면 안가느니만 못하다
(ka-da-mal-myun an-ka-ne-nee-man mot-ha-da)
If you say you're going, don't make excuses later for not going

When deciding to do something, don't think that not doing it is an option; quitting shows you were never really serious about it in the first place. Stick to your word.

가랑비에 옷 젖는 줄 모른다
(ka-rang-bee-ae ote jun-neun jool mo-reun-da)
You don't realize your clothes are soaked when it's only a light drizzle outside

By cooking a frog in progressively warmer water, the frog will never know it's being broiled. By the same logic, small and simple things can lead to great changes, seemingly inconsequential actions can have outstanding results.

같은 값이면 다홍치마
(ka-teun kap-shee-myun da-heung-chee-ma)
If they are the exact same price, choose the crimson colored skirt

When choosing among several options, choose the best one available. In dynastic Korea, young women who were unmarried wore crimson colored skirts as a show of their availability. This proverb refers to this custom, as parents would consider the color of the woman's skirt when looking for a prospective bride for their son.

고생 끝에 낙이 있다
(go-saeng kke-tae na-gi eet-dda)
Happiness lies at the end of suffering

Those who wish to bask in the glory of the rainbow must first suffer through the torment of rain.

한우물만 파라
(han-oo-mool-man pa-ra)
If you're going to dig a well, dig only one

It is the patient person that digs only one well. The impatient person will go around digging well after well, none of which is actually a great well; the jack-of-all-trades is the master of none.

윗물이 맑아야 아랫물이 맑다
(wee-moo-ree mal-ga-ya a-rae-mool-ee mal-dda)
The upper waters must be clear for the lower waters to be clear

What goes on up top will necessarily affect everything under it. This proverb used to be especially poignant when referring to corruption in the government.

서울 김서방 찾기
(saw-oo-rae-saw keem-saw-bang chat-gi)
Like trying to find Mr. Kim's house in Seoul

If you've been to Korea or know anything about the country you know that there are more Mr. Kims than one can count. Thus, trying to find a very non-descript 'Mr. Kim's house in Seoul' is tantamount to trying to locate a needle in the haystack.

사공이 많으면 배가 산으로 간다
(sa-gong-ee man-e-myun bae-ga san-e-ro kan-da)
Too many boatmen send the boat up the mountain

Too many people working on the same project leads to its demise. This is akin to the proverb in English that goes, 'Too many cooks spoil the broth.'

남의 천냥은 내 한푼 가치도 없다
(nam-ae chun-nyang-eun nae han-poon ka-chee-do awp-da)

A thousand yang belonging to another person is not worth one poon of one's own money

The monetary unit of Joseon was the *yang*—something akin to the dollar—and the *poon*—something like the cent. This proverb refers to the fact that no matter how great it may be that someone else has money, for example, their money is not worth a red penny to you. Better to have the object of your desire in hand rather than in mind.

돌다리도 두들겨 보고 건너라
(dol-da-ree-do doo-deul-gyaw-bo-go kawn-naw-ra)
Make sure to tap even the sturdiest of stone bridges

Though stone bridges are generally to be trusted, it is always prudent to make sure that what you are crossing is indeed stone, and safe to cross. This is the same as the proverb, 'Look before you leap,' in English.

공자님 앞에서 문자 쓴다
(gong-ja-neem ap-ae-saw moon-ja sseun-da)
Like teaching Confucius how to use Confucian phrases

This one all but gives itself away—trying to teach Confucius how to use Confucius phrases is like teaching a fish how to swim.

울며 겨자 먹기
(ool-myaw kyaw-ja mawk-gi)
Like eating mustard through tears

It is thought in Korea that eating hot and spicy mustard will bring tears to the eyes. In that way, there are some things we just have to do; bite the bullet and suck it up.

털어서 먼지 안 나는 사람 없다

(taw-raw-saw mawn-gee an na-neun sa-ram awp-da)
There is no person you can shake that dust will not fall off of

Although this proverb uses the word dust, it could just as easily be skeletons, for the phrase means, 'Everyone has a skeleton in their closet.'

제 눈에 안경이다
(jae noo-nae an-kyung-ee-da)
Glasses are made for one person's eyes only

Beauty, as they say, is in the eye of the beholder.

빈 수레가 요란하다
(been soo-rae-ga yo-ran-ha-da)
The empty cart rattles louder than the rest

The weakest wheel causes the most trouble; those that lag behind stick out like a sore thumb.

Family

아내가 귀여우면 처가집 말뚝보고도 절한다
(a-nae-ga gwee-yaw-oo-myun chaw-gat-jeep mal-ddook-bo-go-do chul-han-da)
If the wife is a loving person, the husband must bow down to the house pillars

A truly loving husband will always express his thanks to a loving wife. This means that a good husband will not complain about the smallest things in a harmonious home.

내리사랑이다
(nae-ree-sa-rang-ee-da)
Though there is always love flowing downward, there is never

love flowing upward

Children can never love their parents as much as their parents love them. Children can, however, respect their parents through their language and behavior.

사촌이 땅을 사면 배가 아프다
(sa-chon-ee ddang-eul sa-myun bae-ga a-pe-da)
To develop a stomachache because your cousin bought some land

Though he may be your cousin (and you know how important family is for Koreans), you still turn green with envy at the news of his great fortune. Or, in this case, instead of turning green, you develop stomach pains.

어느 한 손가락도 안 아픈 손가락이 없다
(aw-ne han son-ka-rak-do an a-peun son-ka-ra-gi awp-da)
Any of the ten fingers will hurt if bitten

Every child is dear to his or her parents. No one is of less worth than the other.

Food

계란이냐 달걀이냐
(kae-ran-ee-nya dal-kya-ree-nya)
Is it an egg or an egg?

You say potAto, I say potAHto; tomAto, tomAHto.

금강산도 식후경
(keum-gang-san-do sheek-hoo-kyung)
Never forget to eat, even before visiting Keumgang-san

Physical needs always come first no matter how resolute you are in your determination. Don't ignore the physical to get to the aesthetic.

빨리 먹으면 체한다
(bbal-lee maw-ge-myun chae-han-da)
Rice eaten in haste chokes

Things done too quickly inevitably end in ruin.

김칫국부터 마신다
(keem-cheet-gook-boo-taw ma-sheen-da)
While the host does not entertain thoughts of offering rice cakes, the guests go ahead and drink the juice from the *kimchi* anyway

Rice cakes, *kimchi*, and broth—sound like the perfect party? This proverb teaches us not to count our chickens before they hatch. Don't expect to be offered mouth-watering rice cakes just because someone invited you into their house.

콩으로 메주를 쑨다 하여도 곧이듣지 않는다
(kong-ee-ro mae-joo-reul ssoon-da hae-do ha-yaw-do go-jee-deut-jee an-neun-da)
Even though you say soybeans make soy malt, I do not believe you

It follows that soybean malt, *mae-joo* (메주), is made from soybeans, *kong* (콩). However, someone who has lost all creditability or cried wolf too many times will not be believed by others even if speaking such an implicit truth as the above proverb.

미친 체하고 떡판에 엎드러진다
(mee-cheen chae-ha-go ddawk-pan-ae awp-de-raw-jeen-da)
As if lying on one's back eating rice cakes

Even the laziest and most apathetic person can eat rice cakes while relaxing on his back; easy as pie.

수박 겉 핥기

(soo-bak kawt hal-gi)

Like licking the skin of a watermelon

The best part of the watermelon is on the inside. Doing nothing but licking its distasteful skin is missing the point of eating watermelon in the first place.

남의 떡이 더 커 보인다

(nam-ae ddaw-gi daw kaw bo-een-da)

The other man's rice cake always seems bigger

In this example rice cake is used, but it could just as easily be substituted with grass; the grass is always greener on the other side.

Nature

가랑잎이 솔잎더러 바스락거린다고 한다

(ka-rang-eep-ee sol-eep-daw-raw ba-se-rak-kaw-reen-da-go han-da)

The fallen leaf says the pine needle is noisy

Like the pot calling the kettle black; hypocrisy.

티끌 모아 태산

(tee-ggeu mo-a tae-san)

Dust gathers and makes a big mountain

Dust that is allowed to gather and grow can indeed make a mighty mountain; a penny might be a penny, but saving all those pennies can one day lead to quite a lot of money.

모난 돌이 정 맞는다

(mo-nan do-ree jung man-neun-da)

The ax always falls on the straight tree first

Just as honest men are targeted by scoundrels, so too are the best trees targeted by the lumberjack because of their worth over a bent tree; only the good die young.

하늘이 무너져도 솟아날 구멍이 있다
(ha-neu-ree moo-naw-jyaw-do so-sa-nal koo-mung-ee eet-da)
Though the heavens may fall, there will always be a hole to escape through

While in the eye of the tornado or the center of the storm, man still has the ability to attain salvation. Never give up hope.

하늘에서 별 따기
(ha-ne-rae-saw byawl dda-gi)
Like plucking a star from the heavens above

Though someone with a great deal of hope may think it possible to pluck a star from the sky, everyone knows that it's impossible.

열번 찍어 안 넘어가는 나무 없다
(yul-bawn jjee-gaw an nawm-aw-ka-neun na-moo awp-da)
Give any tree ten strokes and it will fall

The more you keep at something, the more likely it is to come under your control. In a similar way, repeated temptations make even the strongest of hearts surrender. This can be viewed both positively (e.g. love), and negatively (e.g. addictions).

비 온 후에 땅이 굳어진다
(pee on hoo-ae ddang-ee goo-daw-geen-da)
The ground hardens after the rain

This can be taken literally and extended to other parts of life. Good can always be found in bad, from a fight may develop a lasting friendship.

지성이면 감천이라
(gee-sung-ee-myun kam-chun-ee-ra)
A devoted heart can move heaven

Where there's a will, there's a way. Will something hard enough, and the universe conspires to work in your favor.

Relationships

가까운 남이 먼 일가보다 낫다
(ka-kka-oon nam-ee mun eel-ga-bo-da nat-da)
Those nearby are better than those far away from home

Neighbors who are close by are better than relatives who are far away.

가는 정이 있어야 오는 정이 있다
(ka-neun jung-ee ees-saw-ya o-neun jung-ee eet-da)
If affection is to be received, it must first be given

To have a friend, one must first be a friend. The *jung* used in this proverb is the *jung* I refer to often in this book, (정 · 情), affection, love, friendship and devotion.

그 아비에 그 자식이다
(ke a-bee-ae ke ja-sheek-ee-da)
Like father, like son

This says it all.

오래 익은 벼가 고개 숙인다
(o-rae eeg-eun byaw-ga ko-gae soog-een-da)
Even an old straw shoe has its own mate

This proverb is in reference to the Korea of old when the poor wore straw shoes that wore out easily. The rich, on the other hand, wore leather shoes that held up well. This is meant to signify that even the poorest and most destitute of shoes have a second partner; everyone has a second half out there in the world.

Appendices

Useful Phrases

유익한 표현

This is the part of the book that students who are currently studying or living in Korea will appreciate more than anything. I've tried to create a list of phrases in a wide variety of situations that can help those just visiting Korea as well as those living here for the long haul. I can assure you that the situations I have covered are translated with Korean in mind first and foremost. As a result, you'll notice a few sentences, for example, that sound a little odd in English. Don't worry about that. This is a book for native English speakers learning Korean, not the other way around. That's why I've kept the Korean linguistic aspect, the social situations, the role of age and the slang of everyday Korean in mind when coming up with this list.

I hope this list proves useful, and that ultimately it saves you hours of frustration; the world can only be a better place with not as many people like me out there throwing sharp, dangerous objects around because I didn't know the proper way to say something.

<u>Korean/English Translation</u>	<u>Phonetic</u> <u>Transliteration</u>	<u>Situation Explanation</u>

Meeting People/사람들을 만나다/*sa-ram-de-reul man-na-da*

GREETING PEOPLE

안녕. **Hi/Hey**	*an-nyung.*	the most informal, casual greeting between friends or older people to kids
안녕하세요.[1] **Hi/Hey/Hello**	*an-nyung-ha-sae-yo.*	polite, extremely common
만나서 반갑습니다. **It's a pleasure to meet you**.	*man-na-saw ban-kap-seum-nee-da.*	most formal, polite
반가웠어요. **It was nice seeing you again.**	*ban-ka-waws-saw-yo.*	polite, common among strangers and new friends
잘 지내셨어요?[2] **How've you been doing?**	*chal gee-nae-shaws-saw-yo?*	polite, formal
잘 지냈어? **How've you been?**	*chal gee-naes-saw?*	most informal, casual
어디 가세요?[3] **Where are you going?**	*aw-dee ka-sae-yo?*	formal, polite
어디 가는 중이야? **Where are you off to?/** **Where are you headed?**	*aw-dee ka-neun-joong-ee-ya?*	causal, informal

[1] *An-nyung-ha-da* (안녕하다) is the root verb for greetings and good-byes in Korean, both being referred to as the *in-sa* (인사). The Chinese roots for this word are *an* (안 · 安), which means 'peace,' and *nyung* (녕 ·寧), which also means 'peace.' This is why *an-nyung-ha-sae-yo* (안녕하세요) is sometimes translated as 'peace' or 'peacefulness.' In spoken conversation, it's often just pronounced *a-nyo-a-sae-yo*, though.

[2] As I've said in other parts of this book, this phrase is only used when you haven't seen a person for some length of time.

[3] As mentioned before, this is similar to 'How are you?' in some instances in Korean.

Korean/English Translation	Phonetic Transliteration	Situation Explanation
	SOCIAL SITUATIONS	
실례지만 이름이 뭐예요? **Excuse me, but what's your name?**	*sheel-lae-gee-man ee-reum-ee mo-yae-yo?*	between people on an equal social level usually
성함이 어떻게 되세요? **May I ask your name?**	*sung-ham-ee aw-ttaw-kae dwae-sae-yo?*	more formal, especially at a place of business
어떤 일을 하세요? **What do you do?**	*awt-tawn ee-reul ha-sae-yo?*	natural, polite (i.e. work or occupation)
뭐해요? **What do you do?**	*mo-hae-yo?*	informal, casual (i.e. work or occupation)
여자친구 있어? **Do you have a girlfriend?/ Are you seeing anyone these days?**	*yaw-ja-cheen-goo ees-saw?*	informal, casual
남자친구 있어요? **Do you have a boyfriend?**	*nam-ja-cheen-goo ees-saw-yo?*	formal, polite
몇 살이야? **How old are you?**	*myut sa-ree-ya?*	most informal, especially older people to kids
나이가 어떻게 되세요? **May I ask how old you are?**	*na-ee-ga awt-taw-kae-dwae-sae-yo?*	formal, polite—social and business situations

Korean/English Translation	Phonetic Transliteration	Situation Explanation
어느 나라에서 오셨어요? **Whereabouts are you from?**	*aw-ne na-ra-ae-saw o-shaws-saw-yo?*	(i.e. Koreans asking you which country you're from)
고향이 어디세요? **Where are you from?**	*go-hyang-ee aw-dee-sae-yo?*	formal (i.e. foreigners asking Koreans their hometown)
취미가 뭐야?[4] **What do you like doing in your free time?/Any hobbies?**	*chwee-me-ga mo-ya?*	casual, between friends
몇 째에요?[5] **What number child are you?**	*myut-jjae-ae-yo?*	polite
저는 첫째예요.[6] **I'm the first child (of other children).**	*jaw-neun chawt-jjae-yae-yo.*	polite
언니 둘요. **(I have) two older sisters.**	*aw-nee dool-yo*	polite
형 하나하고, 여동생 하나요.[7] **(I have) an older brother and a younger sister.**	*hyung ha-na ha-go, yaw-dong saeng ha-na-yo.*	polite
형제 몇 명 있어요?[8] **How many siblings do you have?**	*hyung-jae myut -myungees-saw-yo?*	polite

[4] A very common question for Koreans to ask people. Technically, *chwee-mee* (취미) means hobby.

[5] As family and age are of the utmost importance in Korea, so is the order of a child's birth.

[6] As in, 'I'm the first of four kids in the family,' for example. The term *chawt-jae* (첫째) is followed by *dool-jae* (둘째), then *saet-jae* (셋째), then *naet-jae* (넷째) and on and on.

[7] Though most English speakers might just say, 'I have one brother and one sister,' age is important in Korean relationships, so that phrases involving siblings always take the person's age into account.

[8] Although some English speakers might just say, 'Do you have any brothers or sisters?' Koreans ask the question with the implication that you have siblings.

Korean/English Translation	Phonetic Transliteration	Situation Explanation
저는 혼자예요.[9] **I'm an only child.**	*jaw-neun hon-ja-yae-yo.*	polite
어떤 철학을 갖고 계세요?[10] **What's your philosophy?**	*awt-tawn chaw-ra-keul kat-go kae-sae-yo?*	extremely polite
명함 있으세요? **Do you have a business card?**	*myung-ham ees-se-sae-yo?*	very polite, extremely common
근무 하시는 곳이 어디세요? **Where are you working?**	*keun-moo ha-shee-neun ko-shee aw-dee sae-yo?*	very polite
뭐 할래? **What do you want to do?**	*mo hal-lae?*	*ban-mal,* casual
뭐 하고 싶어요. **What do you want to do?**	*mo ha-go-shee-paw-yo?*	polite
반말로 해도 되요? **Would it be okay if we switched into *ban-mal*?**	*ban-mal-lo hae-do dwae-yo?*	polite, somewhat common
너 따라서 할께.[11] **I'll follow you.**	*naw dda-ra-saw hal-ggae.*	*ban-mal,* casual

[9] This phrase is also used when referring to marital status or the fact that you're living alone, so it must be used in context.

[10] This question looks weird in English, but occasionally Koreans ask you this if they're looking for your views on life and, well, philosophy.

[11] This expression may not be so common in English, but it's very common in Korean when people don't want to make a decision. Thus, a better translation of this Korean phrase is, 'Whatever (you want),' to someone's suggestion. The phrase *naw ha-neun-dae-ro hal-ggae* (너 하는 대로 할께) can also be used.

<u>Korean/English Translation</u>	<u>Phonetic Transliteration</u>	<u>Situation Explanation</u>

SAYING GOOD-BYE

Korean/English Translation	Phonetic Transliteration	Situation Explanation
또 만나요. **See you again/Take care.**	*ddo man-na-yo.*	polite
안녕. **Good-bye/See ya later/Take care**	*an-nyung.*	*ban-mal*, between friends, older person to a child
안녕히 가세요.[12] **Good-bye/Take care**	*an-nyung-hee-ka-sae-yo.*	formal, polite
안녕히 계세요.[13] **Good-bye/Take care**	*an-nyung-hee-kae-sae-yo.*	very polite
수고하셨습니다. **Good work/Way to go**	*soo-go-ha-shaws-seum-nee-da.*	very polite
수고하세요.[14] **Take Care/Nice work**	*soo-go-ha-sae-yo.*	polite
고생하셨어요.[15] **Good work/Way to go**	*go-saeng-ha-shaws-saw-yo.*	polite

At a Store/가게에서/*ka-gae-ae-saw*

Korean/English Translation	Phonetic Transliteration	Situation Explanation
몇 시까지 영업해요? **What are your store hours?**	*mae shee-kka-gee yung-awp-hae-yo?*	polite

[12] This is only used when the other person is leaving (and you're staying in the same place).

[13] This is only used when you are leaving (and the other person is staying).

[14] I don't believe there's a proper translation for this Korean phrase. Although extremely polite in Korean, there's simply nothing in English that is comparable with this. This phrase is used in situations that range from having finished a project together to leaving a store to saying thank you to a taxi driver for a long ride.

[15] This means the same thing as *so-go-ha-da* (수고하다), but isn't quite as common.

279

Korean/English Translation	Phonetic Transliteration	Situation Explanation
몇시에 문 열어요? **What time do you open?**	*mae-shee-ae moon yaw-raw-yo?*	polite
몇시에 문을 닫아요? **What time do you close?**	*mae-shee-ae moon-eul da-da-yo?*	polite
얼마예요? **How much (is this)?**	*awl-ma-yae-yo?*	polite (most common expression)
그게 뭐예요? **What's that?**	*ke-gaw mo-ae-yo?*	polite (common)
정말 비싸요. **This is really expensive.**	*jung-mal bee-ssa-yo.*	polite
정말 싸요. **This is really cheap.**	*jung-mal ssa-yo.*	polite
깎아 주실 수 있어요? **Can you give me a bit of a deal on this?**	*kka-kka joo-sheel-soo-ees-saw-yo?*	polite (common)
입어 봐도 되요? **Do you mind if I try this on?**	*ee-baw bwa-do dwae-yo?*	polite (at a clothing store)
다른 색깔 있어요? **Do you have this in a different color?**	*da-reun saek-kal ees-saw-yo?*	polite

Korean/English Translation	Phonetic Transliteration	Situation Explanation
더 큰 사이즈 없어요? **Do you have this in a bigger size?**	*daw keun sa-ee-je awb-saw-yo?*	polite
더 작은 사이즈 없어요? **Do you have this in a smaller size?**	*daw cha-geun sa-ee-je awb-saw-yo?*	polite
고맙습니다. **Thanks very much.**	*ko-map-seum-nee-da.*	polite
천만에요.[16] **You're welcome.**	*chun-man-ae-yo.*	polite

At the Grocery Store/슈퍼에서/*shoo-paw-ae-saw*

SHOPPING

실례지만, 감자는 어디 있어요? **Excuse me, where are the potatoes?**	*sheel-lae-gee-man, kam-ja-neun aw-dee ees-saw-yo?*	polite
혹시 샐러드 소스 있어요? **Do you carry salad dressing?**	*hok-shee sael-law-de so-se ees-saw-yo?*	polite
죄송한데요, 다 팔렸습니다. **I'm sorry, we're all sold out (of that).**	*chwae-song-han-dae-yo, da pal-laws-seum-nee-da.*	very polite

[16] Regardless of what Koreans tell you today, this phrase is not useful in most situations in Korea. The only reason I include it here is to alert you of this fact. Koreans don't use this or any phrase like it nearly as much as native English speakers.

281

Korean/English Translation	Phonetic Transliteration	Situation Explanation
봉투에 담아 드려요? **Would you like a bag with that?**	*bong-too-ae da-ma de-ryaw-yo?*	very polite
아니요. 됐어요. **No, that's okay. (I don't need a bag)**	*a-nee-yo. dwaes-saw-yo.*	polite
배달 좀 해 주시겠어요? **Can you deliver this to my place?**	*bae-dal jom hae joo-shee-gaes-saw-yo?*	extremely polite
얼마나 걸릴까요? **How long will it take (to deliver this)?**	*awl-ma-na kawl-leel-kka-yo?*	polite

FOOT ITEMS [17]

VEGETABLES (야채)	*ya-chae*
cabbage (배추)	*bae-choo*
carrot (당근)	*dang-geun*
chili pepper (홍고추)	*hong ko-choo*
chili pepper (청고추)	*chung ko-choo*
garlic (마늘)	*ma-neul*
lettuce (상추)	*sang-choo*
mushroom (버섯)	*baw-sawt*
onion (양파)	*yang-pa*
(green) pepper (피망)	*pee-mang*
(red) pepper (피망)	*pee-mang*
pickle (피클)	*pee-keul*

[17] Food is never pluralized in Korean as it is in English with the addition of the S. Instead, Koreans count the number of items they want or need by using the counting system discussed in **Ch. 14**.

282

English/Korean Translation   **Phonetic**
Transliteration

potato (감자)	*kam-ja*
pumpkin (small) (애호박)	*ae-ho-bak*
pumpkin (large) (늙은호박)	*neul-geun ho-bak*

FRUIT (과일)	*kwa-eel*
apple (사과)	*sa-gwa*
banana (바나나)	*ba-na-na*
Chinese melon(참외)	*cham-wae*
Chinese pear (배)	*bae*
grapes (포도)	*po-do*
kiwi (키위)	*kee-wee*
orange (오렌지)	*o-raen-gee*
peach (복숭아)	*bok-soong-a*
persimmon (감)	*gam*
pineapple (파인애플)	*pa-een-ae-peul*
plum (자두)	*ja-doo*
strawberry (딸기)	*ddal-gi*
tangerine (귤)	*kyool*
tomato (토마토)	*to-ma-to*
watermelon (수박)	*soo-bak*

BEEF, PORK, AND POULTRY(고기), (돼지), (닭)	*go-gi, twae-gee, dak*
ground beef (다진고기)	*da-jeen-go-gi*[18]
breaded fish cutlet (생선까스)	*saeng-sun-kka-se*
breaded pork cutlet (돈까스)	*don-kka-se*
pork cutlet (돼지등심)	*dwae-gee-deung-sheem*
steak (스테이크)	*se-tae-ee-ke*
boneless chicken breast (닭가슴살)	*dak-ka-seum-sal*
samkyupsal (삼겹살)	*sam-kyup-sal*

[18] Ground beef is also called *da-jeen swae-go-gi* (다진 쇠고기) at times.

283

English/Korean Translation	Phonetic Transliteration
Korean-style pork (돼지갈비)	*twae-gee-kal-bee*
Korean-style beef (불고기)	*bool-go-gi*
Korean-style chicken (닭갈비)	*dak-kal-bee*
roast chicken (통닭)	*tong-dak*
SEAFOOD (해물)	*hae-mool*
fish (생선)	*saeng-sun*
lobster (바닷가재)	*ba-dat-ka-jae*
octopus (낙지)	*nak-gee*
(live) octopus (산낙지)	*san-nak-gee*
shrimp (새우)	*sae-oo*
(giant) shrimp (대하) [19]	*dae-ha*
squid (오징어)	*o-jeeng-aw*
sushi- raw fish (회)	*hwae*
tuna (참치)	*cham-chee*
DUMPLINGS (만두)	*man-doo*
beef dumplings (고기만두)	*go-gi-man-doo*
***kimchi* dumplings** (김치만두)	*kimchi-man-doo*
steamed dumplings (물만두)	*mool-man-doo*
fried dumplings (군만두)	*koon-man-doo*
CONDIMENTS	
cooking oil (식용유)	*shee-gyong-yu*
ketchup (케찹)	*kae-chap*
mayonnaise (마요네즈)	*ma-yo-nae-je*
mustard (머스터드)	*maw-se-taw-de*
(Korean) mustard (겨자)	*kyaw-ja*
(ground black) pepper (후추)	*hoo-choo*
salad dressing (샐러드소스)	*sael-law-de-so-se*

[19] Also called *keun-sae-oo* (큰새우).

English/Korean Translation	Phonetic Transliteration
salt (소금)	*so-geum*
vinegar (식초)	*sheek-cho*

At the Bank/은행에서/*eun-haeng-ae-saw*

BANK MACHINE/ATM (FUNCTIONS OFFERED)

There are two basic kinds of bank machines in Korea: the first is for people with credit cards and international bank cards (those found mostly in subways, for example); the second is the standard bank machine found everywhere in Korea. In an attempt to clarify the process of performing transactions at the ATM, I'm including screens from both machines.

Also, bank machines are called a variety of names in Korean just as they are in English. The most common name you see written above an ATM is *hyun-geum-gee-geup-gi* (현금지급기). However, some are called *hyun-geum-ja-dong-eep-chool-geum-gi* (현금자동입출금기). The term *shee-dee-gi* (CD기), which literally means Electronic Cash Dispenser, is occasionally used as well. On top of that, some Koreans actually say ATM, *ae-ee-tee-aem* (에이티엠) with each other, but the few times I've tried saying ATM in Korean nobody understood me.

BANK MACHINE FOR CREDIT CARDS AND INTERNATIONAL BANK CARDS

계좌출금 **withdrawal**	*kae-jwa-chool-geum*
잔액조회 **account balance**	*jan-aek-jo-hwae*
계좌이체 **inter-bank transfer of funds**	*kae-jwa-ee-chae*
현금서비스 **cash advance** (from a credit card)	*hyun-geum-saw-bee-se*

COMMON BANK MACHINES

No two banks have the exact same screen, but all ATMs follow something roughly corresponding to the following examples:

FIRST SCREEN

예금출금 **withdrawal**	*yea-geum-chool-geum*
송금 **send money**	*song-geum*
예금조회 **account balance**	*yae-geum-jo-hwae*
통장정리 **bankbook update**	*tong-jang-jung-nee*
계좌이체 **inter-bank cash transfer**	*kae-jwa-ee-chae*
분실신고 **report a lost or stolen card**	*boon-sheel-sheen-go*
서비스거래 **cash advance**	*saw-bee-se-gaw-rae*
월부금 **monthly installment amount**	*wawl-boo-geum*
취소 **cancel**	*chwee-so*
대출이자 **annual loan rate**	*dae-chool-ee-ja*
입금 **deposit**	*eep-geum*

SECOND SCREEN

명세표 **receipt**	*myung-sae-pyo*
명세표생략 **no receipt**	*myung-sae-pyo-saeng-nyak*
(balance shown on screen)	

THIRD SCREEN

This is usually where you are asked to select the amount of money you wish to withdraw. Although not every bank is the exact same, 700,000 won (70만원) is usually the most you can withdraw at one time from one machine. Be careful, though. Unlike machines in other parts of the world where the actual amount is shown, in Korean ATMs, it's a multiple. Thus your options look something like this:

1만	(10,000)	20만	(200,000)
3만	(30,000)	40만	(400,000)
5만	(50,000)	50만	(500,000)
10만	(100,000)	70만	(700,000)
취소	*chwee-so*	기타	*gi-ta*
cancel		**other** (i.e. another amount which is not specified on the screen)	

FOURTH SCREEN

비밀번호 **enter your PIN**	*bee-meel-bun-ho*

FIFTH SCREEN

현금을 세고 있습니다. **Now counting your money.**

hyun-geum-eul sae-go ees-seum-nee-da

Korean/English Translation	Phonetic Transliteration	Situation Explanation

INSIDE/AROUND THE BANK

가까운 현금지급기가 어디 있는지 아세요? **Do you know where the nearest ATM is located by any chance?**	*ka-kka-oon hyun-geum-gee-geup-ga aw-dee een-neun-gee a-sae-yo?*	very polite, very common question used to strangers on the street

287

Korean/English Translation	Phonetic Transliteration	Situation Explanation
은행에 가야 되요. **I need to run by the bank.**	*eun-haen-ae ka-ya-dwae-yo.*	polite
돈 찾아야지. **I need to grab some cash.**	*don cha-ja-ya-gee.*	informal, *ban-mal*
현금지급기에 제 카드가 끼어서 안 나와요.[20] **The ATM ate my bankcard.**	*hyun-geum-gee-geup-gi-ae jae ka-de-ga kkyaw-saw an na-wa-yo.*	polite
신용카드를 만들고 싶은데요. **I'd like to apply for a credit card, please.**	*sheen-yong-ka-de-reul man-deul go-sheep-eun dae-yo.*	polite
죄송한데요, 제 통장을 잃어버렸어요. **I'm sorry, but I lost my bankbook.**	*chwae-song-han-dae-yo, jae tong-jang-eul ee-raw baw-ryaws-saw-yo.*	polite
해외로 송금하려고 해요. **I'd like to send some money overseas, please.**	*hae-wae-ro song-geum ha-ryaw-go hae-yo.*	polite
해외송금 수수료는 얼마에요? **How much does it cost to send money overseas?**	*hae-wae-song-geum-soo-soo-ryo-neun awl-ma-ae-yo?*	polite

[20] You could also say *hyun-geum-jee-geup-gi-ae jae ka-de-ga kkee-aw-saw an-na-wa-yo* (현금지급기에 제 카드가 끼어서 안나와요).

Korean/English Translation	Phonetic Transliteration	Situation Explanation
통장을 만들고 싶은데요.[21] **I'd like to open an account here, please.**	*tong-jang-eul man-deul-go-sheep-eun dae-yo.*	polite
제 계좌를 해지하고 싶습니다.[22] **I'd like to close my account here.**	*jae kae-jwa-reul hae-gee-ha-go-sheep-seum-nee-da.*	very polite
저에게 돈 보내셨어요? **Have you sent me the money (yet)?**	*jaw-ae-gae don bo nae-shaws-saw-yo?*	formal, very polite
돈 들어왔어요? **Is the money there yet (in the account)?**	*don deu-raw-was-saw-yo?*	polite
카드가 잘 안돼요. **My card doesn't work.**	*ka-de-ga chal an-dwae-yo.*	polite

At a Friend's House/친구집에서/*cheen-goo jeep-ae-saw*

집들이가 언제에요? **When are you having your housewarming?**	*jeep-deu-ree-ga awn-jae-ae-yo?*	polite
집들이 하려고 하는데 다음주 금요일 밤 7시에 초대하고 싶어.	*jeep-de-ree ha-ryaw-go ha-neun-dae da-eum-joo keum-yo-eel bam eel-*	casual, *ban-mal*

[21] You could also say *kae-jwa-reul kae-sul-ha-go sheep-aw-yo* (계좌를 개설하고 싶어요).

[22] This can also be said *tong-jang hae-jee-ha-ryaw-go ha-neun-dae-yo* (통장 해지하려고 하는데요).

289

Korean/English Translation	Phonetic Transliteration	Situation Explanation
I'm having a house warming party and would like to invite you over next Friday night at 7:00.	*gop-shee-ae cho-dae-ha-go-sheep-aw.*	
집들이 갈 때 뭐 사가지고 갈까?[23] **What should I bring to the (housewarming) party?**	*jeep-de-ree kal-ddae mo sa-ka-gee-go-kal-kka?*	*ban-mal*, casual
집들이 잘 했어? **How did your house warming party go?**	*jeep-de-ree chal haes-saw?*	*ban-mal*, casual
집이 너무 멋있다. **Your place looks awesome!**[24]	*jeep-ee naw-moo maw-sheet-ta.*	casual
우와~ 정말 넓다. **Wow! It's so spacious here!**	*oo-wa! jung-mal nawlb-da!*	casual
혼자 여기에서 살아?[25] **Do you live here by yourself?**	*hon-ja yaw-gi-ae-saw sa-ra?*	*ban-mal*, casual
자취하세요?[26] **Do you live on your own?**	*ja-chwee-ha-sae-yo?*	very polite
나는 룸메이트가 있어.[27] **I have a roommate.**	*na-neun loom-mae-ee-te-ga ees-saw.*	*ban-mal*, casual

[23] Also said, *naw-ee jeep-ae-saw mo-eel-ddae nae-ga maw ka-jee-go ka-ya-dwae?* (너의 집에서 모일 때 내가 뭐 가지고 가야 돼?)

[24] The word 'awesome' in this case could also be translated as 'beautiful,' 'amazing,' 'great,' 'wonderful,' 'gorgeous,' or any other such adjective.

[25] Only used when asking the person at the home in question. It wouldn't be used outside the home.

[26] This phrase is usually used outside of someone's home.

[27] You could also say *na-neun ka-chee sa-neun cheen-goo-ga ees-saw* (나는 같이 사는 친구가 있어).

290

Korean/English Translation	Phonetic Transliteration	Situation Explanation
요즘 제일 친한 친구랑 살고 있어. **I'm living with my best friend these days.**	*yo-jeum jae-eel cheen-han cheen-goo-rang sal-go-ees-saw.*	*ban-mal,* casual
월세 얼마나 내? **How much are you paying for rent?**	*wawl-sae awl-ma-na nae?*	*ban-mal,* casual
보증금 얼마야?[28] **How much did you put down for your place?**	*bo-jeung-geum awl-ma-ya?*	*ban-mal,* casual

At an Internet Cafe/PC 방에서/*pee-shee-bang-ae-saw*

여기서 디스켓 팔아요? **Do you sell diskettes here?**	*yaw-gi-saw dee-se-kaet pa-ra-yo?*	polite
인터넷 쓰는데 1시간에 얼마예요? **How much is it for an hour on the Internet?**	*een-taw-naet sse-neun-dae han-shee-gan-ae awl-ma-yae-yo?*	polite
그런데, 칼라프린터 있어요? **Do you have a color printer by any chance?**	*ke-run-dae, kal-la-pe-reen-taw ees-saw-yo?*	polite
출력하는데 1장 얼마예요?[29] **How much does it cost per page (on the printer)?**	*chool-lyuk ha-neun-dae han-jang awl-ma-yae-yo?*	polite

[28] The word *bo-jeung-geum* (보증금) means deposit, if translated literally.

[29] Another way of asking this question is *pe-reen-te ha-neun-dae han-jang awl-ma-ae-yo* (프린트 하는데 1장 얼마에요?).

Korean/English Translation	Phonetic Transliteration	Situation Explanation
제 컴퓨터 잠깐 봐 주실 수 있어요? **Would you mind giving me a little help (on my computer)?**	*jae kawm-pyu-taw cham-gan bwa joo sheel-soo-ees-saw-yo?*	very polite
제 디스켓에 파일 다운받기가 안돼요. **I can't upload a file from my disk.**	*jae dee-se-kae-sae pa-eel da-oon bat-gi-ga an-dwae-yo.*	polite

At the Post Office/우체국에서/*oo-chae-gook-ae-saw*

빠른우편으로 보내시겠어요? **Would you like it sent by special delivery?**	*bba-reun oo-pyun-e-ro bo-nae-shee-gaes-saw-yo?*	polite
아니요. 그냥 보통우편으로 해주세요. **No, there's no rush. Just send it by normal mail.**	*a-nee-yo. ke-nyang bo-tong oo-pyun-e-ro hae joo-sae-yo.*	polite
미국으로 엽서 보내는데 얼마예요? **How much does it cost to send a postcard to the States?**	*mee-gook-e-ro yawp-saw bo-nae-neun-dae awl-ma-yae-yo?*	polite

292

Korean/English Translation	Phonetic Transliteration	Situation Explanation
캐나다에 편지 도착하는데 얼마나 걸리죠? **How long does it take a letter to get to Canada?**	*kae-na-da-ae pyun-gee do-chak-ha-neun-dae awl-ma-na kawl-lee-jo?*	polite
(국제)봉투 10장만 주실래요? **Can I get 10 (international) envelopes please?**	*(kook-jae) bong-too yul-jang-man joo-sheel-lae-yo?*	very polite

On the Go/가는중이다/*ka-neun joong ee-da*

Korean/English Translation	Phonetic Transliteration	Situation Explanation
⋯ 가주세요.[30] **I'm going to/Can you take me to** ⋯	*ka-joo-sae-yo.*	polite
종로 3가 가요?[31] **Do you go to Chongno 3-ga?**	*chong-no sam-ga ka-yo?*	polite
죄송하지만 좀 더 천천히 가 주시겠어요? **Would you mind driving a little slower, please?**	*chwae-song-ha-gee-man jom daw chun-chun-hee ka joo-shee gaes-saw-yo?*	very polite
여기 좀 세워주세요. **Can you let me off here, please.**	*yaw-gi jom sae-waw joo-sae-yo.*	polite

[30] This phrase would be used with a taxi driver, for example.

[31] This phrase would be used with a bus driver, for example.

Korean/English Translation	Phonetic Transliteration	Situation Explanation
(place) 어디인지 아세요? **Do you know where (place) is?**	*aw-dee-een-gee a-sae-yo?*	very polite
차 가지고 왔어? **Did you bring your car?**	*cha ka-gee-go was-saw?*	*ban-mal,* casual
차 가지고 가셨어요? **Did you take your car?**	*cha ka-gee-go-ka-shaws-saw-yo?*	very polite
은행까지 좀 태워 주시겠어요? **Would you mind giving me a lift to the bank?**	*eun-haeng-kka-gee jom tae-waw joo-shee gaes-saw-yo?*	very polite
대사관까지 태워 줄래? **Can you drop me off at the embassy?**	*dae-sa-gwan-kka-gee tae-waw jool-lae?*	*ban-mal,* casual
공덕역 어느 쪽 이에요? **Which way is Gongdeok Station?**	*kong-duk-yawk aw-nee jjok ee-ae-yo?*	polite

On the Telephone/전화할 때/*jun-hwa-hal ddae*

BASIC CONVERSATION

전화 받는 사람 **The person answering the phone.**	*jun-hwa ban-neun sa-ram.*	no conjugation, neutral

Korean/English Translation	Phonetic Transliteration	Situation Explanation
전화 건 사람 **The person phoning /calling.**	*jun-hwa gawn sa-ram.*	no conjugation, neutral
실례지만, 전화 좀 써도 될까요? **Would you mind if I used your phone?**	*sheel-lae-gee-man, jun-hwa jom ssaw-do dwael-kka-yo?*	polite
여보세요?[32] **Hello?**	*yaw-bo-sae-yo?*	polite, standard
안녕하세요? 저 (이름) 인데요. **Hi, there. This is (name) here.**	*an-nyung-ha-sae-yo? jaw (ee-reum) een-dae yo.*	polite, most common
전화받기 괜찮으세요?[33] **Sorry, did I catch you at a bad time?/Can you talk now?**	*jun-hwa-bat-gi kwaen-cha-ne-sae-yo?*	very polite
지금 안 계세요. **He's/She's not here right now.**	*chee-geum an-kae-sae-yo.*	formal, very polite
지금 없는데요. **He's/She's not in right now.**	*chee-geum awm-neun dae-yo.*	informal, polite

[32] This greeting is only used on the telephone, and never when meeting someone in person.

[33] The phrase *jun-hwa-bat-gi kwaen-cha-ne-sae-yo?* (전화받기 괜찮으세요?) literally means, 'Is it okay for you to answer the phone now?' In the interest of translating phrases as naturally as possible, though, I've translated it as I did. Thus, when it's okay for you to talk you would say 'yes,' *nae, nae* (네, 네), or *yea, yea* (예, 예)

Korean/English Translation	Phonetic Transliteration	Situation Explanation
지금 자리 비우셨는데요.[34] **He's/She's not here at the moment**	*chee-geum ja-ree pee-oo-shawtt-neun-dae-yo.*	formal, especially at companies
언제쯤 들어오실까요? **Do you know when she'll/he'll be back?**	*awn-jae-jjeum deu-raw-o-sheel-kka-yo?*	polite
(이름)한테 전화 왔다고 전해 주시겠어요? **Can you tell him/her that (name) phoned, please?**	*(ee-reum) han-tae jun-hwa watt-da-go jun-hae joo-shee gaes-saw-yo?*	very polite
미안. 전화가 꺼져 있었어. **Sorry, but my phone was off.**	*mee-an. jun-hwa-ga kkaw-jjaw-ees-saws-saw.*	*ban-mal*, causal
전화번호가 어떻게 되세요?[35] **May I ask what your number is?**	*jun-hwa-bun-ho-ga awt-tawk-kae dwae sae-yo?*	very polite, especially in business situations and with strangers
이상하다. 내 핸드폰은 켜져 있었어요. **That's weird. My phone was on (at the time).**	*ee-sang-ha-da. nae haen-de-pon-eun kyaw-jyaw ees-saws-saw-yo.*	polite

[34] This Korean phrase actually means 'He's/She's away from his seat.'

[35] Although Koreans usually only use this phrase in formal situations, this could also be translated as, 'Could I get your number?' or 'Do you think I could have your number?'

Korean/English Translation	Phonetic Transliteration	Situation Explanation

TAKING/LEAVING A MESSAGE

Korean/English Translation	Phonetic Transliteration	Situation Explanation
메모 남겨 드릴까요? **Would you like to leave a message?**	*mae-mo nam-gyaw de-reek-ka-yo?*	formal, polite
메세지 남겨 주실래요? **Do you mind if leave a message?**	*mae-sae-gee nam-gyaw joo-sheel-lae-yo?*	very polite
메세지 받으면 나에게 전화해죠. **Call me back when you get the message, okay?**	*mae-sae-gee ba-de-myun na-ae-gae jun-hwa-hae-jo.*	casual
메세지 받으시면 연락 좀 주시겠어요? **Would you mind giving me a call back when you get the message, please?**	*mae-sae-gee ba-de-shee-myun yul-lak jom joo-shee-gaes-saw-yo?*	formal, very polite

PHONE MESSAGE ON CELL PHONES

Korean/English Translation	Phonetic Transliteration	Situation Explanation
안녕하세요? (이름) 핸드폰 입니다. 지금은 전화를	*an-nyung-ha-sae-yo? (ee-reum) haen-de-pon*	polite

297

Korean/English Translation	Phonetic Transliteration	Situation Explanation
받을 수 없으니 삐 소리가 난 후 메세지를 남겨 주세요. 감사합니다. **Hi, you've reached (name's) cell phone. I can't take your phone call at the moment, so please leave a message after the beep. Thanks very much.**	*eem-nee-da. chee-geum-eun jun-hwa-reul ba-deul-soo-awb-se-nee bbee so-ree-ga-nan hoo mae-sae-gee reul nam-kyaw joo-sae-yo. kam-sa-ham-nee-da.*	

ORDERING FOOD ON THE PHONE

배달 되나요? **Do you deliver?**	*bae-dal dwae-na-yo?*	polite
배달 시킬려고요.[36] **I'd like to get something for delivery.**	*bae-dal shee-keel-lyaw-go-yo.*	polite, very common
위치가 어떻게 되시는데요?[37] **Whereabouts is your place?**	*wee-chee-ga awt-tawk-kae dwae-shee neun-dae-yo?*	polite, very common

Sending E-mail/메일 보내기/*mae-eel bo-nae-gi*

메일 주소가 어떻게 되세요? **What's your e-mail address?**	*mae-eel joo-so-ga awt-tawk-kae dwae-sae-yo?*	very polite

[36] This Korean phrase, if translated directly, means 'We'd like to order a delivery.'

[37] The delivery person would ask this.

298

Korean/English Translation	Phonetic Transliteration	Situation Explanation
저에게 메일 보내 주시겠어요? **Would you mind sending it to me by e-mail?**	*jaw-ae-gae mae-eel bo-nae joo-shee-gaes-saw-yo?*	very polite
제가 메일 보내 드릴께요. **I'll send it to you by e-mail.**	*chae-ga mae-eel bo-nae de-reek-kae-yo.*	very polite
메일 확인해 보세요. **Can you check to see if you got it? (by e-mail)**	*mae-eel hwag-een-hae bo-sae-yo.*	very polite

In the Office/사무실에서/*sa-moo-sheel ae-saw*

(이름) 계세요? **Is (name) here right now?**	*(ee-reum) kae-sae-yo?*	extremely polite
(이름)씨 찾는데요. **I'm looking for Mr./Mrs./Ms. (name)**	*(ee-reum) sshee chan-neun-dae-yo.*	polite
커피/차 드릴까요? **Would you like some coffee/tea?**	*kaw-pee/cha de-ree-kka-yo?*	very polite, common
복사해 주세요. **Photocopy this for me, please.**	*bok-sa-hae joo-sae-yo.*	polite

299

Korean/English Translation	Phonetic Transliteration	Situation Explanation
복사 몇 장 해드릴까요?[38] **How many copies do you need?**	*bok-sa myut jang hae-de-ree-kka-yo?*	very polite
양면에(으로) 해 주세요. **Can you do it on both sides, please.**	*yang-myun-ae (e-ro) hae joo-sae-yo.*	polite
한 면만 해 주세요. **Can you do it on just one side, please.**	*han myun-man hae joo-sae-yo.*	polite
회의가 몇 시에 시작하죠? **What time does the meeting/ conference start?**	*hwae-ee-ga mae-shee-ae shee-jak-ho-jo?*	polite
오늘 회식이 몇 시야?[39] **What time's our *hwae-sheek* tonight?**	*o-neul hwae-sheek-ee mae-shee-ya?*	*ban-mal*, casual

[38] You would ask this question when making photocopies.

[39] A Korean *hwae-sheek* is a unique business outing where people from the same office/company go out for dinner and then, often, have many drinks afterwards. I believe it would be unfair to translate this simply as a business meeting at a restaurant, so have kept the original Korean word in place in the translation.

[40] The word *no-rae-bang* (노래방) is known variously by English speakers as a karaoke bar or singing room.

Going Out to Eat/Drinking/외식하고 한잔할 때/ *way-sheek-ha-go han-jan-hal ddae*

AT A RESTAURANT, BAR OR NO-RAE-BANG (노래방)[40]

메뉴판 좀 주세요. **Can I have a menu, please?**	*mae-nyu-pan jom joo-sae-yo.*	polite, common
여기서 드실거예요? **Is that for here?**	*yaw-gi-saw de-sheel-gaw-yae-yo?*	very polite

Korean/English Translation	Phonetic Transliteration	Situation Explanation
포장해 드릴까요? **Is that to go?**	*po-jang-hae de-ree-kka-yo?*	very polite
돼지갈비 4인분 좀 주세요. **Can we get four portions of pork _kalbi_ please.**	*twae-gee-kal-bee sa-een-boon jom joo-sae-yo.*	polite
불판 좀 갈아 주세요. **Can you replace the grill, please?**	*bool-pan jom ka-ra joo-sae-yo.*	polite, used at *soot-bool-kal-bee-jeep* (숯불갈비집)
화장실 어디에요? **Where's the washroom?**	*hwa-jang-sheel aw-dee-ae-yo?*	polite
물수건 주실래요? **Can I have a wet towel, please?**	*mool-soo-gun joo-sheel-lae-yo?*	very polite
공기 밥 2개 주세요. **Can we get two bowls of rice, please?**	*gong-gi-bap doo-gae joo-sae-yo.*	polite
계산서 좀 주세요. **Can we get the bill now, please?**	*kae-san-saw jom joo-sae-yo.*	polite
계산해 주세요. **We'd like to take care of the bill now, please.**	*kae-san-hae joo-sae-yo.*	polite

Korean/English Translation	Phonetic Transliteration	Situation Explanation
제가 대접하겠습니다. **It's on me/Let me get this one.**	*chae-ga dae-jup-ha-gaes-seum-nee-da.*	formal, very polite
내가 사 줄께. **It's on me/Let me get this one.**	*nae-ga sa jool-ggae.*	*ban-mal*, casual
(신용)카드 되요?[41] **Do you take credit cards?**	*(sheen-yong) ka-de dwae-yo?*	polite, very common

DRINKING

버드와이저 2개 주세요. **Can we have two Budweisers, please?**	*baw-de-wa-ee-jaw doo-gae joo-sae-yo.*	polite
맥주 하나랑 소주 하나 주세요. **Can we have a bottle of beer and a bottle of soju, please.**	*maek-joo ha-na-rang so-joo ha-na joo-sae- yo.*	polite
자! 이차 가자![42] **All right, let's get out of here (and on to the next bar).**	*cha! ee-cha ka-ja*	*ban-mal*, casual
주량이 얼마나 되세요?[43] **How much can you drink?**	*joo-ryang-ee awl-ma-na-dwae-sae-yo?*	polite, common

[41] Although in English you'd probably just use the credit card name, in Korean the generic term 'card' or 'credit card' is used instead when asking this at stores and restaurants.

[42] This phrase is used extensively among Koreans when out for a good time. The *ee-cha* (이차), second place to drink and have fun, is followed by the *sam-cha* (삼차), *sa-cha* (사차), and so on and so forth, all following the Chinese derived counting system.

[43] People rarely, if ever, ask this question in English, but in Korean it's quite normal to ask one of his/her drinking capability. When asked in Korean, the assumed drink of choice is *soju* (소주), so you're supposed to answer how many bottles of *soju* you can drink in one sitting or in one night.

302

Korean/English Translation	Phonetic Transliteration	Situation Explanation
뭐 부르고 싶어? **What do you want to sing?**	*mo boo-re-go-shee-paw?*	*ban-mal*, casual
어떤 노래 부르고 싶어요? **What do you want to sing?/Which song would you like to sing?**	*awt-tawn no-rae boo-re-go-shee-paw-yo.*	polite
이 노래 누가 불렀어? **Who sings this (song)?**	*ee no-rae noo-ga bool-laws-saw?*	*ban-mal*, casual

At School/학교에서/*hak-kyo-ae-saw*

김 선생님! **Mr. Kim!**	*Keem sun-saeng-neem!*	polite
죄송하지만, 내일 수업 못 갈 것 같아요. **I'm sorry, but I can't go to class tomorrow.**	*chwae-song-ha-gee-man, nae-eel soo-awp mot kal kawt kat a-yo.*	polite
어제 수업에 못 왔어요. **I couldn't come to class yesterday.**	*aw-jae soo-awp-ae mot was-saw-yo.*	polite
제가, 물어볼 게 있는데요. **I have a question.**	*chae-ga, moo-raw-bol kae een-neun-dae-yo.*	polite

Korean/English Translation	Phonetic Transliteration	Situation Explanation
물어보세요. **What is it?/Go ahead and ask.**	*moo-raw-bo-sae-yo.*	polite
수요일에 시험 있어요. **I have a test on Wednesday.**	*soo-yo-eel-ae shee-hum ees-saw-yo.*	polite
이틀 전에 시험 봤어요. **I had a test two days ago.**	*ee-teul jun-ae shee-hum bwas-saw-yo.*	polite
시험 잘 봤지? **Did you do well on your test?**	*shee-hum chal bwatt-gee?*	*ban-mal*, casual
시험 잘 보셨어요? **Did the test go well?**	*shee-hum chal bo-shaws-saw-yo?*	formal, very polite
몇 점 받았어요? **What did you get on your test/exam?**[44]	*myut jum ba-das-saw-yo?*	polite
영어 하세요? **Do you speak English?**	*yung-aw ha-sae-yo?*	very polite
한국말을 할 줄 아니? **Can you speak any Korean?**	*han-goong-ma-reul hal-jool-a-nee?*	*ban-mal*, casual

[44] This refers to a person's score, mark or average on a test or exam. In Korean, score, mark, and average are all expressed with the same noun, *jum* (점). As an extension of this, *hak-jum* (학점) is a credit in school.

Korean/English Translation	Phonetic Transliteration	Situation Explanation

Traveling/여행하기/*yaw-haeng-ha-gi*

BASIC QUESTIONS

Korean/English Translation	Phonetic Transliteration	Situation Explanation
어디로 가는 거예요? **Where are you going?/** **Where are you off to?**	*aw-dee-ro ka-neun gaw-yae-yo?*	polite
여행할려고요. **I'm planning on going away.**	*yaw-haeng-hal-lyaw-go-yo.*	polite
다음 주부터 휴가예요. **My vacation/holiday starts** **next week.**	*da-eum joo-boo-taw hyoo-ga-yae-yo.*	polite
이 주 동안 중국에 가기로 했는데요. **I'm planning on going to** **China for a couple** **of weeks.**	*ee joo dong-an choong-gook-ae ka-gi-ro haen-neun-dae-yo.*	polite
여행 잘 다녀오세요. **Have a great trip!**	*yaw-haeng chal da-nyaw-o-sae-yo!*	formal, very polite
여행 잘 다녀와. **Have a great trip!**	*yaw-haeng chal da-nyaw-wa!*	*ban-mal*, casual
야! 사진 좀 찍어 줘. **Hey, take a picture of me.**	*ya! sa-geen jom jeek-aw jo.*	*ban-mal*, to a close friend

305

Korean/English Translation	Phonetic Transliteration	Situation Explanation
실례합니다. 사진 좀 찍어 주시겠습니까? **Excuse me, would you mind taking a picture for me/us?**	*sheel-lae-ham-nee-da. sa-geen jom jeek-aw joo-shee-gaes-seum-nee-kka?*	very polite, to a stranger
어느 나라 가 보셨어요?[45] **Where were you?**	*aw-ne na-ra ka bo-shaws-saw-yo?*	very polite
미국에 가 본 적 있어요?[46] **Have you ever been to the States?**	*mee-gook-ae ka bon jawk ees-saw-yo?*	polite
해외에 나가 봤어? **Have you ever been abroad/overseas/ to another country?**	*hae-wae-ae na-ga bwas-saw?*	*ban-mal*, casual
신혼여행은 어디로 가셨어요? **Were did you go on your honeymoon?**	*sheen-hon-yaw-haeng-eun aw-dee-ro ka-shaws-saw-yo?*	polite
일본에 갔다 왔어요.[47] **I just got back from Japan.**	*eel-bon-ae katt-da-was-saw-yo.*	polite
여행 잘 다녀오셨어요? **Did you have a good trip?**	*yaw-henag chal da-nyaw-o-shaws-saw-yo?*	very polite, formal

[45] In this question, the word *na-ra* (나라) means 'country,' so the question would only be asked of someone who has just returned from another country.

[46] It's not true that Korean has a present perfect tense in the same way that English does. Although most Korean textbooks claim that the verb structure VERB 본 적(이) 있다/없다 conforms to the have/has or haven't/hasn't verb structure in English, that is not true. Koreans rarely use this verb structure and certainly never anywhere near the amount it is used in English.

[47] Literally, 'I just went and came from Japan.'

Korean/English Translation	Phonetic Transliteration	Situation Explanation
태국에 몇 번 가 봤어요? **How many times have you been to Thailand?**	*tae-gook-ae myut bawn ka bwas-saw-yo?*	polite

AT THE AIRPORT

Korean/English Translation	Phonetic Transliteration	Situation Explanation
12번 출구가(게이트) 어디예요? **Where's gate number 12?**	*sheep-ee-bawn chool-goo-ga (gae-ee-te) aw-dee-yae-yo?*	polite
타이항공 카운터가 어디예요? **Where's the Thai Airlines counter?**	*ta-ee-hang-gong ka-oon-taw-ga aw-dee-yae-yo?*	polite
비행기 출발 시간은 언제예요? **What time is the flight leaving?**	*bee-haeng-gi chool-bal shee-gan-eun awn-jae-yae-yo?*	polite
대한항공 114번 비행기 도착 시간이 언제예요? **Do you know what time Korean Air flight 114 is arriving?**	*dae-han-hang-gong eel-eel-sa-bawn bee-haeng-gi do-chak shee-gan-ee awn-jae-ae-yo?*	polite
영어 잘 하시는 분에게 얘기했으면 좋겠어요. **May I talk with someone who speaks English, please?**	*yung-aw chal ha-shee-neun boon-ae-gae yae-gi-haes-se-myun-cho-gaes-saw-yo?*	polite

307

Korean/English Translation	Phonetic Transliteration	Situation Explanation
KOREAN NAMES TO CITIES, COUNTRIES, CONTINENTS AND OCEANS		
South Korea (남한)[48]	*nam-han*	Officially, the country's name is *dae-han-meen-gook* (대한민국),the Republic of Korea.
Seoul (서울)	*saw-ool*	
Busan (부산)[49]	*pu-san*	Pusan
Incheon (인천)	*in-chun*	Inchon
Gwangju (광주)	*kwang-joo*	Kwangju
Daegu (대구)	*tae-goo*	Taegu
Daejeon (대전)	*tae-jun*	Taejun
Jeju Island (제주도)	*chae-joo-do*	Cheju Island
East Sea (동해)[50]	*tong-hae*	
West Sea (서해)[51]	*saw-hae*	
South Sea (남해)	*nam-hae*	
North Korea (북한)[52]	*book-han*	Officially, the country's name is *cho-sun-meen-joo-joo-eui een-meen-gong-hwa-gook* (조선민주주의 인민공화국), the Democratic People's Republic of Korea.
Pyeongyang (평양)	*pyung-yang*	
Wonsan (원산)	*wawn-san*	
Gaeseong (개성)	*kae-sung*	
Sinpo (신포)	*sheen-po*	

[48] North Koreans refer to South Korea as either *nam-cho-sun* (남조선), 'South Joseon,' or *nam-jjok* (남쪽), 'south direction.'

[49] Cities listed in this column are how they used to be spelled according to the old M-R romanization system.

[50] Known also as the Sea of Japan.

[51] In Korean, the sea between China and Korea is also known as *hwang-hae* (황해), which means Yellow Sea, the name by which most people around the world know this body of water.

[52] North Korea still refers to the Korean peninsula as Joseon, the name of the last ruling dynasty. It refers to itself as *book-cho-sun* (북조선), 'North Joseon,' but North Koreans sometimes just say *book-jjok* (북쪽), 'north direction,' instead.

Korean/English Translation	**Phonetic Transliteration**	**Situation Explanation**
Africa (아프리카)	*a-pe-ree-ka*	
Antarctica (남극)	*nam-geuk*	
Arctic Ocean (북극해)	*book-geuk-hae*	
Atlantic ocean (대서양)	*dae-saw-yang*	
Australia (호주)	*ho-joo*	
Belgium (벨기에)	*bael-gi-ae*	
Canada (캐나다)	*kae-na-da*	also called *ka-na-da* (카나다)
Montreal (몬트리올)	*mon-te-ree-ol*	
Ottawa (오타와)	*o-ta-wa*	
Quebec (퀘벡)	*kwae-baek*	
Toronto (토론토)	*to-ron-to*	
Vancouver (뱅쿠버)	*baeng-koo-baw*	
China (중국)	*choong-gook*	meaning 'middle country'
Beijing (북경)	*book-kyung*	sometimes referred to as *bae-ee-jeeng* (베이징)
The Great Wall (만리장성)	*mal-lee-jang-sung*	
The Summer Palace (이화원)	*ee-hwa-wawn*	
The Temple of Heaven (천단원)	*chun-dan-wawn*	
The Forbidden City (자금성)	*cha-geum-sung*	
Xian (서안)	*saw-an*	
Shanghai (상하이)	*sang-ha-ee*	
Hong Kong (홍콩)	*hong-kong*	
Europe (유럽)[53]	*yoo-rup*	
Germany (독일)	*dok-eel*	
Indian Ocean (인도양)	*een-do-yang*	
Ireland (아일랜드)	*a-eel-laen-de*	
Italy (이탈리아)	*ee-tal-lee-a*	

[53] Technically the word Europe has Chinese roots, which, when expressed in Korean characters, come out as *koo-ra-pa* (구라파). If taken at face value, Europe is then the place defined as **vomit/arrange/clan** from its Chinese characters. However, I have yet to meet a Korean to this day that knows the Chinese derivative for 'Europe,' and so *yoo-rup* (유럽) remains the only word you need to know when discussing the continent wedged in between Africa and Asia.

Korean/English Translation	Phonetic Transliteration	Situation Explanation
Japan (일본)	*eel-bon*	meaning 'sun root'
Tokyo (동경)	*dong-kyung*	also called *to-kyo* (토쿄)
Kyoto (교토)	*kyo-to*	
Osaka (오사카)	*o-sa-ka*	
Maldives (몰디브)	*mole-dee-be*	
Mongolia (몽고)	*mong-go*	
New Zealand (뉴질랜드)	*nyoo-jeel-laen-de*	
North America (북미)	*boong-mee*	
Pacific Ocean (태평양)	*tae-pyung-yang*	
Philippines (필리핀)	*peel-lee-peen*	
Portugal (포르투갈)	*po-re-too-gal*	
Russia (러시아)	*law-shee-a*	
Singapore (싱가폴)	*sheeng-ga-pol*	
South America (남미)	*nam-mee*	
Southeast Asia (동남아시아)	*dong-nam-a-shee-a*	literally, 'east-south Asia'
Spain (스페인)	*se-pae-een*	
Taiwan (대만)	*dae-man*	
Thailand (태국)	*tae-gook*	
United Kingdom (영국)	*yung-gook*	
England (잉글랜드)	*eeng-gel-laen-de*	
Scotland (스코틀랜드)	*se-ko-tel-laen-de*	
Wales (웨일즈)	*wae-eel-je*	
Northern Ireland (북아일랜드)	*book-a-eel-laen-de*	
United States (미국)	*mee-gook*	see **Ch. 1** for explanation of America's name
Alaska (알래스카)	*al-lae-sa-ka*	
Boston (보스턴)	*bo-se-tun*	
Chicago (시카고)	*shee-ka-go*	

Korean/English Translation	Phonetic Transliteration	Situation Explanation
Dallas (달라스)	*dal-la-se*	
Guam (괌)	*gwam*	
Los Angeles (로스엔젤레스)	*lo-se-aen-jael-lae-se*	
New York City (뉴욕시티)	*nyu-yok-shee-tee*	
Saipan (사이판)	*sa-ee-pan*	
San Francisco (샌프란시스코)	*saen-pe-ran-shee-se-ko*	
Seattle (시애틀)	*shee-ae-tel*	
Washington D.C. (워싱턴 디.씨.)	*waw-sheeng-tun dee. shee.*	
Vietnam (베트남)	*bae-te-nam*	

Appendices

Verb and Adjective Conjugations
동사 + 형용사의 변화

This is something that I've dreamed about for a long, long time. Although Koreans can't always understand the fact that students of the Korean language aren't able to readily conjugate every single kind of Korean verb, those of us who have grown up in the trenches of language warfare know how painful this can be; a dictionary or a friend tells you the root of a verb, then leaves you to fiddle around with it like a caveman looking at a computer. On a personal note, all I ever wanted years ago was a quick reference list by which to check if what I had done to the verb was correct in its conjugation. Some textbooks out there do in fact have a list of verbs conjugated for honorific situations in the present tense, but what I've always wanted was something more. I wanted a list that conjugated verbs for past, present, and future tenses in situations other than the honorific.

GETTING DOWN TO THE NITTY-GRITTY

Now it's time to actually dissect these entities you've been dreading for hundreds of pages. Although there's a system in place that makes the conjugation of verbs in Korean scientific (as opposed to the method in English whereby students have to memorize every single conjugation to a verb independently), it's extremely difficult, time-consuming, and hard to measure if what you've done is correct (when studying on your own, that is). The one critical difference between verbs in English and Korean is that the root to an English verb (e.g. play, wear, see) is simply plugged into a sentence once learned. You look up the word in your dictionary, discover its meaning, and then you're off to the races, so to speak. With Korean, there are a few more complex steps involved that make the whole thing rather taxing. That's why I've created this elaborate system of conjugated verbs. For the newcomer to Korean, and for those out there that simply want a reference to verbs, the following tables allow you once and for all to see how a root is brought to life. Looking up the adjective 'cold,' for example, in the dictionary, you find the word *choop-da* (춥다). However, that root isn't a whole lot of help, as plugging the adjective into a sentence without doing anything to it will lead to confusion and outright misunderstanding most of the time (e.g. *nae cheen-goo-ga choop-da* (내 친구가 춥다)).

FIRST THING'S FIRST

The first thing to know is that Korean has tenses similar to English, three basic tenses loosely translated as past, present, and future.[1] Although the root of the verb is occasionally used as is (i.e. in its stem form, such as *yea-ppe-da* (예쁘다)), it's much more common to conjugate the verb for both tense and situation.

All Korean verbs can be separated into three distinct categories, and with the exception of only one kind of verb, the other two are relatively easy to remember how to conjugate. The first branch of verbs are the ones described in **Chapter 11**. These verbs are almost always derived from Chinese nouns and are known as *ha-da* verbs, *ha-da dong-sa* (하다 동사). These words include both verbs (as we know them in English) and adjectives, and are thankfully the easiest to conjugate. I say thankfully because they clearly represent the largest number of verbs in the Korean language today.

The second branch of verbs is called *o-ah* verbs, *o/ah dong-sa* (오/아 동사).

[1] For an explanation on why I say 'loosely translated,' please see **Ch. 8**.

313

These verbs don't constitute a huge number of Korean action and descriptive verbs, but they are some of the most useful ones around, so knowing how to conjugate them quickly and correctly is essential.

The third branch of verbs is referred to as **irregular verbs**, *bool-kyu-cheek dong-sa* (불규칙 동사). These verbs all come from pure Korean, and though they don't number as many as the *ha-da* verbs quantitatively, they do represent a large number of both the action verbs as well as the descriptive verbs. Irregular verbs also represent the real headache in conjugation because there are so many different types. Therefore mastering them takes a significant amount of time and energy.

BREAKING DOWN THE VERBS

Verbs that fall in the first category, that is the *ha-da* verbs, are all conjugated the exact same way (Hallelujah!), which means you can learn these quickly and proficiently. The second type of verb, *o-ah* verbs, also follows straightforward rules, which makes them fairly easy to learn as well. The third type, however, the irregular verbs, are where the going gets tough and the tough have to get going.

Irregular verbs are broken down based on their final vowel, and, in some cases, their final consonant. Which vowel (and sometimes which consonant) this is determines how the verb will be conjugated on a grammatical level, not counting the situation you are dealing with (i.e. the level of respect that must be given). This means that words with a final vowel *aw* (어) will be conjugated differently than verbs with a final vowel *ooh* (우), for example.

HOW IT'S ALL SET UP

I've set up the verb conjugations to try and give you as simple and effective a table as possible. Let me say before continuing, however, that verb conjugations are never simple and straightforward, so if the following examples look overwhelming, don't be scared. With a little practice this will all become old hat in no time.

With each type of verb, I've included the English phonetic sounding version in *italics*. The Korean spelling of the word follows in (parenthesis), and after that the meaning of the word is offered in **bold**. Below that are examples of other verbs in [another set of brackets] that are conjugated the exact same way. With the other examples, however, I haven't included the meaning in English. The verb list in the next appendix provides the meaning for every verb I use here, though.

The verbs themselves are broken down into simple **past, present,** and **future tenses**. For **Questions**, I've given basic examples in four different situations: high honorific *jon-dae-mal* (존대말), honorific *jon-dae-mal*, everyday polite (perhaps the most common for everyday situations), and familiar *ban-mal* (반말). For **Statements**, I've included basic examples for three different situations when making first person statements: honorific *jon-dae-mal*, everyday polite, and familiar *ban-mal*. These are by no means the only ways to conjugate every verb, but they represent, in my opinion, the three or four most likely conjugations the average speaker will use in the course of a day when speaking the language. Unfortunately, to conjugate every type of verb in every single possible way would be an exercise that beckons its own book; if I were to do that, this appendix would be something like 220 pages longer than it is now.

USE OF VERBS IN EVERYDAY SITUATIONS

I've said this before in other sections and I'll say it again now: this verb guide is nothing more than that—a guide. It's meant to help you figure out if what you've done with a verb is correct for grammar and nothing more. With the verbs I've used in the examples, for instance, some tenses won't be used (e.g. the future tense of *yae-ppe-da* (예쁘다)), and in other situations, certain conjugations won't be used. Other times, one verb will sound more natural in the present continuous than another verb. *It always depends on the situation, the verb in question, the person you're speaking with, and the tense you wish to speak in.* If you keep that in mind, and you ask Koreans about the verb situations all the time, this guide to verbs will help you on your way to learn Korean like nothing else out there.

_ha-da_ verbs : 하다 동사

_ha-da_ (하다): to do [2]

Questions

	High honorific	Honorific	Common	_ban-mal_
Past	하셨습니까?	했습니까?	했어요?	했어?
Present	하십니까?	합니까?	해요?	해?
Future	하실 겁니까?	할 겁니까?	할 거예요?	할 거야?

Statements

	High honorific	Honorific	Common	_ban-mal_
Past	하셨습니다.	했습니다.	했어요.	했어.
Present	하십니다.	합니다.	해요.	해.
Future	하실 겁니다.	할 겁니다.	할 거예요.	할 거야.

_oh/ah_ verbs : 오/아 동사

_o-da_ (오다): to come

[_ka-gee-go o-da_ (가지고 오다), _de-raw o-da_ (들어오다), _bo-da_ (보다), _sso-da_ (쏘다)]

Questions

	High honorific	Honorific	Common	_ban-mal_
Past	오셨습니까?	왔습니까?	왔어요?	왔어?
Present	오십니까?	옵니까?	와요?	와?
Future	오실겁니까?	올겁니까?	올거예요?	올거야?

Statements

	High honorific	Honorific	Common	_ban-mal_
Past		왔습니다.	왔어요.	왔어.
Present		옵니다.	와요.	와.
Future		올겁니다.	올거예요.	올거야.

[2] The verb _ha-da_ (하다) verb is truly unique in Korean because it's one of the most versatile verbs in the language. I translated _ha-da_ as 'to do' because that's the most common way in which it's used, but it's not the only way. Also note that every verb that ends in _ha-da_ can be plugged into this conjugation model (e.g. 공부하다, 출판하다, etc.).

bbop-da (뽑다): **to develop** (*i.e. pictures*),
to get (*i.e. a drink from a vending machine*), **to pull** (*i.e. teeth*)
[*bat-da* (받다), *dat-da* (닫다), *an-ta* (앉다), *kkakk-da* (깎다), *jap-da* (잡다), *no-ta* (놓다)]

Questions

	High honorific	Honorific	Common	*ban-mal*
Past	뽑으셨습니까?	뽑았습니까?	뽑았어요?	뽑았어?
Present	뽑으십니까?	뽑습니까?	뽑아요?	뽑아?
Future	뽑으실겁니까?	뽑을겁니까?	뽑을거예요?	뽑을거야?

Statements

		Honorific	Common	*ban-mal*
Past		뽑았습니다.	뽑았어요.	뽑았어.
Present		뽑습니다.	뽑아요.	뽑아.
Future		뽑을겁니다.	뽑을거예요.	뽑을거야.

nol-da (놀다):[3] to play

Questions

	High honorific	Honorific	Common	*ban-mal*
Past		놀았습니까?	놀았어요?	놀았어?
Present		놉니까?	놀아요?	놀아?
Future		놀겁니까?	놀거예요?	놀거야?

Statements

		Honorific	Common	*ban-mal*
Past		놀았습니다.	놀았어요.	놀았어.
Present		놉니다.	놀아요.	놀아.
Future		놀겁니다.	놀거예요.	놀거야.

[3] Listed as 'to play' in most dictionaries, I find that translation of *nol-da* (놀다) hard to accept as I've never used the verb 'to play' in the same context as it's used in Korean. The verb *nol-da* is used as much with children in Korean (e.g. kids playing with toys), as it is with adults having a fun time. Going out drinking, going singing, enjoying time with someone—these situations can all be referred to as *nol-da*.

ka-da (가다): **to go**
[*ka-gee-go ka-da* (가지고 가다), *de-raw-ka-da* (들어가다),
ta-da (타다) *sa-da* (사다), *man-na-da* (만나다)]

Questions

	High honorific	Honorific	Common	*ban-mal*
Past	가셨습니까?	갔습니까?	갔어요?	갔어?
Present	가십니까?	가세요?	가요?	가?
Future	가실겁니까?	갈겁니까?	갈거예요?	갈거야?

Statements

Past		갔습니다.	갔어요.	갔어.
Present		갑니다.	가요.	가.
Future		갈겁니다.	갈거예요.	갈거야.

al-da (알다): **to know**

[*sal-da* (살다), *nal-da* (날다), *pal-da* (팔다)]

Questions

	High honorific	Honorific	Common	*ban-mal*
Past	아셨습니까?	알았습니까?	알았어요?	알았어?
Present	아십니까?	압니까?	알아요?	알아?

Statements

Past		알았습니다.	알았어요.	알았어.
Present		압니다.	알아요.	알아.
Future		알겁니다.	알거예요.	알거야.

Irregular Verbs/*bool-kyu-cheek dong-sa*: 불규칙 동사

dwae-da (되다): **to be**[4]

Questions

High honorific	Honorific	Common	*ban-mal*

[4] Although *dwae-da* (되다) is sometimes 'to be,' it's not always so.

318

Past	되셨습니까?	됐습니까?	됐어요?	됐어?
Present	되십니까?	됩니까?	돼요?	돼?
Future	되실겁니까?	될겁니까?	될거에요?	될거야?

Statements

Past		됐습니다.	됐어요.	됐어.
Present		됩니다.	돼요.	돼.
Future		될겁니다.	될거에요.	될거야.

ee-da (이다): to be
[boo-chee-da (붙이다)]

Questions

	High honorific	Honorific	Common	ban-mal
Past	이셨습니까?	이셨어요?	이었어요?	이었어?
Present	이십니까?	이세요?	이예요?	야?
Future	이실겁니까?	일겁니까?	일거예요?	일거야?

Statements

Past		이었습니다.	이었어요.	이었어.
Present		입니다.	이예요.	야.
Future		일겁니다.	일거예요.	일거야.

shwee-da (쉬다): to rest, relax/ take it easy, to breathe

Questions

	High honorific	Honorific	Common	ban-mal
Past	쉬셨습니까?	쉬셨어요?	쉬었어요?	쉬었어?
Present	쉬십니까?	쉬세요?	쉬어요?	쉬어?
Future	쉬실겁니까?	쉴겁니까?	쉴거예요?	쉴거야?

Statements

	High honorific	Honorific	Common	ban-mal
Past		쉬었습니다.	쉬었어요.	쉬었어.
Present		쉽니다.	쉬어요.	쉬어.
Future		쉴겁니다.	쉴거예요.	쉴거야.

울다 (ool-da): to cry

Questions

	High honorific	Honorific	Common	ban-mal
Past	우셨습니까?	울었습니까?	울었어요?	울었어?
Present	우십니까?	웁니까?	울어요?	울어?
Future	우실겁니까?	울겁니까?	울거예요?	울거야?

Statements

	High honorific	Honorific	Common	ban-mal
Past		울었습니다.	울었어요.	울었어.
Present		웁니다.	울어요.	울어.
Future		울겁니다.	울거예요.	울거야.

mo-re-da (모르다): to not know
(da-re-da (다르다), ko-re-da (고르다), ma-re-da (마르다), bba-re-da (빠르다)

Questions

	High honorific	Honorific	Common	ban-mal
Past	모르셨습니까?	몰랐습니까?	몰랐어요?	몰랐어?
Present	모르십니까?	모릅니까?	몰라요?	몰라?
Future	모르실겁니까?	모를겁니까?	모를거예요?	모를거야?

Statements

	High honorific	Honorific	Common	ban-mal
Past		몰랐습니다.	몰랐어요.	몰랐어.
Present		모릅니다.	몰라요.	몰라.
Future		모를겁니다.	모를거예요.	모를거야.

sse-da (쓰다): **to use/to write/to wear/to spend/ to be bitter**

Questions

	High honorific	Honorific	Common	*ban-mal*
Past	쓰셨습니까?	썼습니까?	썼어요?	썼어?
Present	쓰십니까?	씁니까?	써요?	써?
Future	쓰실겁니까?	쓸겁니까?	쓸거예요?	쓸거야?

Statements

		Honorific	Common	*ban-mal*
Past		썼습니다.	썼어요.	썼어.
Present		씁니다.	써요.	써.
Future		쓸겁니다.	쓸거예요.	쓸거야.

ka-re-chee-da (가르치다): **to teach**
[*chee-da* (치다), *dang-gi-da* (당기다), *ddaw-raw-gee-da* (떨어지다),
baw-ree-da (버리다), *ma-shee-da* (마시다), *kkee-da* (끼다),
shee-kee-da (시키다), *mo-ee-da* (모이다), *ke-ree-da* (그리다)]

Questions

	High honorific	Honorific	Common	*ban-mal*
Past	가르치셨습니까?	가르쳤습니까?	가르쳤어요?	가르쳤어?
Present	가르치십니까?	가르칩니까?	가르쳐요?	가르쳐?
Future	가르치실겁니까?	가르칠겁니까?	가르칠거예요?	가르칠거야?

Statements

		Honorific	Common	*ban-mal*
Past		가르쳤습니다.	가르쳤어요.	가르쳤어.
Present		가르칩니다.	가르쳐요.	가르쳐.
Future		가르칠겁니다.	가르칠거예요.	가르칠거야.

man-deul-da (만들다): **to make**
[*meel-da* (밀다), *bool-da* (불다), *heun-deul-da* (흔들다)]

Questions

	High honorific	Honorific	Common	*ban-mal*
Past	만드셨습니까?	만들었습니까?	만들었어요?	만들었어?
Present	만드십니까?	만듭니까?	만들어요?	만들어?
Future	만드실겁니까?	만들겁니까?	만들거예요?	만들거야?

Statements

		Honorific	Common	*ban-mal*
Past		만들었습니다.	만들었어요.	만들었어.
Present		만듭니다.	만들어요.	만들어.
Future		만들겁니다.	만들거예요.	만들거야.

pool-da (풀다): **to relieve/to wear/to solve**
[*deul-da* (들다)]

Questions

	High honorific	Honorific	Common	*ban-mal*
Past	푸셨습니까?	풀었습니까?	풀었어요?	풀었어?
Present	푸십니까?	풉니까?	풀어요?	풀어?
Future	푸실겁니까?	풀겁니까?	풀거예요?	풀거야?

Statements

		Honorific	Common	*ban-mal*
Past		풀었습니다.	풀었어요.	풀었어.
Present		풉니다.	풀어요.	풀어.
Future		풀겁니다.	풀거예요.	풀거야.

boo-re-da (부르다): **to tell/to sing/to call (out)**
[*maw-moo-re-da* (머무르다), *o-re-da* (오르다), *koo-re-da* (구르다)]

Questions

	High honorific	Honorific	Common	*ban-mal*
Past	부르셨습니까?	불렀습니까?	불렀어요?	불렀어?

Present	부르십니까?	부릅니까?	불러요?	불러?
Future	부르실겁니까?	부를겁니까?	부를거예요?	부를거야?

Statements

Past	불렀습니다.	불렀어요.	불렀어.
Present	부릅니다.	불러요.	불러.
Future	부를겁니다	부를거예요.	부를거야.

eek-da (읽다): to read

[eet-da (있다), awp-da (없다), sheet-da (씻다), mawk-da (먹다),
jawk-da (적다), eep-da (입다), ddool-ta (뚫다), sheen-da (신다),
mook-da (묵다) nul-dda (넓다), jum-dda (젊다), naw-ta (넣다),
meet-da (믿다), eet-da (잊다), awt-da (얻다)]

Questions

	High honorific	Honorific	Common	ban-mal
Past	읽으셨습니까?	읽었습니까?	읽었어요?	읽었어?
Present	읽으십니까?	읽습니까?	읽어요?	읽어?
Future	읽으실겁니까?	읽을겁니까?	읽을거예요?	읽을거야?

Statements

Past	읽었습니다.	읽었어요.	읽었어.
Present	읽습니다.	읽어요.	읽어.
Future	읽을겁니다.	읽을거예요.	읽을거야.

bo-nae-da (보내다): to send
[nae-da (내다)]

Questions

	High honorific	Honorific	Common	ban-mal
Past	보내셨습니까?	보냈습니까?	보냈어요?	보냈어?

Present	보내십니까?	보냅니까?	보내요?	보내?
Future	보내실겁니까?	보낼겁니까?	보낼거예요?	보낼거야?

Statements

Past	보냈습니다.	보냈어요.	보냈어.
Present	보냅니다.	보내요.	보내.
Future	보낼겁니다.	보낼거예요.	보낼거야.

pee-da (피다): **to bloom** (i.e. flowers)

Questions

	Honorific	Common	*ban-mal*
Past	피었습니까?	피었어요?	피었어?
Future	핍니까?	피어요?	피어?

Statements

	Honorific	Common	*ban-mal*
Past	피었습니다.	피었어요.	피었어.
Present	핍니다.	피어요.	피어.
Future	필겁니다.	필거예요.	필거야.

deud-da (듣다): **to listen**
[*kawt-da* (걷다), *moot-da* (묻다)]

Questions

	High honorific	Honorific	Common	*ban-mal*
Past	들으셨습니까?	들었습니까?	들었어요?	들었어?
Present	들으십니까?	듣습니까?	들어요?	들어?
Future	들으실겁니까?	들을겁니까?	들을거예요?	들을꺼야?

Statements

	High honorific	Honorific	Common	*ban-mal*
Past		들었습니다.	들었어요.	들었어.

| Present | 듣습니다. | 들어요. | 들어. |
| Future | 들을겁니다. | 들을거예요. | 들을거야. |

pee-oo-da (피우다): **to smoke**
[*joo-da* (주다), *ke-man-doo-da* (그만두다), *chae-oo-da* (채우다)]

Questions

	High honorific	Honorific	Common	*ban-mal*
Past	피우셨습니까?	피웠습니까?	피웠어요?	피웠어?
Present	피우십니까?	피웁니까?	피워요?	피워?
Future	피우실겁니까?	피울겁니까?	피울거예요?	피울거야?

Statements

		Honorific	Common	*ban-mal*
Past		피웠습니다.	피웠어요.	피웠어.
Present		피웁니다.	피워요.	피워.
Future		피울겁니다.	피울거예요.	피울거야.

yul-da (열다): **to open**

Questions

	High honorific	Honorific	Common	*ban-mal*
Past	여셨습니까?	열었습니까?	열었어요?	열었어?
Present	여십니까?	여십니까?	열어요?	열어?
Future	여실겁니까?	열(을)겁니까?	열(을)거예요?	열거야?

Statements

		Honorific	Common	*ban-mal*
Past		열었습니다.	열었어요.	열었어.
Present		엽니다.	열어요.	열어.
Future		열겁니다.	열기예요.	열거야.

<h2 align="center">kken-na-da (끝나다): to finish
[na-da (나다)]</h2>

<h3 align="center">Questions</h3>

	High honorific	Honorific	Common	*ban-mal*
Past	끝나셨습니까?	끝났습니까?	끝났어요?	끝났어?
Present	끝나가십니까?	끝나갑니까?	끝나(가)요?	끝나(가)?
Future	끝나실겁니까?	끝날겁니까?	끝날거예요?	끝날거야?

<h3 align="center">Statements</h3>

		Honorific	Common	*ban-mal*
Past		끝났습니다.	끝났어요.	끝났어.
Present		끝나갑니다.	끝나(가)요.	끝나(가).
Future		끝날겁니다.	끝날거예요.	끝날거야.

<h2 align="center">kawl-lee-da (걸리다): to catch/to take (i.e. time)
[beel-lee-da (빌리다)]</h2>

<h3 align="center">Questions</h3>

	High honorific	Honorific	Common	*ban-mal*
Past	걸리셨습니까?	걸렸습니까?	걸렸어요?	걸렸어?
Future	걸리십니까?	걸립니까?	걸려요?	걸려?

<h3 align="center">Statements</h3>

		Honorific	Common	*ban-mal*
Past		걸렸습니다.	걸렸어요.	걸렸어.
Present		걸립니다.	걸려요.	걸려.

<h2 align="center">a-reum-dap-da (아름답다): to be beautiful</h2>

<h3 align="center">Questions</h3>

	High honorific	Honorific	Common	*ban-mal*
Past	아름다우	아름다웠	아름다웠어요?	아름다웠어?

326

	셨습니까?	습니까?		
Present	아름다우 십니까?	아름답 습니까?	아름다워요?	아름다워?

Statements

Past		아름다웠습니다.	아름다웠어요.	아름다웠어.
Present		아름답습니다.	아름다워요.	아름다워.

choop-da (춥다): **to be cold**
[*shweep-da* (쉽다), *dawp-da* (덥다), *meep-da* (밉다),
moo-gup-da (무겁다), *ka-byup-da* (가볍다), *kwee-yup-da* (귀엽다)]

Questions

	High honorific	Honorific	Common	*ban-mal*
Past	추우셨습니까?	추웠습니까?	추웠어요?	추웠어?
Present	추우십니까?	추우십니까?	추워요?	추워?

Statements

Past		추웠습니다.	추웠어요.	추웠어.
Present		춥습니다.	추워요.	추워.
Future		추울겁니다.	추울거예요.	추울거야.

wae-hyang-jawg-ee-da (외향적이다): **to be extroverted**
[*mae-ryawk-jawg-ee-da* (매력적이다), *nae-sung-jawg-ee-da* (내성적이다),
juk-keuk-jawg-ee-da (적극적이다)]

Questions

	Honorific	Common	*ban-mal*
Past	외향적이였습니까?	외향적이였어요?	외향적이였어?
Present	외향적입니까?	외향적이예요?	외향적이야?

Statements

Past	외향적이었습니다.	외향적이였어요.	외향적이었어.
Present	외향적입니다.	외향적이예요.	외향적이야.

ka-da-rop-da (까다롭다): **to be picky/fussy**
[*sae-rop-da* (새롭다), *hae-rop-da* (해롭다), *gwae-rop-da* (괴롭다)
hyang-gi-rop-da (향기롭다), *seul-gi-rop-da* (슬기롭다),
wae-rop-da (외롭다), *heung-mee-rop-da* (흥미롭다)]

Questions

	Honorific	Common	*ban-mal*
Past	까다로웠습니까?	까다로웠어요?	까다로웠어?
Present	까다롭습니까?	까다로워요?	까도로워?

Statements

Past	까다로웠습니다.	까다로웠어요.	까다로웠어.
Present	까다롭습니다.	까다로워요.	까다로워.
Future	까다로울겁니다.	까다로울거예요.	까다로울거야.

jjal-dda (짧다): **to be short** (i.e. time)
[*nat-da* (낮다), *nok-da* (녹다), *nop-da* (높다)]

Questions

	High honorific	Honorific	Common	*ban-mal*
Past		짧았습니까?	짧았어요?	짧았어?
Present		짧습니까?	짧아요?	짧아?
Future		짧을겁니까?	짧을거예요?	짧을거야?

Statements

Past	짧았습니다.	짧았어요.	짧았어.
Present	짧습니다.	짧아요.	짧아.

Future		짧을겁니다.	짧을거예요.	짧을거야.

mawl-da (멀다): **to be far**
[*keel-da* (길다)]

Questions

	High honorific	Honorific	Common	*ban-mal*
Past		멀었습니까?	멀었어요?	멀었어?
Present		멉니까?	멀어요?	멀어?
Future		멀겁니까?	멀거예요?	멀거야?

Statements

		Honorific	Common	*ban-mal*
Past		멀었습니다.	멀었어요.	멀었어.
Present		멉니다.	멀어요.	멀어.
Future		멀겁니다.	멀거예요.	멀거야.

Honorific Verbs

Honorific verbs are used with others or about others (i.e. in the second and third person), so all of the following verbs are never used about yourself. I've included sample lists here for the most common honorific verbs:

de-shee-da (드시다): **to eat/to drink**

Questions

	High honorific	Honorific
Past	드셨습니까?	드셨어요?
Present	드십니까?	드세요?
Future	드실겁니까?	드실거예요?

Statements

	High honorific	Honorific
Past	드셨습니다.	드셨어요.
Present	드십니다.	드셔요.
Future	드실겁니다.	드실거예요.

jab-soo-shee-da (잡수시다): **to eat**

Questions

	High honorific	Honorific
Past	잡수셨습니까?	잡수셨어요?
Present	잡수십니까?	잡수세요?
Future	잡수실겁니까?	잡수실거예요?

Statements

	High honorific	Honorific
Past	잡수셨습니다.	잡수셨어요.
Present	잡수십니다.	잡수셔요.
Future	잡수실겁니다.	잡수실거예요.

do-ra-ka-shee-da (돌아가시다): **to pass away (i.e. death)**

Questions

	High honorific	Honorific
Past	돌아가셨습니까?	돌아가셨어요?

Statements

Past	돌아가셨습니다.	돌아가셨어요.

joo-moo-shee-da (주무시다): **to sleep**

Questions

	High honorific	Honorific
Past	주무셨습니까?	주무셨어요?
Present	주무십니까?	주무세요?
Future	주무실겁니까?	주무실거예요?

Statements

Past	주무셨습니다.	주무셨어요.
Present	주무십니다.	주무셔요.
Future	주무실겁니다.	주무실거예요.

kae-shee-da (계시다): **to be/to have/-ING**[5]
(*an kae-shee-da* (안 계시다): **to not be/to not have**)

Questions

	High honorific	Honorific
Past	(안) 계셨습니까?	(안) 계셨어요?
Present	(안) 계십니까?	(안) 계세요?
Future	(안) 계실겁니까?	(안) 계실거예요?

[5] *kae-shee-da* (계시다) can be used like *eet-da* (있다) in the sense that it transforms the simple present tense into something akin to the present continuous after the addition of the *go* (고) character to the verb. For example, one instance of, 'Are you going?' could be said, *ka-go kae-sae-yo*? (가고 계세요?)

[6] The verb *de-ree-da* (드리다) is an extremely special verb that is used in a host of different situations. The following section should make this last point clearer.

Statements

Past	(안) 계셨습니다.	(안) 계셨어요.
Present	(안) 계십니다.	(안) 계세요.
Future	(안) 계실겁니다.	(안) 계실거예요.

MORE ON *DE-REE-DA* (드리다)

de-ree-da (드리다): **to give**[6]

Questions

	High honorific	Honorific	Common
Past	드리셨습니까?	드렸습니까?	드렸어요?
Present	드립니까?	드릴까요?	드려요?
Future	드리실겁니까?	드릴겁니까?	드릴거예요?

Statements

Past	드렸습니다.	드렸어요.
Present	드립니다.	드려요.
Future	드리겠습니다.	드릴께요.

There are three very useful things to know about the verb *de-ree-da* that make it one of the most versatile verbs in Korean. After each explanation I've provided several examples to highlight the point. They are as follows:

1. The verb *de-ree-da* is used just the same as *joo-da* (주다) when expressing intent on doing something. Thus, any action that you will do (i.e. you have the intention of doing) can be followed by the verb *de-ree-da* to state the thought more clearly and more politely. For example:

English	**Korean** (*ban-mal*)	**Korean** (*jon-dae-mal*)
(I'll) send you an e-mail	메일 보낼 께.	메일 보내 드릴께요.
(I'll) buy it/that for you.	사 줄께.	사 드릴께요.
(I'll) get in touch with you.	연락할께.	연락드릴께요.
(I'll) give you a call.	전화할께.	전화드릴께요.
(I'll) go get you a menu.	메뉴판 갖다 줄께.	메뉴판 갖다 드릴께요.
Let me give you a hand/	도와 줄께.	도와 드릴께요.
Let me give you some help		

2. When going out and being offered something politely at a restaurant or store, for example, you'll often hear the person say, .. 드려요? or .. 드릴까요? In these situations, the person is merely asking you if you'd like something. For example:

English	**Korean** (*jon-dae-mal*)
Would you like a (plastic) bag?	봉투 드릴까요?
Do you want a bag to go with that?	봉투 드려요?
Would you like a cup of coffee?	커피 드릴까요?
Would you like some candy?	사탕 드릴까요?

3. When asking if it would be all right to do something (or if you simply want to ask if you can do something), *de-ree-da* is often used in place of 'can,' as explained in **Chapter 4**. In these situations, not only is it more polite to use *de-ree-da*, but it's much more natural some of the time. For example:

English	**Korean** (*jon-dae-mal*)
Can you do me a favor?	부탁드려도 될까요?
Would you mind giving me a shout?	연락드려도 될까요?
Do you think you could give me a call?	전화드려도 될까요?

Appendices

Useful Verbs and Adjectives
유용한 동사 + 형용사

I've created this list of adjectives and verbs (all considered verbs in Korean) for the student of Korean to expedite his or her learning process. This list can be used as a study guide for those students just starting out with the language, but for those of you further along, it can serve as a quick reference dictionary for many common day-to-day words. There are two things I should point out, though.

First, this list is not inclusive of every verb in Korean. It's approximately 300 verbs that I believe serve most useful in conducting your affairs in Korea, especially if you're just beginning your studies. Also, because I have firsthand knowledge of what it's like to learn these verbs, I've included footnotes and descriptions where necessary to further illuminate any problems that may commonly be faced with a particular word.

Second, as I've mentioned before, many Korean words have more than one meaning. The meaning(s) I've listed with all of these verbs is usually the most common and nothing more. For a complete listing of a specific word's meanings, most notably it's more obscure ones, please refer to a comprehensive dictionary.

One last thing, this list is set up alphabetically according to a Korean dictionary, that is *ka-na-da-soon* (가나다순), which makes referencing words from Korean go quickly if you know how the Korean characters are arranged. (Please see **Chapter 6** for a thorough explanation of how Korean characters are listed in a dictionary.)

Korean	**Phonetic Transliteration**	**Meaning**
가깝다	*ka-kkap-da*	to be close/close by
가난하다	*ka-nan-ha-da*	to be poor (no money)
가다	*ka-da*	to go
가르치다	*ka-re-chee-da*	to teach
가지고 가다	*ka-jee-go ka-da*	to take
가지고 오다	*ka-jee-go oh-da*	to bring
간단하다	*kan-dan-ha-da*	to be simple/basic
갈아입다	*ka-ra-eep-da*	to change (clothes)
갈아타다	*ka-ra-ta-da*	to change/to transfer (e.g. buses, trains, etc.)
감다	*kam-da*	to close (eyes)/to wash (hair)
갔다 오다[1]	*kat-da oh-da*	to go somewhere
강하다	*kang-ha-da*	to be strong/powerful
강의하다	*kang-eui-ha-da*	to lecture
갖다 주다[2]	*kat-da joo-da*	to go and get something to give someone
거짓말하다	*kaw-jee-mal-ha-da*	to lie (not the truth)
걷다	*kawt-da*	to walk
걸리다	*kawl-lee-da*	to catch (sickness, disease)/to take (length of time)
계산하다	*kae-san-ha-da*	to pay (a bill or a check)
계획이 없다	*kae-hwaek-ee awp-dda*	to not have plans
계획이 있다	*kae-hwaek-ee eet-dda*	to have plans
고르다	*ko-re-da*	to pick/to choose
~고 싶다	*go sheep-da*	want to/would like to

[1] Although this is a past tense verb in Korean, it's at times used in what is the present perfect tense in English. That's why it sometimes comes out as, 'I went somewhere,' and sometimes as, 'I've been somewhere,' in English.

[2] More politely expressed as *kat-da de-ree-da* (갖다 드리다).

Korean	**Phonetic Transliteration**	**Meaning**
공부하다	gong-boo-ha-da	to study
괴롭다	gwae-rop-da	to be painful/distressing
구르다	koo-re-da	to roll
구매하다	koo-mae-ha-da	to purchase
구하다	koo-ha-da	to help (i.e. life and death situations)
귀엽다	kwee-yawp-da	to be cute
그리다	ke-ree-da	to draw/to paint
그만두다	ke-man-doo-da	to quit/to stop (i.e. work)
기도하다	kee-do-ha-da	to pray
깊다	keep-da	to be deep
까다롭다	kka-da-rop-da	to be picky/fussy
깎다	kkak-dda	to cut (i.e. cut down in price)
깨끗하다	kkae-kkeut-ha-da	to be clean
끝나다	kkeun-na-da	to finish/to end (intransitive verb)
끝내다	kkeun-nae-da	to finish/to end (transitive verb)
나가다	na-ga-da	to go out (as in outside)/to be out (videos or books that have been rented/borrowed)
나다	na-da	to be born (babies from a mother)/to grow
나쁘다	na-ppe-da	to be bad/ awful/ terrible
나이(가) 많다	na-ee (ga) man-ta	to be old
나이(를) 먹다[3]	na-ee (reul) mawk-da	to be old
날다	nal-da	to fly
날씬하다	nal-ssheen-ha-da	to be thin/skinny
낮다	nat-da	to be low
낮잠 자다	nat-jam ja-da	to have a nap/to take a nap

[3]The honorific form of this verb is *na-ee de-shee-da* (나이 드시다).

Korean	**Phonetic Transliteration**	**Meaning**
내다	*nae-da*	to pay
내리다	*nae-ree-da*	to get out/to get off/to come down (rain, snow)
내성적이다	*nae-sung-jawg-ee-da*	to be introverted
넓다	*nul-dda*	to be wide/spacious
넣다	*naw-ta*	to put on/put in/put into
녹음하다	*no-geum-ha-da*	to record (audio recording)
녹화하다	*nok-hwa-ha-da*	to record (video recording)
놀다[4]	*nol-da*	to have a good time
놀라다	*nol-la-da*	to be surprised
높다	*nop-da*	to be high
놓다	*no-ta*	to lay down
늙다	*neuk-dda*	to be old
닫다	*dat-da*	to close
달다	*dal-da*	to be sweet
당기다	*dang-gi-da*	to pull
더~[5]	*daw*	more/-er
덥다	*dawp-da*	to be hot (weather, body temperature)
도착하다	*do-chak-ha-da*	to arrive
돕다	*dop-da*	to help/to assist
되다[6]	*dwae-da*	to be
듣다	*deud-da*	to listen
들다[7]	*deul-da*	to hold/to give an example
들어가다	*de-raw-ka-da*	to go in/to enter
들어오다	*de-raw-oh-da*	to come in/to enter
등록하다	*deung-nok-ha-da*	to register/to sign up
등산하다	*deung-san-ha-da*	to hike
따뜻하다	*dda-ddeut-ha-da*	to be warm
따라가다	*dda-ra-ka-da*	to follow (going somewhere with a person)

[4] As I explained in the verb conjugation appendix, the verb *nol-da* (놀다) is difficult to translate into English as one verb, and so is usually accompanied with a phrase. Use of it in Korean infers having a good time, though.

[5] In Korean, this is a prefix that serves the same function as the '-er' superlative in English. For example, *daw cho-a-yo* (더 좋아요) means better, greater, or more amazing.

[6] Another common verb in Korean used like 'to be' is *ee-da* (이다).

[7] When you're offering an example to someone, you can say *yae-reul de-raw-saw* (예를 들어서), and when you would like an example provided you can ask *yae-reul de-raw-joo-sae-yo* (예를 들어주세요).

Korean	Phonetic Transliteration	Meaning
따라오다	dda-ra-oh-da	to follow (coming somewhere with a person)
따라하다	dda-ra-ha-da	to follow (repetition)
떠나다	ddaw-na-da	to leave/to get away
떨어지다	ddaw-raw-gee-da	to fall/to drop/to go down/to decrease
뚱뚱하다	ddoong-ddoong-ha-da	to be overweight
뜨겁다	dde-gup-da	to be warm (food and drinks)
마르다	ma-re-da	to be thin/scrawny
마시다[8]	ma-shee-da	to drink
마음에 들다[9]	ma-eum-ae deul-da	to like
마음이 아프다	ma-eum-ee a-pe-da	to have a heavy heart/to feel deeply saddened
마음에 안 들다	ma-eum-ae an deul-da	to not like
만나다	man-na-da	to meet/to get together/to go out with someone
만들다	man-deul-da	to make
만족하다[10]	man-jok-ha-da	to be satisfied
많다	man-ta	a lot/lots of (used as a verb in Korean)
말하다[11]	mal-ha-da	to say/to speak
맑다	mal-dda	to be clear
맛이 없다	ma-shee awp-da	to not be delicious
맛이 있다	ma-shee eet-da	to be delicious
매다	mae-da	to wear (neckties, bow ties, scarves, necklaces)
매력적이다	mae-ryawk-jaw-gi-da	to be attractive
맵다	maep-da	to be hot/spicy
머무르다	maw-moo-re-da	to stay (accommodation)
먹다[12]	mawk-da	to eat
멀다	mawl-da	to be far/to be far away

[8] The honorific form of this is de-shee-da (드시다).

[9] This verb means the same thing as cho-a-ha-da (좋아하다).

[10] A truer translation of this verb is often 'happy.'

[11] The more polite form of this verb is mal-sseum-ha-da (말씀하다).

[12] The honorific form of this verb is technically jap-soo-shee-da (잡수시다), but in its place, de-shee-da (드시다) is more common in spoken conversation.

338

Korean	Phonetic Transliteration	Meaning
모르다	mo-re-da	to not know/to have no idea/to have no clue
묵다	mook-dda	to stay (accommodation)
묶다	mookk-da	to wear (ponytails, hairstyles)
묻다 [13]	moot-dda	to ask/to bury
미끄럽다	mee-kke-rup-da	to be slippery
미안하다	mee-an-ha-da	to be sorry (apologizing)
미치다	mee-chee-da	to be crazy/wild/insane
믿다	meet-da	to believe/to be believable/to be trustworthy
밀다	meel-da	to push
밉다	meep-da	to be ugly/detestable
바꾸다	ba-kkoo-da	to change/to switch
바쁘다	ba-bbe-da	to be busy
받다	bat-da	to get/to receive
배달 되다	bae-dal dwae-da	to deliver
배우다	bae-oo-da	to learn
버리다	baw-ree-da	to throw out
보관하다	bo-kwan-ha-da	to store (locker)
보내다	bo-nae-da	to send
보다	bo-da	to watch/to see
보여주다 [14]	bo-yaw joo-da	to show
부끄럽다	boo-ke-rup-da	to be shy/reserved
부드럽다	boo-de-rup-da	to be smooth
부르다	boo-re-da	to sing (a song)/to tell (i.e. to tell someone your name)
부자가 되다	boo-ja-ga dwae-da	to be rich
부정적이다	boo-jung-jaw-gi-da	to be negative
부지런하다	boo-jee-run-ha-da	to be hardworking/driven
불가능하다	bool-ka-neung-ha-da	to be impossible
불다	bool-da	to blow (a balloon)

[13] The more polite form of this verb is *yaw-jjoo-da* (여쭈다).

[14] The more polite form of this verb is *bo-yaw de-ree-da* (보여 드리다).

Korean	Phonetic Transliteration	Meaning
불친절하다	*bool-cheen-jul-ha-da*	to be mean/unkind
붙이다	*boo-chee-da*	to attach
비싸다	*bee-ssa-da*	to be expensive
빠르다	*bba-re-da*	to be fast/to be quick
빠지다	*bba-gee-da*	to lose (weight), to fall (in love)
빨래하다	*bbal-lae-ha-da*	to wash (clothes)
뽑다	*bbop-da*	to develop (pictures)/to get (something from a vending machine)/to pull (teeth)
사교적이다	*sa-gyo-jaw-gi-da*	to be sociable
사귀다 [15]	*sa-gwee-da*	to get close with someone
사다	*sa-da*	to buy
사용하다	*sa-yong-ha-da*	to use
살다	*sal-da*	to live
새롭다 [16]	*sae-rop-da*	to be new
섞다	*sawkk-da*	to mix
선불하다	*sun-bool-ha-da*	to pre-pay
선택하다	*sun-taek-ha-da*	to choose/to pick
설겆이를 하다	*sul-kaw-jee-reul-ha-da*	to do/wash the dishes
섭섭하다	*sawp-sawp-ha-da*	to be disappointed/to feel sorry about something
세다	*sae-da*	to count (numbers)
세탁하다	*sae-tak-ha-da*	to wash (clothes)
소개팅하다	*so-gae-ting-ha-da*	to go on a blind date
속상하다	*sok-sang-ha-da*	to be annoying/frustrating
송금하다	*song-geum-ha-da*	to send money
쇼핑하다	*show-peeng-ha-da*	to shop/to go shopping
쉬다	*shwee-da*	to rest/relax/take it easy
쉽다	*shweep-da*	to be easy
스케줄이 없다	*se-kae-joo-ree awp-da*	to have no plans/previous engagement/appointment

[15] This is a useful verb in Korean when describing two people becoming close.

[16] This translation is somewhat misleading. The word 'new' in Korean is usually just *sheen* (신) or *sae* (새), from *sae-rop-da* (새롭다).

Korean	Phonetic Transliteration	Meaning
스케줄이 있다	*se-kae-joo-ree eet-da*	to have plans/previous engagement/appointment
슬기롭다	*seul-gi-rop-da*	to be intelligent/wise
슬프다	*seul-pe-da*	to be sad/upset
시끄럽다	*shee-kke-rup-da*	to be loud/noisy
시다	*shee-da*	to be sour (tasting)
시원하다	*shee-wawn-ha-da*	to be cool (weather, food, drinks)
시키다	*shee-kee-da*	to order/to make a person do something
식사하다	*sheek-sa-ha-da*	to have a meal
신다	*sheen-dda*	to wear (socks, shoes, pantyhose)
신이 나다	*sheen-ee na-da*	to be excited
실망하다	*sheel-mang-ha-da*	to be disappointed
심하다 [17]	*sheem-ha-da*	to be extreme/crazy/out of control
심심하다	*sheem-sheem-ha-da*	to be boring/bored
싱싱하다	*sheeng-sheeng-ha-da*	to be fresh
싸다	*ssa-da*	to be cheap/inexpensive
싸우다	*ssa-oo-da*	to fight (physically)
쌀쌀하다	*ssal-ssal-ha-da*	to be a touch cold
쏘다 [18]	*sso-da*	to shoot (a gun)/to treat
쓰다	*sse-da*	to use/to wear (i.e. glasses, hats, sunglasses)/to be bitter (tasting)
씻다	*ssheet-da*	to wash (hands, body, hair)
아름답다 [19]	*a-reum-dap-da*	to be beautiful
아프다	*a-pe-da*	to be sick/hurt/to not feel well
안전하다	*an-jun-ha-da*	to be safe
앉다	*an-ta*	to sit

[17] This is a common expression when describing a situation or a person that has (usually) negative qualities at the extreme end of the spectrum. For example, 'Traffic's a mess,' is *kyo-tong-jung-chae-ga naw-moo* **sheem-ha-da** (교통정체가 너무 심하다).

[18] This verb is very common, especially among younger Koreans, when wanting to treat someone.

[19] Every dictionary I know of translates this word as 'beautiful,' but the truth is that *a-reum-dap-da* (아름답다) is not used nearly as much in Korean as it is in English. That's why I like to think of it as something closer to 'pretty,' an adjective not as common as 'beautiful' in English.

Korean	**Phonetic Transliteration**	**Meaning**
알다	*al-da*	to know
약속 없다	*yak-sok awp-dda*	to have no plans
약속 있다	*yak-sok eet-dda*	to have plans
약속하다	*yak-sok-ha-da*	to make plans/to make a promise/to promise
약하다	*yak-ha-da*	to be weak
양보하다	*yang-bo-ha-da*	to give up a position/to yield
어둡다	*aw-doop-da*	to be dark
어렵다	*aw-ryup-da*	to be difficult
언쟁하다	*awn-jaeng-ha-da*	to fight/to quarrel (verbally)
얻다	*awt-da*	to obtain (information or research)
없다 [20]	*awp-dda*	to not have
여행가다	*yaw-haeng-ka-da*	to go on a trip
여행하다	*yaw-haeng-ha-da*	to travel
연락하다	*yul-lak-ha-da*	to contact/to get in touch with
연주하다	*yun-joo-ha-da*	to play (musical instruments)
열다	*yul-da*	to open
예쁘다	*yae-ppe-da*	to be pretty
예약하다	*yae-yak-ha-da*	to reserve/to make a reservation
오다	*o-da*	to come
올라가다	*ol-la-ka-da*	to go up
올라오다	*ol-la-o-da*	to come up
옮기다	*om-gi-da*	to move (i.e. from one position to another)
외롭다	*wae-rop-da*	to be lonely
요리하다	*yo-ree-ha-da*	to cook
욕하다	*yok-ha-da*	to swear/to curse/to mouth off
운동하다	*oon-dong-ha-da*	to work out/to exercise
운전하다	*oon-jun-ha-da*	to drive

[20] The honorific form of this verb is *an kae-shee-da* (안 계시다).

Korean	**Phonetic Transliteration**	**Meaning**
울다	*ool-da*	to cry
웃다	*oot-da*	to laugh/to smile
웃기다	*oot-gi-da*	to be funny
원만하다	*wawn-man-ha-da*	to be friendly/sociable
원하다 [21]	*wawn-ha-da*	to want
월세를 내다	*wawl-sae-reul nae-da*	to pay rent
위험하다	*wee-hawm-ha-da*	to be dangerous
유감이다	*yoo-gam-ha-da*	to regret/to be sorry
이다	*ee-da*	to be
이사하다	*ee-sa-ha-da*	to move (from one house to another house)
이야기하다 (얘기하다)	*ee-ya-gi-ha-da* (*yae-gi-ha-da*)	to talk/to speak/to tell/ to tell a story
이해가 안 되다	*ee-hae-ga an dwae-da*	to not understand
이해하다	*ee-hae-ha-da*	to understand
일어나다	*ee-raw-na-da*	to wake up/to get up
일하다	*eel-ha-da*	to work
읽다	*eek-dda*	to read
잃다	*eel-ta*	to lose
잊다 [22]	*eet-da*	to forget
입금하다	*eep-geum-ha-da*	to deposit (money)
입다	*eep-da*	to wear (pants, shirts, suits, dresses, skirts)
입사하다	*eep-sa-ha-da*	to start work (get hired at a business)
입학하다	*eep-hak-ha-da*	to start school (begin your studies at a school)
있다 [23]	*eet-da*	to have
자다 [24]	*ja-da*	to sleep
자르다	*ja-re-da*	to cut
자신없다	*ja-sheen awp-dda*	to have no confidence

[21] This verb is not used as much as the suffix *sheep-da* (싶다).

[22] Though this is a verb on its own, when saying, 'I forgot,' in Korean, it's usually combined with the verb *baw-ree-da* (버리다), so that 'I forget/I forgot' becomes *ee-jaw-baw-ryaws-saw-yo* (잊어버렸어요).

[23] The honorific form of this verb is *kae-shee-da* (계시다).

[24] The honorific form of this verb is *joo-moo-shee-da* (주무시다).

Korean	Phonetic Transliteration	Meaning
자신있다	*ja-sheen-eet-dda*	to have confidence
자연스럽다	*ja-yun-se-rup-dda*	to be natural
자취하다	*ja-chwee-ha-da*	to live alone
작다	*chak-dda*	to be small (in physical size)
잡다	*jap-dda*	to grab/to hold on to/to grasp
재미 없다	*jae-mee awp-dda*	to be boring/uninteresting
재미 있다	*jae-mee eet-dda*	to be fun/interesting
저장하다	*jaw-jang-ha-da*	to save (e.g. a computer file)
적극적이다	*jawk-keuk-jawg-ee-da*	to be positive
적다	*jawk-dda*	to write/to write down
전공하다	*jun-gong-ha-da*	to major in (academically)
전화하다	*jun-hwa-ha-da*	to phone/to call/ to make a call
젊다	*jum-dda*	to be young/youthful
젓가락질하다	*chawt-ka-rak-jeel-ha-da*	to use chopsticks
정리하다	*jung-nee-ha-da*	to organize/to arrange/to put things in order
조심하다	*jo-sheem-ha-da*	to be careful
조용하다	*cho-yong-ha-da*	to be quiet
좋다	*cho-ta*	to be good/great/ awesome
주다 [25]	*joo-da*	to give
죽다 [26]	*chook-dda*	to die
주문하다	*joo-moon-ha-da*	to order
준비하다	*joon-bee-ha-da*	to prepare/to get ready
지루하다	*jee-roo-ha-da*	to be boring/bored
지치다	*jee-chee-da*	to be exhausted
징그럽다	*jeeng-ge-rup-da*	to be disgusting/to be heinous/to be gross
짧다	*jjal-dda*	to be short (i.e. length of time), short hair

[25] The more polite form of this verb is *de-ree-da* (드리다).

[26] The honorific form of this verb is *do-ra-ka-shee-da* (돌아가시다).

Korean	Phonetic Transliteration	Meaning
찌다	jjee-da	to gain weight
찍다 [27]	jjeek-dda	to take (a picture)/ to imprint/to stamp
차다	cha-da	to be cold (food and drinks)
창피하다 [28]	chang-pee-ha-da	to be embarrassed/ ashamed
찾다	chat-dda	to search/to look for/to find
채우다	chae-oo-da	to lock/to fill in
청소하다	chung-so-ha-da	to clean
촬영하다	chwa-ryung-ha-da	to film/to shoot (a movie)
출금하다	chool-geum-ha-da	to withdraw (money)
출력하다	chool-lyuk-ha-da	to print
출발하다	chool-bal-ha-da	to leave (on a trip)
출판하다	chool-pan-ha-da	to publish
춥다	choop-dda	to be cold (weather, people, not food and drinks)
충분하다	choong-boon-ha-da	to be enough/to be ample
취소하다	chwee-so-ha-da	to cancel
취직하다	chwee-jeek-ha-da	to look for a job
취하다	chwee-ha-da	to be drunk
치다	chee-da	to hit (a person)/to play (things you hit, such as a piano or billiards)
친절하다	cheen-jul-ha-da	to be nice/kind (people)
친하다	cheen-ha-da	to be close (between friends)
크다	ke-da	to be big/to be large
키가 작다	kee-ga jak-da	to be short (height)
키가 크다	kee-ga ke-da	to be tall (height)
타다	ta-da	to ride/to take (any mode of transportation)
태어나다	tae-aw-na-da	to be born

[27] This verb is used when using a stamp or chops, called *do-jang* (도장) in Korean, to sign a document. Also, people use this verb at stores and supermarkets when scanning items.

[28] This means both 'embarrassed' and 'ashamed' in Korean.

345

Korean	Phonetic Transliteration	Meaning
통통하다	tong-tong-ha-da	to be chubby
통화하다 [29]	tong-hwa-ha-da	to get in touch
퇴근하다	twae-geun-ha-da	to leave work (for the day)
투자하다	too-ja-ha-da	to invest (money)
파티하다	pa-tee-ha-da	to have a party/to host a party
팔다	pal-da	to sell
풀다	pool-da	to relieve/to solve
피곤하다	pee-gon-ha-da	to be tired
피우다	pee-oo-da	to smoke
필요없다	peel-yo-awp-dda	to not need
필요하다	peel-yo-ha-da	to need
하다	ha-da	to do
한턱내다 [30]	han-tawk-nae-da	to treat
해롭다	hae-rop-dda	to be harmful
행복하다 [31]	haeng-bok-ha-da	to be happy
향기롭다	hyang-gi-rop-dda	to be fragrant
혼란스럽다	hol-lan-se-rup-dda	to be confusing/confused
환생하다	hwan-saeng-ha-da	to be reincarnated
환영하다	hwan-yung-ha-da	to welcome
환전하다	hwan-jun-ha-da	to exchange (money)
후불하다	hoo-bool-ha-da	to pay (after receiving item)
휴학하다	hyoo-hak-ha-da	to take a semester/year off
흔들다	heun-deul-da	to shake
흘리다	heul-lee-da	to spill/to lose money
흥미롭다 [32]	heung-mee-rop-dda	to be amazing/incredible/fantastic
힘들다	heem-deul-da	to be hard/to be tough

[29] This is a common verb in Korean when asking if you've been in touch with someone by telephone. The verb literally means 'to communicate through the telephone,' but since you would never say that in English, I've translated it as 'get in touch with (someone).'

[30] This verb does mean 'to treat' (as in a meal), but it's usually only used when the situation comes about as a result of a first paycheck from work, or someone coming into a lot of money.

[31] The adjective 'happy' is not used in Korean nearly as much as it is in English. Depending on the situation, a different adjective is usually used.

[32] This adjective is not used nearly as much in Korean as it is in English.

List of Works and Web sites Consulted

About and About.com. Inventors Library. 2002. <*http://inventors.about.com*>

American Forum for Global Education. China Project Website. 2002.
        <*www.globaled.org*>

Attic World Community Company Ltd. Korean Traditions Page. 1998.
        <*http://english.attic.co.kr*>

Chang, Suk In, and Hong Kyung Pyo, and Ihm Ho Bin. *Korean Grammar for
        International Learners.* Yonsei University Press: Seoul, 1988.

Chinatown.org. Chinese Language and History Page. 1998.
        <*www.chinatown.org*>

Chinatown.org. Chinese Horoscope Page. 1998. <*http://zhongwen.com*>

Choe Yong-shik. Busting out modified hangeul in cyberspace. Korea Herald 8
        Oct. 2002: 16.

Choe Yong-shik. Is hangeul world's first invented alphabet? Korea Herald 9 Oct.
        2002: 16.

Cotterell, Arthur. *China: A Cultural History.* Penguin Books: New York, 1990.

Did you Know History Site. Inventors Library. <*http://www.didyouknow.cd*>

Garlick, Jeremy. A world of animism on Taebaek mountain. Korea Herald 4
        Oct. 2002: 10.

Institute of Korean Language and Culture, Korea University. *Korean,* volume 1
        (한국어1) Korea University press: Seoul, 1991.

Institute of Language Education of Ehwa Womans University. *Pathfinder in
        Korean II.* Ehwa Womans University Press: Seoul, 1999.

Ivillage Inc. Chinese Zodiac Page. 1995-2002. <*http://chinese.astrology.com*>

Kim Jin. Saju: secrets of Oriental fortune-telling. Korea Herald 15 Feb. 2002: 9,
        12.

Korea.com Communications., Ltd. Measurements and Weights Page. 2000-2002.
        http://welcome.korea.com

Korean Insights. Korean Culture Page. <*http://korea.insights.co.kr*>

Korean National Tourism Organization. Korean Language and History Pages.
        <*www.knto.or.kr*>

Korea National Tourism Organization. Korean. Korean Language Page. *<http://english.tour2korea.com >*

Korean Peninsula Energy Development Organization (KEDO), eds. *The Light water Reactor Handbook* (경수로 생활수첩). KEDO (경수로사업지 원기획단): Seoul, 2002.

Lancaster, Lewis R., Yu, C.S., ed. *Introduction of Buddhism to Korea: New Cultural Patterns.* Asian Humanities Press: Berkeley, 1989.

Lee Byung Jun, ed. *Essence Korean-English Dictionary.* Minjungseogwan: Seoul, 1972.

Lee, Peter H., Seo, ed., Dae-seok, complier. *Myths of Korea.* Jimoondang Publishing Company: Seoul 2000.

Life in Korea. Tripitaka Koreana Page. 1997-2002. *<www.lifeinkorea.com>*

Merriam-Webster, eds. *Webster's New American Dictionary.* Merriam-Webster, Inc.: New York, 1995

Ministry of Culture and Tourism. Korean Language Page. 2001. *<www.mct.go.kr>*

National Academy of Korean Language. Korean Language Page. 2001. *<www.korean.go.kr/eng/intro/intro.html>*

National Folk Museum of Korea. Korean History Page. 2002. *<www.nfm.go.kr>*

National Intelligence Service, North Korea Education and Sports Page. 2002. *<www.nis.go.kr>*

Palmer, Spencer J. *Confucian Rituals in Korea.* Asian Humanities Press: Berkeley, 1992.

Park, Francis Y.T. *Speaking Korean- Book II.* Hollym International Corp.: New Jersey, 1994.

Republic of Korea. Republic of Korea. 2000-2001. *<www.korea.net>*

Sangji University. Confucianism Page. April 1, 1998. *< http://cinema.sangji.ac.kr>*

Seligson, Fred Jeremy. *Oriental Birth Dreams.* Hollym Corp.: Seoul, 1990.

State University of New Mexico. Chinese History and Astrology Page. *<http://astro.nmsu.edu>*

Transparent Language. Korean Language Statistics Page. 2002. *<www.transparent.com>*

United Nations Educational, Scientific, and Cultural Organization. King Sejong Literary Prize Website. *<www2.unesco.org>*

Whitlock Jr., James C. *Chinese Characters in Korean*. Ilchokak Publishers: Seoul, 2001.

Yahoo Astrology. Chinese Zodiac Page. 2002. *<http://astrology.yahoo.com>*

Index